West Virginia Histories

Volume 1

⊜⊜⊜

Unique People, Unusual Events, and the Occasional Ghost

Gerald D. Swick

Grave Distractions Publications
Nashville, Tennessee

Grave Distractions Publications
Nashville, Tennessee
www.gravedistractions.com

ISBN-13: 978-1-944066-15-4

In Publication Data
Swick, Gerald D.

Primary BISAC Category: HIS036120
History / United States / State and Local / South

Printed in the United States

For Sheri, always beside me, come what may.

Other Books By Gerald D. Swick

West Virginia Histories Volume 2:
Days of Slavery ✦ Civil War and Aftermath ✦ Statehood and Beyond

Grave Distractions Publications

Historic Photos of West Virginia
Turner Publishing

TABLE OF CONTENTS

SOCIAL CHANGE

4. PIONEERS, RELIGION, WEATHER, SPORTS, MOUNTAIN MELTING POT

PIONEERS

RELIGION

WEATHER

SPORTS

MOUNTAIN MELTING POT

5. INDUSTRY, LABOR, TRANSPORTATION, WEST VIRGINIANS AT WAR

INDUSTRY

LABOR

TRANSPORTATION

WEST VIRGINIANS AT WAR

West Virgina

Counties and Prominent Places

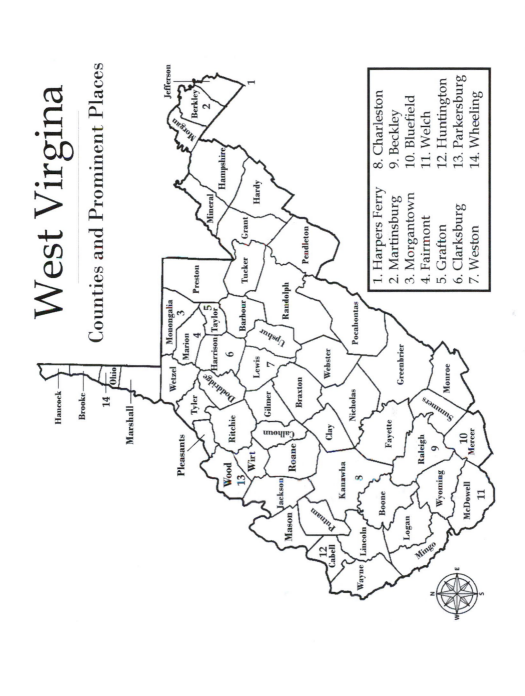

1. Harpers Ferry
2. Martinsburg
3. Morgantown
4. Fairmont
5. Grafton
6. Clarksburg
7. Weston
8. Charleston
9. Beckley
10. Bluefield
11. Welch
12. Huntington
13. Parkersburg
14. Wheeling

Acknowledgments

F irst and foremost, thanks to the staff and publishers of the *Clarksburg Exponent Telegram* for allowing me to share these stories with readers as a weekly column for over sixteen years.

The staff of the West Virginia and Regional Collection at West Virginia University: always friendly, ever helpful.

The West Virginia Humanities Council for compiling the new *West Virginia Encyclopedia* and to all the writers who contributed information and the fact-checkers who made sure all information was accurate. The Encyclopedia has been and continues to be a boon to researchers.

The Wheeling Intelligencer for preserving copies of all its issues, going back to 1851; a tremendous resource for researchers

David Houchin, librarian at the Local History and Genealogy section of the Clarksburg-Harrison Public Library, for his many assists in research.

David Hyman for answering questions about United States currency when they arose.

Gene Larosa for giving me access to his collection of Charles Brinkman's original columns of Taylor County history that appeared in the Grafton Sentinel.

Phyllis Wilson Moore, keeper of the state's literary history, for her frequent assistance on matters related to West Virginia's writers and for pointing me toward some topics for the columns.

And, always, to my parents and siblings for inspiring and teaching me.

Preface: The Lunch

I n the beginning, there was the lunch.

I had been freelancing for *The Exponent Telegram* newspaper in Clarksburg, West Virginia, for a few months when Bill Sedivy, then managing editor, asked me to join him for a midday repast in January 1998 to discuss additional assignments.

Over sandwiches and salads at a Main Street restaurant, he gave me some new projects, and then I asked about something I had been mulling over.

What if I were to write a weekly column of West Virginia history?

His eyes lit up like a man who'd just drawn his fourth ace, and I knew I was onto something. We agreed the column would begin after I returned from South San Francisco, where I was speaking at the Celebrate History! conference in late February.

Oh, goody, I was going to get to write a history column—every week!

Oh, damn, I was going to have to write a history column—every week!

I've researched and written for magazines, encyclopedias and websites, but this was going to be a whole new game. I'd never written a newspaper column before, but I'm a longtime fan of the likes of Molly Ivins, William Raspberry and George Will. Most of all, a fellow from Texas named Mike Kelley inspired me. I eagerly anticipated reading his hilarious, insightful columns in the *Austin*

American-Statesman when I lived there, and I hoped I could create some of that anticipation with my column.

Newspaper readers are a broad audience with diverse interests; many of them would never pick up a history book. If I wanted to entice such readers to this column, I would have to get them past the notion that history is about memorizing names and dates and show them how entertaining it can be. I had to make history come alive for readers, to make it as much fun for them as it is for me.

I wanted West Virginia's history to provide a window on corresponding national and international events and, whenever appropriate, I wanted to draw parallels with the present day. Although we differ from generations who went before us, we also have much in common with them. They, too, struggled with questions about education, gun control, immigration, religion, race, and how to interpret the Constitution.

I hoped to avoid parochialism and make this column something that even non-residents of dear old West-by-god might find entertaining and informative. Some weeks, it would explore major historical events. Other times, it would provide a glimpse into daily life of the past. Some stories would come from the time when the area was still part of Old Virginia; we got divorced but we kept the memories.

Weekly deadlines would preclude the depth of research I give to longer-range projects, but the column still had to be informative and accurate. There's enough misinformation out there; I don't need to contribute to it.

(That said, many of my columns are based on newspaper articles published before the American Society of Newspaper Editors, or ASNE, established the first codes of journalistic ethics in the United States in 1923. Before such codes became widely accepted reporters — usually known as "correspondents" — sometimes made up stories they thought sounded good and accepted others at face value without attempting to verify facts. Whenever I could find additional information to supplement what was in the original article I have done so, but that was not always possible.)

Finally, in determining what my column would be like, I knew humor would be part of the mix. I regard words not just as tools to work with but as toys to play with: NBC Radio once dubbed me the National Pun Champion after a string of victories in the annual O. Henry Pun-Off in Austin, Texas. Besides, history is mostly about human beings, and there's nothing funnier. I'm convinced we were created because monkeys proved insufficiently entertaining.

The column, titled "Once, Long Ago," debuted on the front page of the "Celebrations" section in the Sunday edition of the *Exponent Telegram*, March 8, 1998, with a story titled "Confederates raiders rampage on the Monongahela." Over the years it explored everything from military actions to Mother's Day. Every Halloween, I'd take a break from history to examine Appalachian folklore, like the legend of a headless ghost said to have once haunted the railroad cut behind where we lived when I was a boy.

Along the way, the columns won a Lifestyles excellence in journalism award and helped me earn a literary fellowship. My hope that they might appeal beyond the state's borders was fulfilled: a few of them were reprinted or quoted in the *Columbia* (Tennessee) *Daily Herald, Business Horizons* magazine, and *Haunted Palace: Danvers Asylum as Art and History* by Michael Ramseur (ARTSHIPpublishing, 2005), a book about a New England mental asylum. You can find some of my columns cited as sources on Wikipedia.

One reader told me that when she read my column she felt like I was sitting in her living room, telling her a story. If so, that's because my love of history began with my parents, Harold and Iona (Phillips) Swick, telling me stories about their lives in bygone times: skating down a creek to a one-room school; labor strikes; watching the appalling behavior of the crowd when victims of a serial killer were discovered.

My older brothers and sister—Howard, Clinton, Theron and Linda—fed my love of learning by telling me what they had studied in school and always challenged me to learn more, for which I am eternally grateful.

I certainly learned a great deal while researching these columns. Despite the popular image of West Virginia as a place filled with illiterate, moonshine-swilling, inbred hillbillies, it has, in fact, been home to a number of nationally and internationally known heroes and heroines, inventors, social reformers and writers—a surprising number considering its small size and population. Of course, it has also produced its share of twits and rapscallions. You'll find them all represented in these pages.

In places, I've added some information to clarify references to then-current news events. A few typos have been corrected, a couple of sentences rewritten for better clarity (Dang those short deadlines!), and references to upcoming local events deleted, but otherwise these stories are as they appeared in the *Exponent Telegram* with one notable exception: since the columns were going to appear in a newspaper I used the *AP Stylebook*, which calls for putting titles of books, movies and the like in quotation marks; when preparing this book I italicized those titles instead, as called for in *The Chicago Manual of Style*, to better denote longer works like a book from shorter ones such as articles. Also, for this book, I chose to italicize both the names of newspapers and the town in which they was published, e.g., *Buckhannon Delta*.

In some cases I learned additional information after a column was published, and I have appended that information. The original date of publication appears after each article's title. There are also a few stories included that have never been published before.

Researching and writing "Once, Long Ago" was a joy, and I am grateful to the staff of the *Exponent Telegram* for allowing me to share it with their readers for so many years.

But in the beginning, there was the lunch.

And it was good.

DAYS OF SLAVERY

CIVIL WAR AND AFTERMATH

STATEHOOD

THE SLAVE LUCY BAGBY'S UNFORTUNATE FOOTNOTE IN HISTORY

October 14, 2012

S ara Lucy Bagby Johnson, generally remembered simply as Lucy Bagby (Bagbe) became an unfortunate footnote in American history. She is believed to be the last runaway slave ever returned to the South under the Fugitive Slave Law. She was brought back to Wheeling after a few months freedom in Ohio.

Lucy was born around 1833 and sold in Richmond to William S. Goshorn of Wheeling, according to an online article from the Library of Virginia. In October 1860, she escaped and made her way to Cleveland where abolitionist sentiment was strong. She must have felt she'd reached the Promised Land, but national events conspired against her.

At first, she stayed with the family of W. E. Ambush, before finding employment with George A. Benedict's family, according to *North into Freedom: The Autobiography of John Malvin, Free Negro, 1795–1880* (The Press of Western Reserve University, 1966). The Library of Virginia article says she was a domestic servant for Republican Congressman-elect A. G. Riddle, but left for a similar position in the household of a jeweler, L. A. Benton.

On January 19, 1861, federal officers forcibly entered Benton's home and "carried away Lucy Bagby, a young mulatto servant," according to *Cleveland: The Making of a City*, by William Ganson Rose (Kent State University Press, 1950).

Her owner and his son had learned her whereabouts from a black woman in Cleveland, according to Wheeling's *Daily Intelligencer*, January 23, 1861, citing reports in the Cleveland newspapers.

Abolitionists hired Rufus Spalding as Lucy's attorney, and he secured a habeas corpus hearing. Probate Judge Daniel R. Tilden found no legal reason to release her but ruled that she could not be held in the local jail. A room was temporarily fitted out for her in the post office building.

Spalding went to Wheeling seeking information to help his client but found nothing. Lucy was taken from the post office to the jail until her hearing under United States District Judge Hiram V. Willson (or Wilson).

The day of her trial, a crowd assembled outside the post office building where the trial was to be held, and violence soon broke out. An unfortunate freeman of color, C. M. Richardson, a long-time Cleveland resident, was knocked to the ground by a blow to the head from a man who thought Richardson was there to free the defendant. Another black man named Munson was nearly clubbed, but Hon. Jabez M. Fitch, who was passing by, interceded.

Inside the courtroom, Ambush, with whom Lucy had first stayed in Cleveland, exchanged words with the younger Goshorn, and both drew pistols, according to Malvin's autobiography. Others in the room broke up the argument.

Abolitionists offered Goshorn twice Lucy's value to free her, but he refused. A few months earlier they might have done more to intercede, but by January 1861 four states had withdrawn from the Union. Many feared that any attempt to prevent enforcement of the Fugitive Slave Law would be seized on by Southern firebrands and cause more states to break away. Even the Republican *Cleveland Leader* advised forbearance in the interest of preserving the Union.

Goshorn, in thanking the people of Cleveland for the treatment he had received there, said, "It may be oil poured upon the waters of our nation's troubles ... The South had been looking for such a case as this."

Lucy was returned to Wheeling, placed in jail and severely punished. Freemen of color reportedly had intended to intercept the train that was taking her to Wheeling, but the engineer didn't stop.

If national events worked against Lucy in January 1861 they turned in her favor not long after. At some time after Federal troops occupied Wheeling in June she was freed and her owner imprisoned. The abolitionists of Cleveland held a Grand Jubilee for her on May 6, 1863.

She married a Union soldier, George Johnson, in Pittsburgh but returned to Cleveland late in her life, dying there in 1906.

TWO YOUNG SLAVES FLED LUMBERPORT FOR MANNINGTON AND A BETTER LIFE

October 7, 2001

An unknown number of runaway slaves traveled the shadowed paths of the "Underground Railroad" from safe house to safe house until they reached a free state or Canada. Many escapees found ways to freedom on their own. One account I've seen told of a man who had his friends pack him in a small crate and ship him to an abolitionist's address. The clandestine roads from servitude to freedom were usually long and dangerous, but sometimes the flight to liberty was much shorter.

A case in point involves two young boys who fled Harrison County into neighboring Marion where they found refuge from a cruel owner. R. Emmett Mockler related their story in *Footprints at the Foot of Buffalo: An Early History of Mannington, West Virginia* (WFY, Inc. 1985).

One day in 1862 or 1863, Loss Nay looked out from his place of business, known as the Old Furbee Mill. Two black boys he did not recognize were fishing near the dam on Mannington's Buffalo Creek. Through the afternoon, they sat there, happily pulling perch from the stream.

Nay noticed they carried with them a stuffed pillowcase and a package wrapped in a red bandanna. When the workday ended the boys were still fishing, so he stopped to speak with them. Nay discovered the lads, aged ten and twelve, had run off from neighboring Harrison County.

The area of what is now North Central West Virginia had few slaves compared with the Shenandoah, Greenbrier and Big Kanawha valleys, but Harrison County had perhaps the largest enslaved population in this region. One estimate, made by Nettie Southworth Herndon, in her 1926 West Virginia University Master's Thesis, "History of Clarksburg to 1860," estimated blacks accounted for about one-fourth of Clarksburg's population, which totaled 1,000, around the time the town was incorporated in 1849. Dorothy Davis's *History of Harrison County* (American Association of University Women, 1970) used the 1860 census to show 582 slaves and thirty-two freemen of color resided in the county just before the Civil War.

That population had just been reduced by two. The young fellows fishing on Buffalo Creek told Nay their owner, who had "a small plantation" near Lumberport, was a cruel and demanding man who instilled in all his slaves a fear of disobedience or error. Any mistake was punished with a leather "blacksnake" whip.

One of the boys had accidentally broken a knob on a bureau drawer. Their mother, fearing what punishment awaited the child when their owner returned, made the heartbreaking choice to send them away. She had heard that the residents of Mannington, approximately twenty miles north, were more sympathetic to members of her race than many other communities were, so she wrapped up their few belongings and sent them there.

Regardless of whether or not Mannington was more enlightened than its neighbors, Loss Nay was not a man who would send the boys back to an owner who beat them. He took them into his home and found work for them.

One boy remains nameless in Emmett Mockler's account, but the other was known as Dick. Slaves were not given surnames, but often took their former owners' last names upon emancipation. Mockler claimed that is how Dick wound up as Dick Rittenhouse, but it is entirely possible the lad found another source for his surname.

Dick continued in the employ of Loss Nay and became an efficient horse handler. His brother later found work in Clarksburg, but Dick stayed in Marion County. When the oil and gas fields opened there, he handled teams of heavy draft horses for W. D. Smith (later W. D. Smith and Son). He died in 1944 at the age of 93, a well-known and highly respected man, Mockler wrote.

How a Slave Named Jack Came to and Fled from Gauley Bridge

September 26, 2010

That the "peculiar institution" of slavery had many peculiari-
ties is an understatement. Images of slave auctions are often
employed in books and documentaries, but in point of fact, trans-
ferring ownership of human property was more often conducted
between individuals than at the auction block. At any time an enslaved individual might be informed he or she had been sold or
traded to a new owner in a different part of the state or a different
state altogether.

Case in point: A slave identified only as "Jack," since slaves
weren't given surnames, came to Gauley Bridge, Fayette County,
as payment for a debt. Such facts as are known in the matter were
discovered by W. T. Lawrence, a historian of that area, who found
them in the transcript of a trial held in 1880, nearly fifteen years
after slavery had been outlawed in the United States. Lawrence's
findings were reported in the *Charleston Gazette*, September 9, 1995.

In that trial, Elizabeth Sturgeon testified that before she was
married she had loaned money to a man in her home state of South
Carolina. Following her wedding, she called in the loan, and he
offered to transfer ownership of his slave Jack to her in place of

money, and she accepted. Her trial testimony states that she "kept him in my possession as my individual property," indicating he did not become part of her husband's holdings.

As noted above, trading slaves to repay debts was fairly common practice and added significantly to the insecurity of the enslaved, who never knew when they might be traded away from friends, family and perhaps the only home they had known.

Sturgeon did not state the amount of the loan for which she received Jack in payment, but he developed such a reputation as a good worker and a bright fellow that other slaveowners tried to buy him from her. She claimed that she once turned down $1,000 in gold from a Daniel Stalnaker of Lewisburg.

Having already refused such an impressive offer, she wasn't particularly receptive when Colonel James B. Muncy came to her in 1861 and offered to would give her land he owned near Gauley Bridge in exchange for Jack.

Muncy had been among the men appointed by the Virginia legislature on March 25, 1848, to collect "subscriptions" to pay for constructing the Weston and Gauley Bridge Turnpike, according to "Acts Passed at a General Assembly of the Commonwealth of Virginia," 1848. Said subscriptions were shares sold at $25 each to raise $30,000 for construction costs. By 1861, Muncy had been a toll-taker on the road for some years.

He was, he told Elizabeth Sturgeon, getting on in years and needed someone to work for him. He offered her a tract above Sand Branch and fifty acres on the Gauley's west side if she would just sign over the slave papers to make him Jack's owner.

No deal, she replied, but Muncy was a persistent man. Apparently, Jack had a very good reputation, because the toll-taker came to Sturgeon again the next day and the day after that. Following the third visit, she gave in and traded Jack to him.

Possibly, she accepted his offer in part due to family ties. A James B. Muncy married an M. A. Sturgeon in Fayette County on August 2, 1830 or '31, according to Fayette County marriage records, suggesting a link between the families. However, she also used the land for farming and to build houses on, which indicates she did all right by the exchange.

Muncy, as it turned out, didn't fare so well. When war came to the Kanawha Valley, Gauley Bridge changed hands three times. Somewhere in the chaos Jack disappeared. It was believed he escaped to Ohio and freedom. If so, it marked the first time in his life that he changed places of residence by his own free will.

THE 1860 PRESIDENTIAL ELECTION IN WESTERN VIRGINIA

November 2, 2008

H ang in there; just two more days and this two-year-long campaign will be over.

It's been a strange and interesting one, but it can't compete with what happened in 1860 when voters had four presidential candidates and the future of slavery and of the Union were the burning questions.

Candidates then didn't campaign directly because that was considered beneath the dignity of the office. Hoo-boy, how things have changed.

The 1860 election saw a sharply divided Democratic Party. In Virginia, one faction supported Governor Henry A. Wise as the Democratic nominee for president, while the other, under R. M. T. Hunter, declared it would support whomever the Democratic Party nominated during its national convention in Charleston, South Carolina, in April.

The Charleston convention split ideologically over slavery. The majority report from the Committee on Resolutions stated that Congress had no power to abolish slavery in the territories; neither did any territorial legislation have the power to abolish slavery, prevent the introduction of slaves, or to impair the right of property in slaves.

A minority report simply held that the Supreme Court should determine all rights of property in states or territories.

The minority report passed, presumably on the strength of many non-Southern Democrats. Virginia cast one vote for it and fourteen against; one Virginia delegate declared the slave trade to be "the noblest of philanthropy, and the most Christian civilizer in the world."

Outvoted, virtually every Southern state walked out of the convention, but Virginia did not. Ultimately unable to elect any candidate, the party agreed to meet in Baltimore in June to try again.

That meeting split into two conventions, with one nominating Stephen A. Douglas and the other choosing John C. Breckinridge.

A month earlier, the National Constitutional Union Party's convention had also been held in Baltimore. It named John Bell of Tennessee as its nominee for president and stated its creed as "the Constitution, the Union, and the Laws." Among the NCU delegates were two from Virginia, A. H. H. Stuart and Waitman T. Willey. The latter, born near Farmington, would become one of West Virginia's first two United States Senators.

Meanwhile, the fledgling Republican Party held its convention in Chicago that May. It was the smallest party in Western Virginia, and its disagreements with Eastern Virginia's Democrats had more to do with economics than ideology, even on the issue of slavery.

The region's Republicans had a vociferous spokesman in A. W. Campbell, editor of the Wheeling *Intelligencer*, who fought a losing battle to have the party hold its national convention in Wheeling instead of Chicago.

Campbell backed the expected Republican nominee, William H. Seward. Two delegates from Brook County were responsible for presenting Abraham Lincoln's name to the Virginia delegation for approval, according to "Brooke County Virginia and West Virginia Official Centennial Program."

To Campbell's surprise—and that of a good many other people—Lincoln won the nomination on the third ballot.

The national race was on between the four candidates. In Western Virginia, the *Intelligencer* was the only major paper to endorse Lincoln. The *Kanawha Valley Star* backed Breckinridge. In many counties, voters were forbidden to vote Republican and were intimidated with death threats.

When the votes were counted, John Bell carried Virginia with 74,555 to Breckinridge's 74,242. Waitman T. Willey could take much of the credit for Bell's victory. The Western counties—including Harrison, according to Dorothy Davis's *History of Harrison County* (American Association of University Women, 1970)—clearly preferred Breckinridge. Douglas got the Miss Congeniality award with 16,361. Lincoln garnered a whopping 1,962, virtually all of them in the Northern Panhandle.

Most of today's information comes from "The Presidential Election of 1860 in Western Virginia," by Robert Franklin Maddox, *West Virginia History*, Vol. XXV No. 3, April 1964.

To state the obvious, in less than 150 years—little more than a nanosecond in human history—we have gone from debating slavery to having an African American as a contender for the presidency. That is dramatic social change.

HARPERS FERRY SITE OF ATTEMPTED ARSENAL SEIZURES

November 7, 2004

L ocation, location, location. In the spring of 1861, Harpers Ferry was arguably America's most prime piece of real estate.

North and South, everybody in the recently divided nation wanted the little town at the junction of the Shenandoah and Potomac rivers, but not because of its inspiring vistas of steeply rising, wooded hills accented by high, rocky outcroppings. The town had other attractions.

For one thing, the Baltimore & Ohio ran through it, the direct rail link between the Union-loyal states of the eastern seaboard and their like-minded sister states west of the Ohio River.

Then there were the guns. Lots of guns.

Back when the nation was unified and young, a testy situation developed with France, which had been our ally during the glorious Revolution of '76. Yep, the on-again, off-again, love-hate relationship between our two countries goes back that far. To make matters worse, France was a major source for our military's small arms.

To insure our armed forces would indeed be armed, President George Washington authorized the establishment of national armories at Springfield, Mass., and Harpers Ferry, Virginia.

In 1859, radical abolitionist John Brown attempted to seize the Harpers Ferry arsenal to arm a slave rebellion. He was hanged for his trouble. At the time, Virginia's governor was Henry A. Wise

Two years later, ex-governor Wise no longer regarded seizing the national armory as a hanging offense. Matter of fact, he'd decided it was a pretty good idea and was conspiring with several other secessionists to do that very thing, according to *The Southern National Armory and The Civil War*, by Phillip R. Smith, Jr., *West Virginia History*, Vol. XXV, No. 1, October 1963.

All that stood in the secessionists' way was a small guard of troops under the command of Lieutenant Roger Jones.

First came a propaganda war, with the armory's superintendent, Alfred M. Barbour, trying to convince skilled laborers there to side with the newly formed Southern Confederacy. In return, Jones tried to win their hearts and minds for the Union. On April 18, his sentinels reported a Confederate force under Turner Ashby was within twenty minutes' march of the town, and the time for talking was over.

Jones had already removed large quantities of powder. With news of Ashby's approaching rebels, he ordered all buildings of the armory and its arsenal burned, then marched his troops safely out of town.

Soon after, Ashby arrived. Workers from the armory doused the fires in the workshops, but the arsenals were a total loss.

Even if the Confederates had captured them intact, they would have been disappointed. Wise and his co-conspirators had estimated up to 100,000 muzzle loaders could be seized for the Southern cause. Lieutenant Jones reported only 15,000 stands of arms were at the arsenal when he ordered it torched. The Confederates managed to salvage less than 4,300.

Many of the guns they'd hoped to find had already been sent to Dixie during the administration of President James Buchanan, the man who preceded Abraham Lincoln in the White House. Buchanan's secretary of war, John Buchanan Floyd, sympathized with the South and had quietly shipped arms there from northern arsenals. Floyd would become a Confederate general during the Civil War and seemed to go to any lengths to avoid capture by Federal troops, probably believing he would be hanged as a traitor for his pre-war arms re-distribution.

Machinery retrieved from the armory at Harpers Ferry was sent to Richmond. Some skilled workers chose to go with it and aid the Confederacy. Others departed for points north, where munitions factories were implementing mass-production techniques designed by Eli Whitney, creator of the cotton gin. Seems Southerners had cheated him out of his gin royalties, and he had gone north to find work. Ouch.

Over the next four years, Harpers Ferry switched hands more often than a belle at a square dance, and many residents left. The Southern National Armory lay in smoldering ruins, never to be rebuilt.

Confederate Raiders Rampage on the Monongahela

March 8, 1998

This article was the first "Once, Long Ago" column.

Every Sunday this column will explore the people and events that made history—or at least sparked conversation—in North Central West Virginia prior to 1900.

On April 30, 1863, the Wheeling *Daily Intelligencer* proclaimed that, based on the predictions of Nostradamus, "the date of the end of the world is satisfactorily fixed for the year 1889."

The folks in Harrison County figured the end was coming sooner; say, any minute.

In this case, the horsemen of the apocalypse were Confederate cavalry under General William E. Jones, and there were a lot more than four of them. Reports varied from 5,000–15,000 depending on the hysteria of the eyewitness.

Actually, "Grumble" Jones, who had succeeded Jeb Stuart as commander of the 1st Virginia Cavalry early in the war, had crossed the Blue Ridge on April 21 with 2,100 men or less, but they were raising Holy Ned along the Monongahela.

They swooped into Morgantown and helped themselves to all the shoes and boots they could carry out of the shops, along with any horses they could lay hands on, then rode out.

Immediately, curiosity-seekers from the countryside rode to town to see what had happened. They found themselves caught in a replay when the Rebels returned and captured all the newly arrived mounts.

Jones crossed over Buffalo Creek to Barrackville in Marion County, prompting the bank at Waynesburg to burn $60,000 in cash.

Around 7 a.m. on the wet morning of April 29, the Rebels rode out of the fog to attack a detachment at Fairmont.

Union troops from West Virginia and New York, along with local militia, made a surprisingly strong stand, with men and women of the town taking up arms to fight for both sides.

By early afternoon the small garrison had surrendered, and the victors gleefully burned the library of Governor Francis H. Pierpont for his "disloyalty to Virginia."

They poured black powder into the cylindrical iron towers supporting an iron railroad bridge that had cost $486,333 to build and blew it into nearly as many pieces.

Next stop, Bridgeport, where the graybacks gathered up some unfortunate Union cavalry, wrecked the railroad, and according to one account, captured a locomotive.

All along the way they were seizing every horse or mule they could lay hands on, reportedly 500 in Marion County alone.

Ironically, most of the liberated livestock belonged to local "secesh," citizens in sympathy with the Southern cause.

Unionists had hidden their horses, knowing what was coming. Secessionists assumed their sympathies would protect them, but

Jones's men believed that was all the more reason to contribute to the cause.

Abraham Lincoln had proclaimed April 30 a day of "national humiliation and prayer."

His soldiers in Clarksburg were feeling pretty humiliated, and their commander Brigadier General Benjamin S. Roberts was praying up a storm.

A second and larger Confederate force under General John D. Imboden had caused Roberts to fall back all the way from Beverly to quiver under the protection of guns atop Pinnickinnick and Criss's (Lowndes) Hill.

Some of the more cynical of Roberts's subordinates expected orders to fall back to Wheeling, if not Cleveland.

Lieutenant Colonel John J. Polsley of Ohio thought Roberts "a perfect antiquated fizzle" and thought if he remained in command there wouldn't be enough property or population left to make this part of West Virginia worth holding.

Fortunately, Roberts wasn't along when Lot Bowen led 62 men of the 3rd West Virginia Cavalry reconnoitering between Clarksburg and Shinnston that day.

At Lambert's Run, the bluecoats met 300 of Jones's raiders. Instead of withdrawing, Bowen's men drew sabers and charged.

"Every gun of both commands was emptied," according to reports, without spilling enough blood to fill a teacup.

The raiders raced back toward Shinnston, their attackers in hot pursuit. At Maulsby's Bridge (near Gypsy), a second skirmish started. The 3rd West Virginia lost one private killed and two wounded and returned triumphantly to Clarksburg with thirteen prisoners—and nineteen horses that had just joined the United States Cavalry.

Next day, another affair took place (near where Lost Creek now stands), and the great raid was over in Harrison County.

Jones linked up with Imboden, but they decided Clarksburg was too tough a nut to crack. Jones burned 150,000 barrels of oil in Wirt County, and the raiders went home richer by over $100,000 in goods and livestock.

In the wake of the Jones-Imboden Raid efforts stepped up against local secesh, and the "violent rebel" sisters Lizzie and Maggie Copeland of Bridgeport were shipped off to jail in Wheeling.

Within days, Union officers felt so safe, some were talking of sending for their wives, but no accommodations were available in Bridgeport.

A West Virginia Regiment Rose to Glory on America's Bloodiest Day

September 17, 2000

T he morning of September 17, 1862, started off with the lads of the 7th Virginia Infantry, Union Army Volunteers, standing in the cold water of Antietam Creek, waiting for the order to advance. The Federal Army of the Potomac and the Confederate Army of Northern Virginia were slaughtering each other among the low, rolling hills outside Sharpsburg, Md. Before sunset, 22,000 Americans would lie dead and wounded, more than on any other day in the nation's history.

The order to advance came. The 7th Virginia—renamed 7th West Virgina when the western counties became a state—moved forward, along with the rest of General Nathan Kimball's brigade, the 14th Indiana, 8th Ohio, and the green troops of the 132nd Pennsylvania.

Sharpshooters plunked at them from farm buildings. A cannon-ball landed among some beehives, sending the 132nd Pennsylvania scattering for cover from angry bees and providing the rest of the brigade their only laugh of the morning.

The rolling hills of Antietam concealed opposing forces from each other until battlelines topped ridge crests 50–100 yards from the muzzles of waiting muskets. Twice, Union brigades crested a ridge above Confederates standing behind piles of fence rails in a sunken wagon road; twice, the Federals stumbled back in disarray, the bodies of their comrades covering the slope behind them like a blue blanket.

Kimball's Brigade was called up. With the 14th Ind. on the right, 8th Ohio beside it, 7th Virginia beyond them, and the 132nd Pennsylvania on the left flank, the brigade crested the hill. A wall of fire greeted them, but unlike the previous brigades, they did not retreat. Instead, they lay on the downslope, rolling on their sides to load their muskets. Bullets flew in such profusion the grasses on the hilltop never stopped waving. Three times the regiment's colors were shot down.

The commander of the 7th Virginia was granite-faced, thick-bearded Colonel Joseph Snider of Morgantown. A delegate to the statehood convention at Wheeling, he was the only member to vote against continuing slavery in the new state, according to Samuel T. Wiley's *History of Monongalia County* (Preston Publishing Co., 1883). Second in command was Lieutenant Colonel Jonathan Lockwood, a fiery, fifty-four year old farmer from Moundsville.

Both officers had their horses shot from under them. Adding insult to injury, Lockwood's horse was later stolen while it was recuperating at a nearby farm.

A white flag waved among the rebels, and the 7th Virginia held their fire; then, seeing the Confederates attempting to flank them, extended their line along with the 132nd Pennsylvania and refused the attempt. A charge against the brigade's center was also repelled, according to Kimball's official report.

The 7th was out of ammunition, 145 of its men killed or wounded, when they saw the green and gold flag of Ireland and the Stars and Stripes advancing toward them through the cornfields. The Irish Brigade from New York relieved them, and they fell back to resupply. A Union charge captured the sunken road, where blood had turned the dust to mud. Ever after, it was called Bloody Lane.

That day, Kimball's Brigade earned a nickname: The Gibraltar Brigade, so called because they stood like the Rock of Gibraltar. The 7th Virginia (7th West Virginia) went on to glory and death at Fredericksburg, Gettysburg, and other fields. Maj. Theodore F. Lang, in *Loyal West Virginia* (The Deutsch Publishing Co., 1895), called them "the banner regiment that served from the State," fighting in a greater number of large battles and losing more men than any other West Virginia regiment. Ironically, many of its soldiers were recruited from Pennsylvania and Ohio because Western Virginia couldn't get enough volunteers.

Among the 7th's wounded at Antietam was my own great-grandfather, Joseph Phillips of Morgantown (later of Wirt County). Shot through the neck and shoulder, he was so disfigured when he arrived home, his wife didn't recognize him and barred the door to keep him out.

"The 7th West Virginia Volunteer Infantry 1861-1865," a Master's Thesis by Katherine O' Brien, is on file at Wise Library, West Virginia University.

A West Virginian Recorded the 'Rebel Yell' for Posterity

October 21, 2007

I magine standing shoulder-to-shoulder with several hundred of your closest friends. Thousands of muskets crackle continuously, like fire sweeping through dry brush, punctuated by deep booms from smoothbore artillery and sharp cracks of rifled guns. Then, rising even above this cacophony comes a weird, unearthly cry as if hell is disgorging all its demons.

That was the experience of Union soldiers hearing the notorious "rebel yell" from thousands of Southern throats as Confederates made or received a charge.

Some historians say the haunting cry was a spontaneous expression to release tension and fear in combat. Others have called it nineteenth century "psy ops," a psychological warfare weapon intended to instill fear in the enemy.

Harvie Drew, late of the 9th Virginia Cavalry, Confederate, described it as beginning with a short, low WHO, followed by a long, high WHO-EY WHO-EY.

After the war was over, no one seemed able to replicate it, even at veteran reunions. Many said it was born of a situation that couldn't be duplicated in peacetime.

The United Daughters of the Confederacy—realizing the old veterans were disappearing like passenger pigeons—set out in 1929 to find someone who could replicate it for a recording. Mrs. Charles Reed of West Virginia was charged with finding that someone. She had about as much luck as Diogenes did searching for an honest man.

Enter Metro-Goldwyn-Mayer movie studio. Five years after Mrs. Reed began her fruitless search, a movie producer decided he needed to find an old rebel whom he could record giving the cry, in order to lend authenticity to a Civil War film.

The desire for such authenticity is a trifle bizarre, considering the film was *Operator 13*, which had blonde-haired, blue-eyed Marion Davies disguising herself as a black laundress in order to carry out a spying mission for the Union. The film also starred Gary Cooper and featured Hattie McDaniel in an uncredited role as Annie, a cook.

The studio found veteran Sampson Sanders Simmons, 90 years old and living in California, and recorded his "authentic" rebel yell. A copy was given to the UDC.

He originally hailed from what is now Cabell County, West Virginia, where he j'ined up with the Cabell County Border Rangers. That group became Company E, 8th Virginia Cavalry, Confederate, according to "West Virginia Man Recorded Famed Rebel Yell," by Terry Lowry, which appeared in *Images of the Civil War in West Virginia* (Quarrier Press, 2000), a book Lowry authored with Stan Cohen.

Simmons saw combat, evidenced by the fact he was wounded at Morristown, Tennessee, in 1863. Captured at Moorefield, West Virginia, August 7, 1864, he ended the war as a prisoner at Camp Chase, Ohio.

Was the yell he recorded the real McCoy? Probably not. As noted above, entire groups of veterans failed to recreate the sound in peacetime, and their throats were younger than Simmons' was when MGM found him.

W. A. Love, an old soldier from Columbus, Miss., wrote in *Confederate Veteran*, Vol. XXXV, December 1927, "It is impossible to describe the sound."

He compared one person giving the yell to acorns dropping individually onto a roof, versus "when a brisk wind arose they fell in showers, making a sound indescribable. So with the rebel yell of thousands of earnest and excited men."

Love said the yell derived from fox hunting cries, which before the war had already morphed into an excited yell used by any Southern hunter. He claimed Confederates used it whenever they became excited, even away from the battlefield.

Alexander Hunter of Washington, D.C., disagreed in *Confederate Veteran*, Vol. XXI, May 1913. He said the cry in battle was different. He had joined in it himself during combat, but only when he was wounded at Thoroughfare Gap did he remain silent and realize the full effect as his enemy would have, with thousands of voices baying.

Simmons' recorded version may not be quite accurate, but it is the closest thing we have.

ABRAHAM LINCOLN WRESTLES WITH WEST VIRGINIA STATEHOOD

June 2, 2013

If the final days before Christmas 1862 passed slowly for children, time crawled for West Virginians waiting for Abraham Lincoln to sign the bill admitting their state to the Union. The controversial measure had passed the United States Senate in July and the House of Representatives on December 10.

On December 18, Francis Pierpont, governor of the Restored Government of Virginia, telegraphed Lincoln that a veto "will be death to our cause." Two days later, Pierpont wired, "Great feeling exists … in reference to your delay in signing the bill for the new state."

Lincoln had a few other things on his mind. On December 13, a futile, lopsided slaughter at Fredericksburg, Virginia, had cost 12,600 Federal casualties. On December 20, his secretary of the treasury and his secretary of state both tendered their resignations — which the president refused to accept.

His Emancipation Proclamation, one of the most controversial actions of his administration, was going into effect on January 1. Recognizing West Virginia as a state would be just as controversial.

Finally, on December 23, Lincoln gave the statehood bill to one of his secretaries, John Nicolay, with a note requesting Nicolay "please read over this & tell me what is in it."

The same day, he asked his cabinet members for their opinions on two questions: Was the statehood bill constitutional and was it expedient? The latter related to whether admitting the state would help or hinder efforts to bring Virginia and others of the rebelling states back into their "natural relationship" with the Union.

Attorney General Edward Bates had written to the government in Wheeling in August 1861, calling the creation of a new state a "new and hazardous experiment." He maintained it was "a mere abuse ... hardly valid under the flimsy forms of law."

The New York Times noted Bates' opposition on December 27 and predicted Lincoln would veto the measure. On December 30, the newspaper reported the cabinet members had not yet replied to the president and again predicted, "the bill will most likely be vetoed."

On the last day of the year, the *Times* wrote, "The Cabinet met to-day two hours earlier than usual, and was principally occupied in discussing the admission of West Virginia." Cabinet members' opinions "though materially differing in regard to the probable results of the admission of the new State, were nearly unanimous in opposition."

The *Times* reported the cabinet felt that if Virginia was still a state of the Union, then division was illegal and approving West Virginia statehood "was a virtual acknowledgment of the legality of secession."

Actually, the cabinet split fifty-fifty. Secretary of State William H. Seward maintained, "The first duty of the United States is protection to loyalty wherever it is found."

As the last sands of 1862 trickled out of the hourglass and reports of another bloody battle—along Stones River near Murfreesboro, Tennessee—came in, Lincoln signed the statehood bill, contingent upon West Virginians amending their constitution to permit emancipation of slaves.

In an opinion explaining his decision he wrote, "We can scarcely dispense with the aid of West-Virginia in this struggle; much less can we afford to have her against us … It is said that the admission of West-Virginia is secession, and tolerated only because it is our secession. Well, if we call it by that name, there is still difference enough between secession against the constitution, and secession in favor of the constitution."

The *Times* wasted little ink in reporting its predictions had been wrong, barely mentioning that Lincoln had signed the bill.

On April 20, 1863, after the state had amended its constitution in regard to slavery, Lincoln gave his final approval. West Virginia would become the 35th star in the flag on June 20.

Today's information comes from *The Collected Works of Abraham Lincoln*, Roy P. Basler, editor (The Abraham Lincoln Association, 1953), and *The New York Times*.

DECIDING ON THE NEW STATE'S BOUNDARIES AND CONSTITUTION

April 7, 2013

O n May 23, 1861, the majority of Virginia's voters decreed the state would leave the Union; however, west of the mountains an "I won't leave and you can't make me" attitude coalesced into a convention in Wheeling that declared the Richmond government void. The Restored Government of Virginia, also called the Reorganized Government, was established at Wheeling to replace it.

That government gave its blessing to forming a new state called Kanawha out of "certain territories" of Virginia, and voters approved the proposal on October 24. Nearly 18,500 voted in favor versus less than 800 voting against, a turnout that can charitably be called skimpy since the 1860 census found a white population of nearly 430,000 in the west.

Nonetheless, the people had spoken, and what they said was, "Form a new state but nix the name Kanawha." There was already a county named Kanawha, and some felt that might lead to confusion. Others strongly identified their region with the long-used name Western Virginia. Some said Kanawha was too hard to spell.

When a convention to write a constitution convened in November 1861, the names Allegheny, Augusta, New Virginia, and one or two other options were discussed before adopting West Virginia, which previously had been rejected when Chapman Stuart of Doddridge County first suggested it. The full debate is in "What's In A Name?" at wvculture.org.

Determining the boundaries of the new state was another can of nightcrawlers. One proposal encompassed everything from Alexandria County (now Arlington County) across the Potomac from the nation's capital all the way to the Tennessee border. Some thought the Alleghenies made a good eastern boundary, while others favored extending that eastward to include the Blue Ridge Mountains and the Shenandoah Valley, with the Big Kanawha River as the southern boundary.

Ultimately, a committee recommended 39 counties that essentially included most of what is now West Virginia. The eastern panhandle and Greenbrier Valley weren't included, but provisions were made to allow those areas to vote on which Virginia they wanted to be part of.

Pro-Union sentiment in most counties that now comprise the eastern panhandle was tepid at best, but the Baltimore & Ohio ran through there. That rail line was the economic lifeblood of the northern section of the proposed new state and a military necessity for the Union; it could not be ceded to Virginia. When the affected counties voted to join West Virginia, there were charges of military intimidation to control the voting, especially in Berkeley and Jefferson counties, but all were appended, and the B&O with them.

In the new constitution, Article 1 declared, "The state of West Virginia is, and shall remain, one of the United States of America." That sentence has never changed.

The constitution provided for free schools. All property, real and personal, would be taxed in proportion to its value—a rejection of Virginia's system that put a much lower tax on slaves than on other property.

Despite some efforts to incorporate gradual emancipation, slavery remained in place; however, no "person of color, slave or free" could enter the state for permanent residence. Apparently, descendants of slaves within the state's boundaries at the time of statehood were going to be the sole source for propagating the peculiar institution.

All of that was rendered moot when the United States Senate balked at admitting a slave state. Waitman T. Willey, our senator from Morgantown, proposed an amendment providing for gradual emancipation of slaves under the age of twenty-five; children born to slaves after July 4, 1863, would be free from birth. The status of slaves older than twenty-five remained unchanged.

Voters approved the new constitution with Willey's amendment, but before the Civil War was over a new amendment abolished slavery in the state. The 13th Amendment to the United States Constitution abolished it nationwide.

Francis H. Pierpont, the 'Father of West Virginia'

June 20, 2010

T his year Father's Day and West Virginia Day fall on the same day. It seems an appropriate time to look at the life of Francis Harrison Pierpont, often called the "Father of West Virginia."

Ironically, he initially did not favor creation of a new state, recognizing that doing so without permission of the mother state would be at odds with Article IV, Section 3 of the United States Constitution. He preferred restoring all of Virginia to the Union but came to see that was not going to happen.

He was born January 25, 1814, near Morgantown, a community founded by his great-grandfather, Colonel Zackquill Morgan. The family moved to a Marion County farm while Francis was still a babe, then moved into Middletown (Fairmont) when he was 13, where his father operated a tannery.

Francis graduated from Allegheny College in Pennsylvania and taught school for a time in Harrison County while studying law. In 1842, he was admitted to the Marion County bar.

Six years later, the Baltimore and Ohio Railroad hired him as a right-of-way lawyer in Marion and Taylor Counties, the beginning of a relationship between Pierpont and the railroad that would be significant during the Civil War.

In the 1850s, when coal was beginning its rise in importance as a fuel, he started a mine on his property and went into partnership with James Otis Watson to form the American Coal Company, forerunner of Consolidation Coal, according to the Marion County Web site. Their partnership dissolved after the Civil War due to political tensions: Pierpont was Republican, Watson a Democrat.

When Virginia seceded from the Union, Pierpont ardently opposed that secession but also worked with other conservatives to cool the fervor for creating a new, Union-loyal state west of the Alleghenies. On June 20, 1861, representatives at the pro-Union convention at Wheeling unanimously elected him governor of the Restored Government of Virginia.

Over the next four years, his efforts to raise funds and troops and protect the B&O Railroad in the state often brought him into contact with President Abraham Lincoln.

Union-loyal states responded to the call for volunteers to suppress the Southern rebellion. They responded so enthusiastically that the War Department had to issue an order to all governors to cease raising regiments, as the government couldn't afford to equip any more.

Pierpont, concerned about guerrilla activity, the proximity of Confederate Virginia, and the need to protect the important B&O rail line appealed to Lincoln for an exemption from the War Department's order, according to the Francis Harrison Pierpont Papers, a transcription of which appeared in *West Virginia History: A Journal of Regional Studies*, Vol.1, No.1 (2007).

Lincoln directed him to complete the regiments that were partly raised, and the president would order them to be mustered in.

Lincoln and members of his cabinet had the same qualms about the constitutionality of creating a new state out of Virginia that Pierpont had felt earlier. Things had changed, however, and the governor worked hard to get West Virginia admitted to the Union, which occurred two years to the day after he had been named Governor of the Restored State of Virginia.

Arthur I. Boreman became West Virginia's governor, and Pierpont moved the capital of the Restored Government to Alexandria, Virginia, an later to Richmond. Pierpont was replaced by a military government in 1868.

Afterward, he served a term in the state legislature. Apart from his work in establishing the state, perhaps his greatest legacy was helping to found the West Virginia Historical Society.

He died at the home of his daughter in Pittsburgh, March 24, 1999. In April 1910, his granddaughter Frances Pierpont Siviter unveiled a marble statue of him in Statuary Hall in the United States Capitol building.

Unless otherwise noted, today's information comes from the entry on Pierpont by Philip Sturm of Ohio Valley University, in *The West Virginia Encyclopedia*, edited by Ken Sullivan (West Virginia Humanities Council, 2006).

Governor A. I. Boreman Guided West Virginia's First Years

July 28, 2013

The first governor of the newly minted state of West Virginia faced a unique situation: chief executive of the only state ever admitted to the Union during wartime in which fighting between armies and guerrilla wars between neighbors was still playing out.

Under such circumstances, a flamboyant, hard-charging leader — perhaps a war veteran — might seem the most likely choice for governor. Instead, West Virginians elected Arthur I. Boreman.

A newspaper of the time, quoted in John G. Morgan's *West Virginia Governors 1863–1980* (Charleston Newspapers, 1980), described him as, "not an especial genius, or a man of par excellence rhetoric, or a man of any show in particular, but a man of good, evenly-balanced parts, a thorough West Virginian, earnest, true and upright."

In times of crisis, a calm, balanced leader is often preferable to a dynamic one.

Arthur I. Boreman — the "I" stood for Ingraham or Ingram, depending on who was spelling it — was born July 24, 1823, in Waynesburg, Pennsylvania , and brought to Middlebourne in

Tyler County while very young, according to Bernard. L. Allen, *The West Virginia Encyclopedia*, edited by Ken Sullivan (West Virginia Humanities Council, 2006).

He studied law under his brother and brother-in-law and hung out his shingle in Parkersburg soon after being admitted to the bar in 1845. Ten years later, he became a Whig delegate to Virginia's General Assembly, a position he still held at the time of secession in April 1861. He'd traveled widely speaking against secession, which he said nearly got him lynched in Charleston.

Shortly after secession, he went to Cincinnati to appeal for United States military protection of Parkersburg's Unionists. He was elected president of the Second Wheeling Convention—the one that declared Virginia's previous government void, installed the Reorganized Government with Francis Pierpont as its governor, and approved the West's separation from Eastern Virginia.

He was elected as a circuit judge in October 1861. At the Constitutional Union Party's convention in Parkersburg May 6–7, 1863, he became one of the party's four nominees for the state's first gubernatorial election. In the first round he came in a distant third behind future senator Peter Van Winkle, but none of the four candidates got a majority. In the second round of voting, Boreman emerged as the clear winner.

He also won the general election—not surprising, since he was unopposed—and took the oath of office on June 20. In his inaugural address he pledged to "do everything within my power" to advance the state's agricultural, mining, manufacturing and commercial interests and to assist in establishing an education system for all children within the state.

His first message to the legislature called for free schools and the establishment of a superintendent of public works to oversee collections on toll roads and maintenance of highways—the latter being an issue that would bedevil a long line of his successors. West Virginia University was established during his tenure.

He called for twelve to fifteen armed men to organize in every neighborhood to oppose Confederate guerrillas and raiders. He reiterated that call on December 23, 1864, as a means of hunting down outlaws who were "roaming the state, stealing, robbing and murdering." During and shortly after the war he sometimes appealed for federal troops to put down anti-Union activity in Glenville, Ceredo and elsewhere.

His most controversial action was securing passage of a law in February 1865 that effectively disenfranchised any citizens who could not prove past and present loyalty to the Union.

Boreman was elected to three terms as governor, more than any of his successors. He left office seven days early in 1869 to serve a single term as a United States Senator.

He and Laurane Tanner Bullock, a war widow he'd married in 1864, settled in Parkersburg for the rest of their lives. At the time of his death on April 19, 1896, he was in his eighth year as a circuit judge.

CRIME

POLITICS

AND OTHER DISASTERS

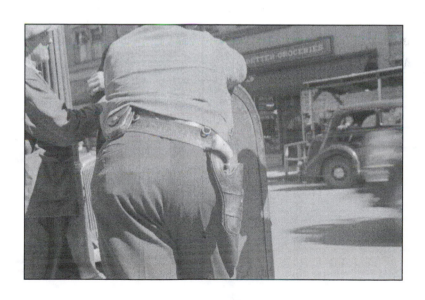

Bad Behavior Brought Reactions in Volcano and Elkins

July 1, 2007

To paraphrase Winston Churchill, there are some things up with which we will not put. As a case in point — two cases actually — consider community response to bad behavior in Volcano and Elkins.

The editor of *The Volcano Lubricator* was about to erupt. Certain individuals were showing disrespect during worship services in the town, and by jingo, he'd had enough of it.

"We have been informed that two young bucks, named Ord and Lee, amused themselves on Sunday night last at the M. E. Church by whispering, much to the annoyance of the clergyman and congregation and only refrained when publicly repremanded (sic) by the Rev. Wayman," the paper announced on October 7, 1873.

That wasn't all that was spoiling religious services in the oil town.

"We also, while we are on this theme, wish to notify our young gentlemen (?) who take prostitutes to church and stand in the porch while the soiled doves walk in, that we shall in future give them the benefit of our columns (i.e., the editor was going to start naming names) so they might just as well walk in with there (sic) women. We don't want to do this, but 'you must not go up the chimney if you do not want to get covered with soot.'"

The *Volcano Lubricator* (my all-time favorite name for a newspaper) was also seeking the identity of a young woman "who took occasion to advertise herself at the same church on Sunday last; and we are sure to get it, and when we do we will make the fur fly."

One-hundred-thirty-four years ago, most people in a small town had some connection to each other, and the prospect of public humiliation to self and family was a barrier to bad behavior. In the anonymity of today's society, we seem to have lost any sense of shame.

While the town of Volcano may have depended on its splendidly named newspaper to effect change, a group of ladies in Elkins decided to take matters into their own hands with a social problem thirty years later.

An *Elkins News* story was repeated in Fairmont's *Free Press*, October 22, 1903, under the headline "The Loafing Evil at Elkins."

"So much severe criticism has been hurled from time immemorial at the more or less beautiful ladies of Elkins who congregate at the depot when the evening trains are due, and crowd the lobby at the postoffice (sic) while the evening mails are being distributed, that it has come to be felt as a reflection upon the sex by many who only visit either place under the greatest necessity," according the newspaper.

While this may appear to be a complaint about groups of soiled doves looking for a nest for the night, so to speak, other information in the article implies they were simply women of the town whose presence among so many men made crowding worse and was not considered ladylike.

The women responded by holding up a mirror to male behavior.

They pointed out that "crowds of young men who congregate on the steps of the Elkins National Bank and the corner adjacent and smoke cigarettes, eat peanuts and make remarks about ladies that pass are as objectionable to respectable ladies as the crowds at the depot and post office are to business men."

According to "one of the conspirators" who claimed to "have no sympathy with those who needlessly crowd the depot platform and post office and finds it as objectionable and inconvenient as the business men (do)," a scheme was afoot take back the bank corner.

The women congregating at the depot and post office were going to move their meeting place to the aforementioned street corner and give the loafers a taste of their own medicine, "leaving out the rough language, coarse jokes, cigarettes and peanuts."

They didn't expect to reform the miscreants, but hoped to get a break from their behavior "while the weather remains pleasant enough for ladies to be on the streets after work hours."

A Camera Led to Murder on a Sunday Afternoon

May 16, 2004

In the Gay Nineties, advances in technology made cameras lighter, and cumbersome photographic plates gave way to more manageable film.

George Eastman gave away cameras to encourage people to buy his film, which worked so well he was soon in the business of manufacturing and selling cameras under the name brand Kodak.

People were snapping pictures everywhere, including West Virginia, where a young man from Upshur County got into the hobby. It cost his life.

The Buckhannon Delta of June 29, 1899, angrily reported the details based on the account of an eyewitness whom the newspaper did not identify except to say he was "one of Clarkburg's most reliable and prominent business men, whose character is above reproach."

According to this account, a youthful fellow named Edward A. Young from Buckhannon was visiting Clarksburg. On Sunday afternoon, June 25, he attended a ball game here with friends and took his Kodak along.

While he was happily snapping pictures, a crowd of rowdies taunted him. One reprobate in particular, last name of McClung, kept insulting Young and using "dirty slang" to provoke a fight.

What put a bee in McClung's bonnet is anybody's guess. Maybe Young, the son of a prominent businessman in Buckhannon, was too well dressed to suit him. Maybe he was just bored with the game and figured a fight would be more interesting. Maybe he was jealous of Young's camera.

When Young ignored his taunts, McClung walked up to him and "deliberately kicked the Kodak out of his hand," according to the *Delta*.

That got Young's attention. He decked the bully. Immediately two or three of McClung's friends joined in the fracas, but Young managed to hold his own until the entire group of toughs swarmed him. Recognizing the greater part of valor, he ran for the river, the mob howling after him.

A police office named Waldo joined the pursuit, apparently thinking Young was guilty of some legal violation. When the Buckhannon youth jumped into the West Fork and swam toward the far shore, officer Waldo reportedly told Valley Boughner, one of the toughs in the crowd, to shoot him.

Whipping out his .32 caliber, Boughner fired. The third shot passed through Young near the heart. He died almost instantly.

The *Delta* decried the shooting as "A crime without parallel in the history of the State of West Virginia. An infamous bloody crime that will blotch the pages in the history of Clarksburg so indelibly that ages will not erase it."

This righteous anger arose not only from the crime, but the way newspapers had reported it in Clarksburg, Cincinnati and Pittsburgh, depicting Young as "a tramp and from a low family," according to the *Delta*.

Young's body was brought home to his parents' house on Kanawha Street for services. Spring turned to summer, the leaves of autumn fell, and in the bleak month of January, his killer came to trial.

It was an ugly affair, according to the account in the *Delta*, January 18, 1900. The paper claimed Boughner's defense attorney "injured his own side of the case by his disgraceful, unbecoming and personal behavior toward the prosecution, and was called down several times by his collegue (sic)."

The prosecuting attorney, a Maj. Moore, persisted, with assistance from attorney Miller Snyder. The jury found the defendant guilty of second-degree murder. Only then did Boughner, himself a young man, seem to realize the gravity of his situation, according to the *Delta*: "(S)eemingly the words chilled every drop of blood in his veins."

Boughner got seven years in the penitentiary. Policeman Waldo was to face trial in the next term of the court. What the outcome of that trial was, I cannot say, but I have been told that after Boughner was released from prison he met an early death under suspicious circumstances.

LINCOLN COUNTY FARM WIVES FORMED FRAUD RING

September 10, 2006

O h, my. Oh, dearie me. Another American icon shattered, it's shiny particles tinkling as they scatter across the pavement.

If you can't trust a farmer's wife, whom can you trust? I mean, these are the women who made motherhood and apple pie synonymous with America. Everybody trusts them — well, except for certain blind mice.

Imagine then, the seismic shock rippling out of Southern West Virginia when a whole group of the wholesome ones were arrested for fraud.

Send the children out of the room while we explore this sordid bit of history. Let them hold onto whatever innocence they can in our jaded age.

The disheartening facts leapt from the pages of *The Charleston Mail*, August 3, 1914.

"The story of how a number of West Virginia women, the wives of farmers and mountaineers, conceived a scheme and 'put it over' on one of the largest manufacturing concerns in the United States is recalled by the arrest of Lena King by the Federal authorities at Lexington, Kentucky," the *Mail* began its squalid tale.

"Lena King, along with six or seven other women living in Lincoln county, was indicted by the federal grand jury at Huntington last April on a charge of using the United States mails to defraud."

Lincoln County? They added insult to injury by operating from a place named for old Honest Abe himself? I may never be able to eat apple pie again.

And they used the United States mails to carry out their nefarious scheme. Oh, dissimulation and duplicity, was there no depth to which these pie-baking Bonnie Parkers would sink?

"It is said the defendants defrauded the Larkin Company, soap manufacturers of Buffalo, New York , of thousands of dollars by buying goods of the firm and never paying for them," the *Mail* continued.

"Their scheme was to fill out an order blank for the quantity of goods wanted and then forge the name of a well-known local merchant or business firm in a space allotted for the endorser's signature on the margin of the order blank. This gave the impression that the merchant or firm guaranteed the goods would be paid for in due time, and the Larkin Company failed to scent the deception."

Perhaps the cagey criminals ordered scented soaps to camouflage the stench of their deception.

"As a result, thousand of dollars worth of goods were shipped to Lincoln County on accounts that had absolutely no guarantee.

"After receiving one shipment, some of the women, it is alleged, would assume a fictitious name and send in an order for delivery at a nearby town, knowing the freight agent would detect the fraud were they to call for freight under both their real and assumed names.

"The Larkin Company finally learned that fraud was being practiced, and sent one of its attorneys to Huntington to confer with Mr. Barnhart (District Attorney William G. Barnhart) while the April term of court was in progress. The indictments followed. Papers were served on all the women except Lena King, who had previously left for Kentucky."

How were these felonious females able to dupe a major corporation long enough to steal thousands of dollars worth of a low-priced product? The answer lay in the Larkin Company's own marketing strategy.

Founded in 1875 by John Durrant Larkin in Buffalo, the soap company incorporated in 1892. His brother-in-law Elbert "Bert" G. Hubbard pioneered mail-order merchandising, offering premiums and bonuses in order to eliminate its sales force, according to a history of Buffalo at freenet.buffalo.edu. These premiums ranged from pottery to chautauqua desks.

By 1910, the Larkin Company was receiving nearly 10,000 requests a year. A scam could easily slip in unnoticed.

The record at hand leaves lingering questions. In obtaining the soap in this manner, were the defendants working a money-laundering scheme? Did they try to soft-soap the judge at trial? Were they convicted or did they get off clean?

We'll probably never know.

Train Robbery in Doddridge Country Led to Long Chase

January 27, 2013

O n October 8, 1915, at Central Station, Doddridge County, a band of robbers hit Baltimore & Ohio passenger train No. 1. It was the first train robbery in northern West Virginia, according to Chapter 500 of Charles Brinkman's "The History of Taylor County," as originally published in the *Grafton Sentinel*.

Whether or not that was the case I can't say, but the holdup sparked a manhunt that covered much of the United States. As with most sensational crimes, sources disagree about details, but it was certainly one of the most famous — or infamous — crimes ever committed in the Mountain State.

The leader of the gang was either Charles Jefferson Harrison (aka Charles John Harrison) or Henry Grady Webb. *The New York Times*, December 23, 1916, claimed Harrison's criminal career "for a quarter of a century has been the dread of express companies and the postal authorities … in many respects one of the most remarkable in the criminal history of the country."

Allegedly, he robbed the star mail route in Alabama in 1891 before taking up train robbery as his chief vocation the following year. Sentenced to life imprisonment, he was pardoned eight years later, after which, according to the *Times*, he was blamed for at least seven train holdups in Alabama, Louisiana, Tennessee and Texas between 1910 and 1915.

After the Central Station robbery railroad detectives rushed to Doddridge County, where a Miss Duckworth gave them a description of a man she had seen come out of the woods near her house to fill a coffee pot with water. Detectives disguised as tramps, peddlers and, in one case, an insurance salesman spread out across West Virginia. Their break came, however, in San Antonio, Texas, when a woman of modest means went on a spending spree with money believed to have come from the robbery.

The robbers had gotten $102,000, according to a September 12, 1916, wire service story during their trial. Unfortunately for them, the bank notes weren't signed. The bills showing up in shops in San Antonio were either unsigned or signed by means of a rubber stamp the thieves had made.

The woman spreading the bills around was a sister of one Jeff Harrison who owned what some sources called "a well-equipped machine shop" and others described as an automobile repair shop.

After shadowing Harrison for several days, the detectives arrested him. The *Times* said $50,000 was found under a gasoline tank; Roy C. Long, in his "Railroad Recollections" column in *The Hinton News*, December 20, 1994, said it was $28,000 found in a glass jar buried under the floor of the shop. Long's description of events matches with some newspaper accounts from the trial and is probably the most accurate version.

With Harrison's arrest, the dominos started to fall, and over the coming months his confederates and other parties were arrested in Denver, Atlanta, Chicago and Grand Rapids, Mich. The last captured was Webb, in Kansas City, Kan. Harrison claimed Webb was the mastermind behind the job.

Their trial at the federal court in Martinsburg began September 12, 1916. As details came out, it was determined the gang had lived in Grafton for a time. One of them, Eugene W. Diez (also spelled Dietz and Dies), stayed in Grafton while Harrison and Webb came to Clarksburg for two weeks to finalize plans for the job. Harrison had lived near Central Station some years earlier, according to Long, where his family had a bad reputation. The *Times* report claimed the gang had camped south of Parkersburg just before pulling the robbery.

Among the prosecution's best witnesses was Harrison's brother Richard. Dying of an incurable disease, he was held in a Martinsburg hospital during the trial. He apparently was only an accessory after the fact, not part of the gang.

On April 5, 1917, Webb pleaded guilty and was sentenced to twenty-five years; Harrison got twelve and Diez ten.

GLENVILLE'S VICTORY DOOMED THE TOWN OF DEKALB

February 5, 2006

C hoosing the location of a county seat has led to interesting events in a number of our counties, but for high drama, Gilmer County may have them all beat.

The story was chronicled in "Gilmer: The Birth of a County," No. 7 in the Folk Studies compiled and written by the Writers' Project of the Work Projects Administration and published October 1940.

A century earlier, in the 1840s, the county was just getting organized. A jail was under construction at DeKalb, so that town was where the first session of the county court met, too.

One of the court's first tasks was to examine the poll books and see what piece of Gilmer County heaven voters had selected for their county seat in a recent contest.

Interestingly, a motion to scrutinize the polls and invalidate any votes that appeared to be illegal was defeated. One ponders, doesn't one?

The unscrutinized poll books showed a majority of 66 voters wanted the county seat not at DeKalb but at "The Ford," where the old highway between Weston and Charleston crossed the Little Kanawha.

The road and river were strong arguments in favor of The Ford. Samuel L. Hays had already laid out a town there and named it Glenville because it lay in a glen.

(Hmmmm. Ford. Glen. Think of the possibilities if he had named it Glenn Ford. But I digress …)

When Glenville was selected as the county seat, a question was raised: Should the court continue meeting at DeKalb or move to the future place of government?

The court decided to finish out the term in DeKalb, then meet in Glenville at the beginning of the June session, a Solomon-like decision that failed to take into account sore losers.

Among the sorest was clerk of the court, James Camp. As May faded and arguments arose for keeping the court at DeKalb, he refused to take its records to Glenville.

We've discussed the glorious Texas Archive War in this column before. You may recall that some Texians (they hadn't gotten around to dropping the "i" from the middle of their name yet) loaded the state's records onto a wagon one night in Waterloo (Austin) and lit out for Washington-on-the-Brazos, which they thought would make a much nicer capital. Got as far as Round Rock, they did.

Camp didn't have to move anything. He just sat on the records. Those members of the court who agreed with him met in DeKalb on June 12, 1845. The others convened in Glenville but had no records to work with.

Later that day, news arrived that some members of the court then in session at DeKalb were willing to vote to move. That would give the pro-Glenville members a majority, providing they could get to DeKalb before the court adjourned.

From this point on, the story sounds like a Hollywood movie, maybe starring Glenn Ford.

The fellows in Glenville rounded up horses and rode a circuitous path to avoid detection, re-crossing the river opposite DeKalb. They hurried into the courtroom just as a motion was made to consider adjournment.

(Can't you hear the music swelling as the camera pans the room?)

The newcomers did move to adjourn—to Glenville. The motion passed, and the court met there in Thomas Marshall's home the next day.

Hollywood would roll the credits at this point, but it didn't quite end the saga. A legal challenge was initiated against property that William H. Ball and his wife, Christian, conveyed to the county for a courthouse site in Glenville. Back to DeKalb the court went on February 23, 1846.

In April, it returned to Glenville to stay. That town prospered while DeKalb faltered. Brambles reclaimed what had been town lots. Structures weathered and fell. By 1940, only the wind passed through DeKalb, according to "Birth of a County," but a community of that name is still on the map along Route 5.

How West Virginia Got Its State Flower

January 8, 2006

T he long-awaited West Virginia quarters, depicting the New River Gorge and its bridge, are finally in circulation.

You probably know that twelve graduates of the Governor's School for the Arts narrowed some 1,800 suggestions for the coin's design down to five.

The United States Commission of Fine Arts reviewed the students' design choices and decided, "high school students were not usually that well-trained or mature enough to act as judges," according to an excerpt of their report found on www.money.org. Some design modifications were made; hence, we don't have a parachutist jumping off the bridge on the coin.

This isn't the first time young people were asked to choose a symbol for our state. In 1902, they selected our state flower.

State flowers were all the rage back then. I have not been able to determine for certain what started this posey populism, this run for the roses so to speak, but I strongly suspect it began with the Columbian Exposition, the 1893 World's Fair in Chicago.

The blowout in the Windy City was the biggest thing of its kind since the United States Centennial celebration at Philadelphia in 1876. Chicago's festival drew massive crowds. Every state had exhibits boasting of agricultural, industrial and/or cultural achievements.

How many displayed blossoms associated with their region I can't say, but Idaho showed off the *Philadelphus Lewisii*, otherwise known as Syringa or Meriweather Lewis's mock orange, to the crowds in Chicago. The good people of Idaho had already incorporated that shrub into their state seal in 1890, although they didn't get around to officially making it their state flower until 1931.

Right after the Columbian Exposition, people in pretty much every state got het up about choosing an official blossom.

One of Montana's first statewide referendums was the one to designate its state flower, according to an article by Bob Gilluly in the *Great Falls Tribune*, August 1, 2004. The referendum came in 1894, just a year after the Columbian Exposition.

The bitterroot, a flower Montana had exhibited at the Exposition, was the state's budding star. (I once made flower puns for over fifteen minutes in the O. Henry Pun-Off. Things are going to get ugly before I finish writing this.)

You can read Gilluly's article at greatfallstribune.com, about bitterroot and how the 1894 floral referendum was an early victory for the temperance and women's suffrage movements. In response to my email query, Gilluly agreed that the Columbian Exposition "must have been a focal point for selection of state flowers."

Clearly, something led West Virginians down the garden path in the 1890s. Various groups and speakers promoted the notion of establishing a state flower. Governor George W. Atkinson recommended in 1901 that the legislature select the rhododendron or big laurel, according to *History and Government of West Virginia*, by Virgil A. Lewis (American Book Co., 1912 edition).

State Superintendent of Schools Thomas C. Miller thought a state flower was a wonderful idea. Not one to beat around the bush, he proposed letting school children of the state select which plant would win the laurels. (Don't say I didn't warn you.)

Many a floral banner was raised as competing groups lobbied in hopes their favorite blossom would be picked.

The vote was taken November 26, 1902.

Charleston's *The Daily Gazette* reported the next day, "All the indications are that the laurel or rhodendron (sic) received a big majority of the votes in all parts of the state."

The *Gazette* claimed several parents had voted along with the children.

The final tally made it clear the bloom was off the rose. Rhododendron triumphed with 19,131 of 35,854 votes cast, according to Virgil Lewis. Honeysuckle was a distant second with 3,663, trailed by the wild rose (3,387) and goldenrod (3,162). Other blossoms received only scattered votes. (Favorite sonflowers, I suppose.)

On January 8, 1903, the legislature made the students' choice official, and we had the first of our state emblems.

In 1902, Political Conventions Were a Cause for Real Excitement

May 7, 2000. At the time this column was written, the pending presidential race between George W. Bush and Al Gore looked to be a snoozefest. Before it was over, it was a nail-biter.

Well, the primaries will soon be behind us. The political signs that cover yards and highway intersections like flocks of starlings will come down, to quickly be replaced by others as we enter the l-o-o-o-o-ooong stretch of political advertising between now and the election.

According to recent Associated Press stories, West Virginians feel less than invigorated about this year's contests. On the national level, we've long known the presidential race will be between George Bush and Al Gore.

And there was much rejoicing.

Back at the turn of the last century, politicos knew how to make campaigns exciting, by golly. Before the 17th Amendment was added to the United States Constitution in 1913, state legislatures appointed senators, a process that was time-consuming and rife with opportunity for political patronage. A convention held in the town of Welch to name a senatorial candidate was arguably the Nintendo of its day: it provided entertainment by letting the citizenry vicariously enjoy people beating up and shooting at each other.

First of all, you've got to question the wisdom of holding a political convention in Welch. That's just begging gadflies to say candidates were Welching on their promises. But I digress ...

On June 9, 1902, the *Parkersburg Sentinel* opined "Every Senatorial convention held in the state so far has been exciting, but none heretofore will compare with the Sixth District Senatorial Convention held (in Welch) Saturday. Revolvers, knives, clubs and other weapons were used during the progress of the convention's deliberations, and as a result Colonel J. M. Fuller, one of the wealthiest citizens of Wayne County, lies at a hotel here probably fatally injured, and a dozen or more persons have black eyes and sore heads."

Now, ladies and gentlemen, *that's* entertainment!

"The miniature riot came about," the *Sentinel* continued, "over the selection of a Chairman of the convention. The Scott people selected R. B. Smith, of McDowell, while the Caldwell forces named Colonel Fuller. A vote was taken and the temporary chairman claimed that Mr. Smith was elected, but the Caldwell followers claimed to have more than three fourths of the delegates present and could not see it that way, so they refused to abide by the delegation. Both Mr. Smith and Colonel Fuller went forward and an effort was made to hold two conventions in the same hall at the same time."

Oh, yeah, now there's a plan — dueling conventions held in the same place! It just gets better from here on out, so if you want to run to the kitchen for a snack and a drink to enjoy with this, go ahead. We'll wait.

"In a very few minutes a general fight began, during which Colonel Fuller was knocked from the platform in the convention hall with the butt end of a revolver and was picked up unconscious. His wounds bled profusely and his skull is thought to be fractured. Medical aid was called for him and the Caldwell forces immediately named another Chairman and proceeded. Fighting continued. A pistol shot would occasionally ring out and oaths could be heard above the din of the proceedings of the rival conventions. Finally the Scott people told the Caldwell delegates that unless they vacated the hall it would be a battle to the finish.

"Twenty revolvers were brandished in the air, and in a general rush that was made for doorways a number of people were knocked down and trampled upon. The Caldwell delegates stopped in the hallways downstairs and named H. M. Cline, of Wyoming, for State Senator, while the Scottites remained inside and named B. Randolph Bias, of Mingo. More trouble is expected."

Say what you will about this method of choosing senators, at least the citizenry didn't snooze through the process.

THE SAD TALE OF WILLIAM C. MARLAND'S ROAD FROM GOVERNOR TO TAXI DRIVER

April 1, 2001

O ne day you're West Virginia's 24th governor. A few years later, you're an anonymous Chicago taxi driver. That, ladies and gentlemen, is one long fall from grace.

I am not demeaning cabdrivers. I pleasantly recall the night I picked up Jimmy Buffet's Coral Reefer band in my own taxi—but that's another story.

The political rise of William Casey Marland was nothing short of meteoric. Born in Illinois, he came to Wyoming County, West Virginia, at age seven with his coal-mining family. After serving in the Pacific during World War II, he entered law school at West Virginia University and was named assistant attorney general in August 1948, just fourteen months after receiving his degree. When the attorney general resigned December 1, 1949, young Marland was appointed to succeed him, according to *West Virginia Governors 1863–1980*, by John G. Morgan (Charleston Newspapers, 1980).

He quit that position January 30, 1952, to run for governor. Rumor had it he was the handpicked successor of Governor Okey

L. Patteson, who reputedly headed a Democratic "Statehouse machine." Marland ran a plain-talk, common-folks campaign, greeting voters with a big grin, a swagger and, "Howdy. I'm Bill Marland."

He won a four-way Democratic primary, then edged out his Republican opponent by 27,269 votes. At age thirty-four, Marland was the youngest governor in West Virginia's history up to that time.

Three days into office, he tried to make hamburgers from the state's sacred cows. He saw West Virginia's dependence on coal as self-defeating; the economy had to diversify. (This was near the beginning of the Great Coal Depression.) He committed political heresy by asking the legislature for a severance tax on coal, oil, gas, sand, and other natural resources to pay for better schools and roads. Politically inexperienced and unwilling to compromise, he saw his proposal go down to defeat.

Marland spent much of his term crisscrossing the country, touting the state's advantages to industrialists, with some success. Unfortunately, charges of nepotism rose when his father got the state's St. George wine account and his brother became assistant director of the purchasing office. The state Road Commission built a limestone highway past his Dutch Ridge farm in a sparsely settled part of Kanawha County, fueling further allegations of abuse of office.

He didn't run for reelection. Instead, he made unsuccessful bids for the United States Senate. In 1959, Marland left the Mountain State for Chicago, to become director of sales for the West Kentucky Coal Corporation's northern district. Shortly after, he stopped attending functions with other former governors; at times, he couldn't even be located to receive an invitation. Soon, he blipped off the radar screen completely.

A reporter for the *Chicago Daily News* found him in early March 1965, chewing a $1.25 fried chicken special in a YMCA where

Marland rented a $12-a-week room. The former governor candidly admitted he drank while in office and within a few months of moving to Chicago he was drinking 'round the clock, which led to his departure from the coal company. After a thirty-day hospital rehab, he started driving cab in the summer of 1962, drawn by the anonymity and independence that career offered.

His forthright discussion of his problems brought an outpouring of public sympathy and a new job in West Virginia, as associate director of a company that worked primarily at training and racing thoroughbred horses. He stood on the threshold of a new life, but only briefly. Four months after taking his new position, he was diagnosed with pancreatic cancer that quickly metastasized to his lungs.

Marland died November 26, 1965. His ashes were scattered over his beloved Dutch Ridge farm, dropped from the personal plane of Governor Hulett Smith.

For more information, see *From Governor to Cabby (The Political Career and Tragic Death of West Virginia's William Casey Marland: 1950-1965)*, by Paul F. Lutz, Ph. D. (The Marshal University Library Associates, 1996).

FLOOD WATERS ROLLED DOWNHILL TO CRUSH PARKERSBURG IN 1909

September 26, 1999

Parkersburg is a river city; it expects flooding from the Ohio and Little Kanawha. At least rising rivers give warning. The flood of March 19, 1909, struck abruptly, the water roaring down from a hilltop above the city.

Heavy rain lashed Parkersburg that Friday morning, accompanied by peals of thunder and flashing lightning. Only the earliest risers were up and about at 5 a.m.

Squatting atop Prospect (Quincy) Hill, were two large water tanks, forty feet high and sixty feet in diameter. They held the reserve for the city's water works.

Built in 1883, the tanks were made of iron and rested on stone foundations. To casual observers, they were solid as the Rock of Gibraltar.

Don't judge a book by its cover. Iron and water had cohabited for a quarter century in those tanks, and the water was looking for a divorce.

Every night a million gallons of water was pumped into each tank. Rivets on the one nearest Seventh Street had weakened under the strain; its bottom plates were corroded.

No one was around in the predawn hours to give warning when the weakened plates began to loosen. Any foreboding sound was lost in the night's thunder.

At 5:10, the tank's side burst. Flying debris smashed into the other tank, cracking its side like an eggshell.

A roar, louder than the thunder, rolled through the sleeping town. Two million gallons of water rushed downhill, demolishing a cottage above Avery at Tenth Street. Tangled among debris that swept down the hillside were the bodies of a couple named Wigal, newlyweds who had recently moved into the little house.

Another home nearby was destroyed in seconds, but its occupants were lucky. Search parties found all three badly injured but alive.

On Avery Street stood St. John's Evangelical Lutheran Church, a magnificent stone structure with a grand, circular window. Within moments, the stately house of worship was a pile of toothpicks, an angled portion of its roof lying slanted above the wreckage.

A house beside it was home to a widow and her daughter. It disintegrated around them, but left them safe among what was left.

Dennis Jones, a young black man, was swept away on his bed. Halfway down Tenth Street he was rescued from beneath a pile of rubble.

Townspeople rushing to the scene were greeted by strange sights. A ladder from one of the tanks was twisted around a tree halfway down the hill. Other trees had rammed through Sumner School's brick walls.

A barber shop in the Blennerhassett Hotel on Fourth and Market streets had two inches of mud oozing over its floors. In an underground stable on William and Mary streets a cow drowned.

Tenth Street was completely jammed with timbers, furniture and other debris that had been homes minutes earlier.

With the sort of quirky fate that seems to accompany every disaster, two houses on Shattuck Avenue that stood closest to the tanks suffered little harm.

City council met twice that same day, approving $2,000 for a relief committee, appointing a group to investigate the cause of the disaster and earmarking $2,500 to build four wooden tanks with 1,600 barrel capacity each to insure the town's water supply. In three days the first of those tanks was in place.

Claims for damages totaled over $40,000, which was a tad more than the city had in petty cash. Council ruled claims would be paid after the city collected its share of back taxes on a prominent estate. The first payments were made in April 1913, four years after the deluge.

A small shrine of circular hedges was created on the site where the tanks had stood.

Today's column comes from *Parkersburg: An Early Portrait*, by James Dawson and Gary Null (self-published).

West Virginia's Capitol Building Burned Twice in a Decade

February 1, 2004

I n the early 1920s, West Virginia had a majestic capitol building, a three-story, red-brick edifice which had graced the city of Charleston since 1885.

It featured pairs of peaked windows nestled inside arches across its face and a clock tower that soared 194 feet above the city's bustling streets. All in all, it was a capitol West Virginians could point to with pride.

That ended January 3, 1921.

A fellow named James Arthur Jackson is believed to be the first to realize something was wrong. He was working as law librarian across the street in the capitol annex around 3:15 p.m. when he saw smoke curling from the capitol.

Flames quickly spurted from the roof, then the fire spread downward. Governor John J. Cornwell was among those who fled into the streets.

The city's fire engine, pulled by galloping horses, came barreling through the crowds, its heat-driven pump billowing steam and spewing sparks.

The men of the fire company fought a losing battle as the winter afternoon stretched toward dusk. One fireman would never respond to another alarm; he died when a wall collapsed. Debris scattered near the onlookers, nearly striking State Tax Commissioner Walter S. Hallanan.

Throughout the night coals glowed from charred timbers and blackened walls, all that remained of the once-proud capitol.

While the fire burned, sharp explosions echoed from inside that didn't sound like the usual crackle and pop of wood and windows bursting from heat.

According to a book written some eighteen years later by Governor Cornwell, a small arsenal had been stored in the capitol's attic. In the autumn of 1919, an enterprising arms dealer had sent two truck loads of discounted munitions, including high-powered rifles and soft-nosed bullets, for Boone County's miners to use in the mine wars. State officials had intercepted and confiscated the weapons, stashing them in the attic of the capitol.

In a twist of irony, after the fire the governor's office was temporarily moved to the state armory. Why the munitions hadn't been stored there in the first place is not in the record at hand.

Other government agencies also needed temporary homes and found them in such places as the Elks Club, Methodist Episcopal Church, Virginia Land Bank Building, Scottish Rite Cathedral and the Red Cross shop and tea room. The legislature convened that year with the Senate debating inside the YMCA and the House at the Baptist Temple. So much for separation of church and state.

A new capitol was commissioned, with internationally known Cass Gilbert as the architect. He used a rather thin material called "beaver board" on its exterior, leading Charleston wags to dub the new building the "pasteboard capitol."

On the afternoon of March 2, 1927, fire broke out in the new capitol and tore through the thin beaver board like a weasel through a henhouse. In half an hour, West Virginia had lost its second capitol building in just over six years.

Mercifully, this time around there were no casualties. Public Service Commissioner C. E. Nethken tempted fate by going back into the burning building to retrieve his hat and coat, but he escaped with just some singed hair.

This second conflagration had an odd side effect, one that may have brought smiles to more than one witness.

The horse-drawn fire company was no more. The department became motorized on May 5, 1923, a couple of years after the first capitol burned. When the 1927 conflagration erupted, fire fighters motored to the scene. Meanwhile, a minor blaze broke out in the Yellow Pine Lumber Company plant on Wilson Street.

With its motor vehicles at the capitol, the fire company hitched up two remaining white horses and galloped to the lumber company. It was the last time horses would pull a fire engine to extinguish a blaze in Charleston.

Today's information comes from *Charleston 200*, by John G. Morgan and Robert J. Byers (The Charleston Gazette, 1994.)

WHEELING IN THE TIME OF THE CHOLERA

February 4, 2007

D uring 1833–4, Death went on a world tour. Burial rates in London doubled within a week of his arrival and quadrupled the following week.

After playing in cities across South America, he made a sweep through Mexico that would not soon be forgotten—18,000 died around Mexico City, according to Stephen F. Austin, who was visiting there.

In the vast northern Mexican province of Tejas (Texas), Death focused on the Anglo-American settlements along the Brazos in 1833, nearly wiping them out while giving only token attention to Mexican settlements. The following year he made a return engagement that added the Mexican towns he'd skipped.

He gave a memorable performance in New Orleans, then stopped in every city and town along the Mississippi and Ohio rivers.

By summer 1833, Death had arrived in Wheeling, where he presented the citizens with the star performer in this world tour: Asiatic cholera.

The disease had been a terror for centuries, but this worldwide outbreak was unprecedented.

Cholera is an intestinal infection caused by bacteria, according to the Web site for the Centers for Disease Control and Prevention (CDCP). It produces such severe loss of body fluids that death can come within twenty-four hours.

Primarily originating from contaminated food or water and spread by human waste, it can't be contracted by casual contact, according to CDCP, yet it somehow managed to spread like wildfire around the globe in 1833–4.

Even then, people knew "cleanliness is one of the best preventatives of the devastating disease," as the *Ayuntiamento* (city council) of Nacogdoches noted. It ordered all buildings occupied by Mexican troops to be cleaned after word arrived cholera was in New Orleans, according to "Epidemic Cholera in Texas, 1833-1834," by J. Villasana Haggard, *Southwestern Historical Quarterly Online*, Vol. 40, No. 3.

Wheeling employed every known precaution when the disease reached there. Streets were cleaned and lime spread in cellars, according to *History of Wheeling City and Ohio County, West Virginia and Representative Citizens*, edited and compiled by Hon. Gibson Lamb Cranmer (Biographical Publishing Co., 1902).

The sale of vegetables and fruits was forbidden. In the belief sulphur helped protect against the illness, coal fires were kept going constantly on street corners, creating a funereal pall that hung over the city continuously.

Many residents fled to the countryside or less-populated towns in hopes of avoiding contagion, but the disease often followed and they died among strangers.

With some Wheeling families, "departure was so hurried that the remains of the food which they had hastily partaken and the dishes used by them were left upon the cumbered tables," according to Cranmer.

Scores of coffins awaited internment while gravediggers worked to exhaustion.

A local poet, Thomas J. Lees, wrote, "And all was desolate, fear and flight … Dark days of trouble, closed in nights of woe."

One Sunday afternoon, bells on boats at the wharf began to peal. Word had arrived from across the river in Bridgeport that so many had fled the sick were being left untended and the dead unburied, a situation that wasn't going to make things any better.

A ferry filled with volunteers of both genders went to Bridgeport's relief and found it decimated. A hospital had been set up in the old Point Cotton Factory, and the volunteers were gratefully received there.

Eventually, the crisis of 1833–4 passed into dark legend. In modern America, cholera epidemics have been eliminated by public sanitation programs, but a current epidemic in Africa has lasted 30 years, according to CDCP.

We now know the most effective treatment is to rehydrate the patient with large doses of water mixed with sugar and salt. Indigent Mexicans used a similar treatment in 1833, according to Haggard, giving cholera victims limewater mixed with strained peyote juice, followed every two hours by tea and laudanum. The drugs relieved leg cramps and abdominal pain, but the fluids saved lives.

Blight Swept Through The State's Chestnut Forests

November 29, 2009

So did you stuff yourself on Thanksgiving? Speaking of stuffing, what was your turkey stuffed with—cornbread, oysters, mushrooms?

I have no doubt that in some homes people dined on chestnut stuffing. At one time, this may have been the predominant dressing for Thanksgiving's guest of honor, the turkey, but that began to change around the time of World War I when the mighty American chestnut tree suddenly faced extinction.

The "chestnut belt" stretched from Louisiana to Maine. In West Virginia, they constituted as much as a fourth of all trees in the state, according to John Rush Elkins of Concord University, *The West Virginia Encyclopedia*, edited by Ken Sullivan (West Virginia Humanities Council, 2006).

Valued for their beautiful grain, the trees were often used to make decorative items like fireplace mantles, but their straight trunks and sturdy nature also made them a natural for telephone poles, railroad ties and the like. The Meadow River Lumber Co. in Rainelle, the world's largest hardwood mill, produced chestnut coffins, according to "Meadow River Lumber Company" by Ben Crookshanks, *Blue Ridge Country*, January 2005.

Apart from their value as lumber, the "spreading chestnut tree" under which Henry Wadsworth Longfellow's village blacksmith stood was admired for its size and beauty. Deer, squirrel, swine and other animals dined on its nuts.

Humans loved them, too—"Chestnuts roasting on an open fire," and all that.

They were so popular that a single West Virginia railway depot shipped 155,092 pounds of them in 1911, according to Elkins' *Encyclopedia* article. That would stuff a lot of turkeys.

Gathering all those nuts for export provided many a rural family in the state with extra income.

So when *The West Union Record* informed its readers on February 7, 1913, that chestnut blight had reached the Mountain State, it must have caused a great deal of alarm. The *Record* said it plainly: "Unless prompt and vigorous measures are taken to check the distribution of the blight before it becomes widespread, there is little hope that the vast quantity of chestnut timber in the state can be saved."

The news story said, "The disease known as Chestnut Blight first appeared on Long Island in 1904. During the eight years since then it has spread into a dozen states and has destroyed forty million dollars' worth of chestnut timber."

Pennsylvania's legislature had already appropriated $275,000 to fight blight there, but West Virginia's forests had largely been free of the nuisance, the *Record* reported.

But it had appeared in Jefferson County and was "killing trees at a rapid rate on the west face of the Blue Ridge Mountains."

Hope had existed that the twenty-mile-wide Shenandoah Valley, which had no chestnuts, the *Record* said, would form a barrier against the blight's spread, but by January 1913 the orange-colored killer had been found in "our great chestnut belt in Berkley and Morgan counties."

Six years later, the state still managed to mill 118 million board feet of American chestnut lumber, but just ten years after that the chestnut had become scarce. The blight killed chestnut trees at a rate even worse than the death rate of people during the 1918 flu pandemic.

The blight probably arrived on Asian chestnut trees imported in the late 1800s, which suffer only mild effects from it, but American chestnuts had no resistance to this alien invasion. Its progression through forests couldn't be checked; it produces airborne fungal spores that attach themselves to birds and animals, then spread to wounds in host trees.

The fungus bores its way through the bark, and soon a blighted tree displays a belt around its trunk, with orange blisters that block sap flow; everything above the belt dies.

There is a ray of hope for future chestnuts. A strain of trees combining American and blight-resistant Asian chestnut has been developed and is being planted. In about twenty years, we'll know if it worked.

WOMEN'S HISTORY

THE ARTS

MEDICAL MATTERS

SOCIAL CHANGE

IS THE ROMANTIC TALE ABOUT ULYSSES S. GRANT'S AUNT TRUE?

January 2, 2005

A h, a new year dawns, teasing us with promise and hope. This is the year we'll lose that weight, write that novel, throw away those cigarettes, enjoy life more.

We mean it, we really do. But years are like oceans. Daily, the currents eddy around us, eroding the ground on which we stand but also uncovering unexpected delights among the flotsam and jetsam that washes by us.

As 2004's tide ebbed, it washed up something I had promised to a reader, Garnette Turner McGee of Stonewood. She contacted me a couple of years ago regarding a legend she heard while growing up in the Big Kanawha Valley. Could I find out if it was true?

I started researching it, but when my briefcase was stolen I thought that information was part of what I lost. To my surprise, I found the materials just before Christmas, stuck inside a folder in my files.

The legend McGee told me concerned an aunt of Ulysses S. Grant, the victorious Civil War general and president of the United States.

According to the legend, the aunt, Rachel Maria Grant, was already married to a man in the Kanawha Valley when another chap, one William F. Tompkins, Jr., fell in love with her.

Seeing the woman he loved already married to another man would have been painful enough, but the legend says her husband was a hairy-legged no-account who didn't treat Rachel right.

Tompkins parleyed with the husband, who agreed to divorce Rachel in exchange for a fine horse, a saddle, rifle and four or five gallons of whiskey. He rode off into the sunset, Tompkins and Rachel married, and they lived happily ever after, the end.

Histories of the Kanawha Valley do not record any such transaction, but I'd be mighty surprised if they did. Proper decorum and all that.

History of Charleston and Kanawha County West Virginia, by W. S. Laidley (Richmond-Arnold Publishing Co., 1911) says Rachel was born September 6, 1805, in Washington County, Pennsylvania Her brother, Jesse Root Grant, was the father of the famous general.

Her family moved to Maysville, Kentucky , when she was but an infant. There, she grew up and got her education — probably a good one since Kentuckians generally believed in educating their daughters properly.

During a visit to Malden, east of Charleston she "met and married Mr. Tompkins," according to Laidley. He makes no mention of a previous husband.

Kanawha County marriage records show she wed Tompkins December 28, 1831.

Tompkins was a prominent man in the valley. He owned some 600 acres at Burning Springs, near Malden, where he made a chunk of money operating a salt furnace, according to Laidley. (Both of our Kanawha rivers have had a town named Burning Springs nearby.)

Tompkins had been married before, to Jane M. Grant of Kanawha County. She died at age twenty-seven, the mother of five children, a year before he met and married Rachel Grant. Presumably Rachel and Jane were related, and that likely is how twenty-five-year-old Rachel met thirty-seven-year-old Tompkins.

So, is the romantic legend true?

Probably not. Marriage records list Rachel's surname as Grant. A woman could have her name restored after a divorce in the 1830s, especially if the marriage had been annulled, but such instances were rare. One version of the legend suggests Rachel wasn't actually married to the other man.

Possibly, the woman whose husband Tompkins bought off was Jane, his first wife, and the names have been confused, but that is speculation on my part.

Tompkins built a fine brick home for Rachel in 1844. During the Civil War, Union cavalry came to burn the house, according to Laidley, but Rachel produced a letter from nephew Ulysses saying her property was to be left alone. Reportedly, he visited his aunt in 1873 during his first term as president.

Her home still stands at Cedar Grove, or did two years ago when I was permitted to tour its first floor.

A Quick-Thinking Young Woman Saved a Train

August 29, 2010

B ad luck seemed to be hovering over the West Virginia Short Line Railroad a couple of years after it opened for business. On October 6, 1902, an engine attached to a freight train blew up at Bard while traveling at twelve miles per hour, according to the *Wetzel Democrat*, October 10, 1902.

"The engine was blown to atoms, the track torn up and several cars were blown to pieces," the *Democrat* reported, and three men were injured, two seriously.

That was a tragedy, certainly, but nothing compared to the one that almost occurred to a passenger train that was going to Clarksburg from New Martinsville a few days later, on the evening of Sunday, October 12. This report appeared in the *Fairmont Free Press*, October 23, 1902.

The West Virginia Short Line had opened to traffic just two years earlier, according to the West Virginia Railroad Web site, wvall.railfan.net. It formed a route northwest from the Baltimore & Ohio's main line at Clarksburg to New Martinsville, twisting and curving its way between small towns in Harrison and Wetzel counties.

During the autumn weekend in question, some farmers were cutting timber on a hillside. Sometime Saturday night a large log they'd cut rolled down the hill, lodging against the WVSL tracks near the whistle stop of Minnie Post Office, six miles east of New Martinsville.

While the Short Line had some relatively straight track in the area of Minnie, there were also some curves that were real doozies, and the log lay in one of the bends. The engineer wouldn't be able to stop by the time he saw it.

Minnie could scarcely be called a town at the time, although it had been established way back in 1815 by Aaron Morgan, according to *History of Wetzel County West Virginia*, by John C. McEldowney. When McEldowney penned that work, published in 1901, he wrote of Minnie, "The only place of business is a store owned by Rueben Yoho."

Let's just say there weren't a lot of people around to notice a log had rolled onto the tracks. Fortunately, someone did happen upon it. Young Minnie Martin, who loved to wave to every train crew that passed her home, knew a train was due and recognized the danger the log posed.

She jumped on a horse, swam it across Fishing Creek and flagged the train "just in time to save it from being wrecked," the *Free Press* wrote.

Around the first of December, the young heroine received a letter from the railroad company with a check for $50, according to Charleston's *The Daily Gazette* of December 3.

In the *Gazette*'s story, the log from lumber cut by farmers, as the *Free Press* reported, became a large rock dislodged by heavy rains. Log or rock, the result would have been the same if a speeding train slammed into it. If indeed there were heavy rains that weekend,

Fishing Creek would have been swollen, making Minnie's crossing of it all the more hazardous.

If $50 sounds a bit skimpy for saving a train and its passengers, consider that, adjusted for inflation, today she could buy a 64-giga-bit iPad and still have half of her reward left.

I'd love to know more about Minnie. Did she go on to have other adventures? Did she keep her love of trains?

All I was able to discover is that she was the daughter of Sarah Morgan and Ben Martin, and that she married a man named Sanford Brookover. That information comes from the "Descendants of Morgan Morgan," William Dallas Morgan pages on FamilyTreeMaker. Her father was mentioned in the news articles as a "prominent citizen," and his name appears as a board of education commissioner in the 1914 *Report of the Attorney General*.

The newspaper accounts never mentioned her age, referring to her only as "a country maiden," suggesting she was in her late teens or early adulthood when she saved the train.

Trying to Unravel the Lineage of Abraham Lincoln's Mother

June 29, 2003

Whenever I mention to fellow West Virginians that I am writing a book about Abraham Lincoln and his in-laws, almost invariably someone says, "You know, his wife was born in West Virginia."

No. She. Was. Not.

Lincoln's wife, Mary Ann Todd, was born in Lexington, Kentucky , in her parents' home or possibly at her maternal grandmother's residence next door. Lincoln's mother, Nancy Hanks, may have been born in what is now the eastern panhandle of West Virginia; hence, the confusion.

Where Nancy Hanks was born has long been debated, but that's understandable. The circumstances of her birth have been a matter of contention for well over a century. Most recently, an article on the subject appeared in the Winter 2003 edition of *New England Ancestors*. Nancy Ervin Butterfield, a New Hampshire resident with ties to West Virginia, graciously sent me a copy of the article.

"The Maternal Ancestry of Abraham Lincoln The Origins of Nancy (Hanks) Lincoln: A Study in Appalachian Genealogy," written by Christopher Challender Child, examines several of the conflicting Nancy Hanks stories. Child concluded the two most plausible are:

1. Lincoln's mother was the illegitimate daughter of Lucy Hanks by an unknown Virginia planter, or

2. She was the legitimate daughter of James Hanks and Lucy Shipley.

The first version provides the greatest likelihood she was born somewhere in Virginia, but if the other is true, Nancy Hanks may have been born as far south as Mecklenburg County, No. Car., according to Child.

A Taylor County legend claims Lincoln's great-grandfather almost settled near present-day Grafton, but word of his daughter's illegitimate child preceded them, so the family continued on to Kentucky. Lincoln himself reportedly claimed his mother came to Kentucky with relatives other than her parents, and the Taylor County story probably came into existence after Lincoln's former law partner, William Herndon, claimed Nancy Hanks was the child of an unwed mother.

According to Herndon, Lincoln confided to him around 1850 that Nancy was the illegitimate daughter "of a nobleman so called of Virginia. My mother's mother was poor and credulous, etc. and she was shamefully taken advantage of by the man." (This purported conversation is also where we get the line, "All I am or ever hope to be I owe to my mother," which is a close approximation of something Herndon claimed Lincoln said to him.)

Herndon claimed a great many things about his law partner; some of them were even true. Sharing such intimate information about his mother seems very out of character for Lincoln, who was reticent about his family and always showed great respect for women.

That brings us to the second of Child's preferred theories, that Lincoln's mother was the legitimate daughter of James Hanks and Lucy Shipley. When Nancy Hanks wed Thomas Lincoln in Washington County, Kentucky , in 1806, she was living with the family of Richard Berry, Jr. and Sarah Shipley.

Nancy Hanks's mother's name was Lucy, but Lucy's last name is in question. Those who believe she had an illicit liaison with a Virginia planter maintain her surname was Hanks, until she married Henry Sparrow in 1790. Other researchers claim Lucy was a Shipley. When she married Sparrow, the witnesses who signed for her were Shipleys, not Hanks.

Lincoln's family Bible says his mother, Nancy Hanks, was born February 5, 1784 (six years before her mother's marriage to Sparrow), but the information was written about 1851, long after her death. Child believes Lucy Shipley wed James Hanks (possibly his name was Joshua). James died young, and she remarried in 1790. Child based his opinion on genealogical research and an oral tradition within the Shipley family.

So was Lincoln's mother born in our eastern mountains? A historic marker in the Eastern Panhandle marks the place many scholars believe she came into this world, but like so much of what is written about Lincoln and those around him, the circumstances and location of his mother's birth will likely never be proven definitively.

Addendum

The Charleston Gazette of April 30, 1938, ran a wire story from Pennsboro reporting the death of William E. Dell, age 89, "born in the same cabin which Nancy Hanks, mother of Abraham Lincoln was born." According to the story, the cabin stood on property "which as been in possession of the Dell family for 150 years" near the Devil's Saddle in Mineral County. William Dell was the last of eleven children, four of whom reportedly were born in the cabin.

Is this accurate? As I've noted in other columns, people like to claim connection to historic people and events and believe what they are saying is true but 'taint necessarily so. Anyone in Mineral County want to try verifying the story?

A Wooden Leg, a Glass Eye, and a Woman Lawyer

November 26, 2006

The day before Christmas, 1913, James Edwards, who was visiting from Kentucky, went into a Summers Street bar in Charleston and consumed so much holiday spirit that he went to sleep on the barroom floor.

He had a wooden peg leg. While he was snoring, a prankster slapped paste and horsehair on it so it appeared to have grown hair.

When Edwards awoke, he demanded to know who was responsible. Someone blamed Alex James of Paint Creek, though later reports said he was not the guilty party.

Edwards stumped over to where James sat at the bar, calmly unstrapped the hair-covered peg leg and whacked him over the head.

If the weapons in this duel were to be artificial limbs, James was a mite short on ammunition. All of his appendages were original equipment. He did, however, have a glass eye, which he popped out and used to lambaste Edwards upside the head.

Other patrons then pulled the two combatants apart, according to the *Charleston Mail*, December 24, 1913.

If any legal action ever resulted from this strange little bar-room brawl, James, the West Virginian, should have engaged as his attorney Georgia McIntire-Weaver. She was our state's first female lawyer, and she appreciated a good scrap herself.

She had hung out her shingle in Berkeley Springs just 11 months before, after passing the bar exam at West Virginia University in January, according to the *Keyser Tribune*, January 24, 1913.

She was sister to former Senator A. C. McIntire of Morgan County.

An article at http://womenslegalhistory.stanford.com, said she was "a former dressmaker, stenographer, and honors graduate of Atlanta Law School."

The state of Georgia, like Arkansas and Virginia, still refused to admit women to the bar at that time. McIntire-Weaver, along with another female attorney, Minnie Anderson Hale, testified before the Georgia legislature in 1911 in an unsuccessful attempt to change that situation.

McIntire-Weaver then determined to return to her native West Virginia and practice law here, according to *Women Lawyer's Journal*, February 1913 edition.

She was not someone to trifle with, as demonstrated in a *Charleston Mail* story, June 26, 1914. She successfully defended some clients in litigation filed by Charles E. Casler, a farmer of Morgan County. When he found her alone in her office later, he "became abusive" and ignored her demands that he leave.

She flung Hogg's *Pleadings and Forms* at him, cutting him above the eyebrow, then broke a vase of roses over his head and put him out of her office.

In another incident, she was indicted by a Berkeley Springs grand jury under a seldom-used statute prohibiting intimidation, according to Clarksburg's *Exponent*, April 28, 1918.

She had "browbeat a defenseless male witness" with a tongue-lashing in which "she turned loose a flood of oratory of such a character as to upset the magistrate's judicial dignity."

Let it be noted, however, that West Virginia's "first woman lawyer" was neither the first nor the feistiest female attorney ever to be born in this state.

That honor surely goes to Kate Kane, whose Irish parents took her from her birthplace among our fair hills to Wisconsin while she was still a child. On March 8, 1879, at the age of twenty-five, she became Milwaukee's first woman lawyer, according to www.wisbar.org.

Young and pretty, she was the darling of the press until long-standing tensions between her and a Judge Mallory of the Municipal Court climaxed in February 1883 after he appointed another attorney to defend an indigent.

Kane left Mallory's courtroom in tears but returned and threw a glass of water in the judge's face. She went to jail rather than pay a $50 fine.

The story made national news, and afterward she became a media joke. She had made her mark, though. For many years, women seeking a legal career were told, "Oh, you're going to be a lawyer like Kate Kane."

West Virginia's First Poet Laureate Had a Brilliant Mind Inside a Twisted Body

August 20, 2000. This column was written in honor of the publication of
Wild Sweet Notes: Fifty Years of West Virginia Poetry 1950–1999,
*the first collection of West Virginia poets ever published. Obligatory
disclosure: two poems I wrote are included in that anthology.*

D espite our state's image as a place where *Fun with Dick and
Jane* is considered great literature ("Did you hear West
Virginia's state library burned? Destroyed both books, and one
of them hadn't even been colored in yet," the old joke goes.), the
truth is our fog-shrouded hollows have produced a long list of
award-winning authors, songwriters and poets, who have often
overcome great odds to succeed at their craft.

A case in point is the state's first official poet laureate, Karl
Dewey Myers of Tucker County. When he was born in the early hours of February 2, 1899, in the town of Moore, his body was
so misshapen he was not expected to live till sundown. His close
friend, Homer Floyd Fansler, told his story in Fansler's *History of
Tucker County, West Virginia* (McClain Printing, 1962). The two men

agreed to write each other's biographies and appear to have been remarkably honest in their depictions.

Myers never weighed over sixty pounds. His twisted legs wouldn't allow him to walk, so he never attended school. Maybe his legs couldn't run, but his mind would have won the gold if they held mental Olympics.

According to Fansler, Myers could recite the Declaration of Independence, the Constitution of the United States, the Mayflower Compact and the Magna Carta, word for word. He could name every state and nation, along with their capitals. Every president, every king of England, their terms and reigns, their vital statistics — he knew them all.

Give Myers a newspaper and ten minutes to read through it, and he could summarize every story. Bear in mind that during Myers' lifetime, a single newspaper story could run a page or more, with myriad short reports making up most of the news.

He loved poetry, particularly the work of Edgar Allen Poe. Perhaps he related to those dark verses. His life was filled with many friends, but after his last family member died, he spent nearly twenty years living in nursing homes, on charity and wherever he could find a place to sleep, dulling his pain with alcohol, Fansler wrote.

In spite of his own loss and limitations, Myers helped organize boys clubs and baseball teams and promoted community service organizations. Each year, he mailed daily memorandum books to other poets; they would write a daily couplet or quatrain in the booklets and mail them back to him at year's end.

His own poems appeared in respected publications. In 1926, his friends paid to publish a collection titled *The Quick Years*, but not until 1951 did another of his poetry books, *Cross and Crown*, became available.

When the West Virginia legislature authorized the position of Poet Laureate of the State, Myers was the first to fill that post, from June 9, 1927, to March 10, 1937.

Poetry's rewards are not financial. Myers lived in poverty until his death December 4, 1951, in the home of friends near Elkins. His was buried in an unmarked grave in the Odd Fellows cemetery there, but a monument to West Virginia's first poet laureate was placed in Tucker County a few years ago, according to information the late poet and historian Cleta M. Long provided to Phyllis Wilson Moore, the unofficial historian of West Virginia's writers.

Two Wheeling Brothers in the Early Film Industry

May 1, 2011

The recent article in this newspaper about how West Virginia is enticing filmmakers and television producers to shoot here reminded me of two brothers from West Virginia who played a major role in establishing California's film industry.

New Jersey, home base of Thomas Edison's studios, was the first movie capital of America, but films were being made elsewhere as well. In 1913, Herbert M. Horkheimer purchased a former Edison Company studio in Long Beach, Cal., and with his brother Elwood co-founded Balboa Amusement Producing Company, AKA Balboa Studios. The company would establish Long Beach as a movie-making center.

The Horkheimer brothers were born in Wheeling—Elwood on February 8, 1881, and Herbert on July 9, 1882, according to International Movie Database (IMDb).

Herbert is credited with producing 144 titles, directing five, and writing the script for *The Stolen Play*, which starred Ruth Roland, one of the queens of early movie serials.

Elwood's name is attached to far fewer productions, but he developed efficient methods that would help the company create over 1,000 films during its five years of existence.

Long Beach was already a theater town with a modest movie business: eight theaters and two stock film companies were located there, according to "Before Hollywood—There was Long Beach," by Anna V. Alcott at hollywoodmotionpicture.com. Balboa Amusement would make the seaside community into a center for filmmaking.

The studio reportedly began with a single building but soon expanded to twenty buildings on eight acres, with eleven more acres for outdoor filming in Long Beach's Signal Hill township. It became America's largest independent studio of the time, according to *Balboa Films: A History and Filmography of the Silent Film Studio*, by Jean-Jacques Jura and Rodney Norman Barden II (McFarland & Co., 1999).

Long Beach grew with Balboa. From 17,000 residents in 1910, it burgeoned to over 55,000 by 1920, a growth spurt largely credited to its movie industry.

Balboa not only made innovations in studio management, its cinematographers developed new ways of shooting night scenes and creating in-camera effects, as well as new techniques for color tinting.

Performers were rewarded "for faithful and loyal services," as stated in a letter to actress Myrtle Reeves that said her salary was being increased to five dollars a week. Reeves would become Oliver Hardy's second wife.

The studio was also a tourist attraction. Nathan B. Scott, a former United States Senator from West Virginia, visited it and reported the company was worth a half-million dollars and employed nearly 400 people, according to Clarksburg's *Sunday Telegram*, March 18, 1917.

Scott mentioned that Balboa's productions included the famous *Little Mary Sunshine*, which created the first child star, curly-headed "Baby Marie" Osborne.

The studio issued written instructions not to shout at or tease "Baby Marie" or address her in slang, according to "The movie capital of yore," by Steve Harvey, *Los Angeles Times*, October 25, 2009.

Attractive, talented "tomboy star" Jackie Saunders, married Elwood Horkheimer in 1916. They divorced in 1920, according to Looking for Mabel Norman.Webs.com. Henry Ford's *Dearborn Independent Magazine* wrote that though Saunders was ill with pleurisy during one filming, "out of devotion to her husband she kept on working ... (running) on foot in tattered old shoes down a rocky mountain."

The brothers lived well. Herbert had a large home in elegant Bluff Parks and entertained lavishly, according to "The Development of Bluff Park" by Stanley Poe on the Long Beach Heritage Web site.

The world was stunned, therefore, when Herbert declared Balboa bankrupt in 1918. Some mystery still surrounds the studio's demise, but contributing factors included too many unprofitable films; expenses had topped $2,500 a day by 1915, to create 15,500 feet of film weekly. Expensive lawsuits, including one against author Jack London over film rights to *The Seawolf*, compounded the problem.

Too, the company's main distributors were British and French; World War I disrupted distribution.

For five glorious years, though, two West Virginians were among filmdom's biggest names.

WAS BARBOUR COUNTY'S IDA L. REED THE MOST PROLIFIC SONGWRITER OF ALL TIME?

August 30, 1998

F ew West Virginians realize one of the most prolific songwriters of all time — possibly the most prolific — lived out her life in the hills of Barbour County. Well over 2,000 of Ida L. Reed's hymns and carols were published, as well as her nature lessons, stories, religious exercises and seasonal services.

She was born November 30, 1865, the sixth of Harrison and Nancy Willard Reed's eight children. Her parents had come to Barbour County prior to the Civil War, where they established a hard-scrabble farm on a stony hillside near Moatsville. The war wiped out the notes and accounts her father held back in eastern Virginia, and poverty followed Ida throughout her life.

Although Ida would gain world renown with songs of her Christian faith, she found her earliest experiences with religious instruction anything but uplifting. In a self-published autobiography titled *My Life Story*, she recalled attending "Old Ebeneezer" Methodist Episcopal Church, a log cabin with bare walls where night services were carried out amid the flickering shadows from tallow candles. Seats were rough-hewn logs resting on heavy pins with no backs for parishioners to lean against.

She recalled, "How utterly weary we (children) used to grow as we sat through the long lesson hour, too small to understand or have any part in the service as it was read."

Nature and a love of reading were what defined and guided her childhood. "I almost lived outdoors," she declared, in the beauty and freedom of the fields and forest. Her childhood nickname was "Tom," short for tomboy.

She discovered the wonder of the printed page very early. Her father gave her a small hymnal he owned, and it was among her most precious childhood possessions. When it disappeared, she was heartbroken. Later, she learned one of her brothers had secretly given it to his girlfriend as a present.

The children's books of Ida's day — what few there were — filled their pages with didactic stories of children she described as "flawless, faultless … perfect from the beginning in amazing wisdom and judgment, a constant reproach to their more sinful playmates and elders."

The stories often ended with the child's triumphant death, the soul borne sweetly to heaven by angels, leaving "a very large circle of subdued, and saddened, and saved relatives and friends. I could not hope to attain that high state of angelic goodness," she declared.

By the time she was ten, she began to suffer blinding headaches. Being in a crowd was almost certain to bring them on, she noticed, so she began to avoid "crowds and everything that taxed strength … I went from home more and more seldom."

At first, the severe stress-induced headaches were only a source of pain to her, but eventually she came to feel "God touched with

His love that which seemed to be a great deprivation and it became the source of untold blessing, for I learned to love, more and more, to read ... eager to develop to the highest reach all the powers of my mind and heart."

If illness was indeed a blessing for Ida, she was greatly blessed. As a teenager, she was attacked by diphtheria, and she developed spinal fever as a young woman. Her health would never be robust. Yet she prepared herself to be a teacher, tested for and received the required certificate and taught until ill health forced her to quit.

While she was still teaching, her younger brother made the suggestion that would ultimately spread this gentle lady's name around the world. He encouraged her to write something for the *West Virginia Protestant* newspaper published at St. Mary's. Her very first manuscript was accepted, and she continued to free-lance for that paper. Her work came to the attention of an editor of Methodist Sunday School periodicals in Pittsburgh, and he asked her to write for them.

Guileless and naive, she asked only for reimbursement to cover the cost of paper and postage. That was her pay during the two or three years she wrote for those publications with a circulation of 30,000–35,000.

When she was forced from teaching, she used money she had intended to further her own education to buy an organ. She later said it was the best purchase she ever made, for writing became her life's work, and songwriting came to be the most important part of that work. When no words would come, she would sit at the organ, playing some melody over and over until words "sung themselves to me."

Among the songs she wrote this way was her most successful piece, "I Belong to the King," published by the Hall-Mack company.

She wrote the publisher in curiosity sometime prior to 1911 to ask how many copies had been published.

They told her the song had been used in thirty to thirty-five songbooks, thousands of which were sold in England alone. It had appeared in pamphlets and had been translated into Scandinavian and German. In all, they estimated four million copies were in circulation.

Ida was thrilled to learn she had touched so many people. From her account, it appears she never realized the monetary value of a song that successful. She received no royalties on her music or prose, just minuscule flat fees. She supplemented her meager income selling vegetables from her garden.

When she died at the home of a nephew in Arden on July 8, 1951, she had never received the financial rewards her work deserved. For Ida, perhaps touching people's hearts was reward enough. The state erected a historical marker to her that stands along Route 250 near Philippi.

A Controversial "Moon" in West Virginia's Mountains

November 4, 2007

Did you see the news wire article a couple of weeks ago about how demand for "modern" or at least less-traditional art is supplanting more conventional art forms in West Virginia?

Perhaps that's true in the Eastern Panhandle, where the article was written, but I suspect most West Virginians still prefer Winslow Homer and George Bellows to Jackson Pollack and Andy Warhol.

The story reminded me of the time when West Virginia and surrealism stared each other in the face and West Virginia said, "Huh?"

As Michael Lipton wrote in the *Charleston Gazette-Mail* on June 20, 1993, thirty years after the fact, the incident "thrust an unsuspecting Mountain State into the world of modern art."

The year was 1963 and the occasion was the state's centennial celebration. Among the festivities and special programs was an art competition. Its grand prize was based on the year of the centennial — $1,963 for the best artwork.

Now, what the Centennial Organization envisioned when it proposed this contest I do not know, perhaps a painting of a coal miner being welcomed home by his family at sunset or a woman hanging quilts on a line.

Whatever they were hoping for, the organizers simply left the door open to the "best" artwork.

I am reminded of an old joke about an artist who was commissioned to depict on canvas the last thoughts of General Custer at the Little Big Horn. Unfortunately, I can't tell that joke in a family newspaper, but I can tell you my favorite light bulb joke.

Question: How many surrealist painters does it take to change a light bulb?

Answer: A fish.

If that punch line befuddles you, you know how the Centennial Organization felt when the blue ribbon was hung on the winning entry at Huntington Galleries (later named Huntington Museum).

The impartial judge, one James Johnson Sweeney, director of the Museum of Fine Art in Houston, Texas, and later director of the Guggenheim Museum in New York, awarded the $1,963 to work titled *West Virginia Moon*.

It consisted of a half-dozen planks that, fastened together, looked like a worn-out shipping palette some warehouse had discarded. On its right-hand side was the outline of a person, probably male, like a chalk drawing you might find on a sidewalk in front of an elementary school. In the upper left was a circle that looked like someone had set a large can down on the beat-up shipping palette and sprayed paint around it.

Reactions ranged from "Slander to the state" to "A monstrosity" to "Atrocious and sickening"—the latter coming from John Shanklin, then mayor of Charleston.

Naturally, newspapers printed photos of the controversial piece. The papers of Washington, D.C., and Baltimore accidentally printed the picture sideways.

Some wag hung a sign on an old barn: "Not a barn. West Virginia art."

Not everyone was displeased. Delia Brown Taylor, chair of West Virginia State's art department thought, "We need to be aroused from our artistic lethargy."

The work did that. Crowds thronged to see it when it was displayed, first in Huntington, then in Charleston.

The creator of *Moon* was Joe Moss, an art professor at West Virginia University, who grew up in Lewis and Harrison counties. Later, he went on to a twenty-eight-year tenure at the University of Delaware and was an Artist Fellow at the Massachusetts Institute of Technology's Center of Advanced Visual Studies, according to the Kemper Art Museum Web site.

Moss became known for creating what the Kemper site calls "multi-sensory environments," blending visuals with sound. For example, West Virginia governor Hulett Smith asked him to come up with something to dramatize the effects of strip mining. Moss unveiled a painting of a pristine landscape, then blew it to smithereens with dynamite. He titled it *West Virginia Boom*, a play on his other title.

The notoriety of *Moon* eventually forced him to leave the state; otherwise, he said, he would never be known for anything else.

West Virginia's Influence on a Comic Genius

April 16, 2006

F ew West Virginians will ever be as widely known or as beloved as the late Don Knotts. His genius for comedy created memorable characters from tall-tale spinner Windy Wales on radio's *Bobby Benson and the B-Bar-B* Western program to *The Incredible Mr. Limpet* in the movies to swinger-wannabe Ralph Furbee of television's *Three's Company*.

His most beloved character, of course, was hyper, bug-eyed Deputy Barney Fife of Mayberry, whom he played for five seasons on *The Andy Griffith Show*. Originally, Griffith was to be the comic character, but Knotts proposed playing his deputy, and Griffith chose to play straight man to the manic Fife.

In his autobiography, *Barney Fife and Other Characters I Have Known*, written with Robert Metz (Berkley Boulevard Books, 1999), Knotts mentioned one childhood incident that spawned a comic moment on that program.

During Sunday visits to relatives on farms outside Morgantown, after-dinner conversations were punctuated with long silences between sentences. Once, after some ten minutes passed without a spoken word, an uncle asked, "Anybody want to walk down to the gas station and get a bottle of pop?"

In a Mayberry sketch, Knotts recreated the scene but with Fife repeating his intentions to walk over to the filling station and get a bottle of pop as if he was planning the D-Day invasion. Finally, an exasperated out-of-towner shouted at him to go do it.

This is the only specific event Knotts mentioned, but his autobiography tells of numerous events and characters from his Morgantown years that he almost certainly drew from for *Andy Griffith*. Not long after joining the show, he was invited to help with script rewrites, and one wonders how his early experiences helped shape story lines.

There was the time he and his friend Jarvey Eldred bragged they would climb Cooper's Rock in the dark. Trapped by their Barney-Fife-like bravado, they made the long, long climb, terrified every moment that they would fall from the steep cliff to the water below.

His father had been a farmer until illness made the elder Knotts into a virtual invalid. The family moved to a large house on University Avenue so their mother could rent out rooms for income. Don, by far the youngest, slept in the kitchen so the family could have another room to rent.

Several guests tried to slip out without paying. Some succeeded. His account of this sounds remarkably like the episode in which the Darlings try to sneak an entire family into Mayberry's hotel while paying for just one person.

Even lovable town drunk Otis Campbell touched very close to home. Knotts's brothers William Earl and Ralph, better known as Shadow and Sid, were on familiar terms with ol' John Barleycorn. When Sid was in his cups he would enter the house singing loudly, then go to the kitchen where Don was trying to sleep and fry himself an egg.

Shadow was jailed once on a drunk and disorderly charge. Their mother, Elsie L. Moore Knotts, sent Don to deliver food to him but instructed Don not to enter the jail. He had to take it to the back of the building to toss it up to Shadow's cell window. That invokes images of Aunt Bea delivering food to prisoners and of episodes in which characters slipped into the alley behind Mayberry's jail to talk to prisoners through the cell window.

Knotts got his love of entertaining and comedy from his movie-loving mother and from a family in which humor was part of everyday conversations.

He began his career as a ventriloquist, performing at social clubs and events around Morgantown. A West Virginia University professor made a dummy for him. At Morgantown High School he wrote a humorous column, scripted sketches for shows and MC'd assembly programs, laying the groundwork for a lengthy and remarkable career.

The characters he created will keep people laughing for a long time to come. That is no small accomplishment.

DISCUSSING OLD-TIME CURES, WARTS AND ALL

June 18, 2006

Happy Father's Day, dads. Today especially, I find myself recalling things my father taught me, such as how to plant tomatoes or how to wire dynamite. A father never knows what his children may need on their journey through life.

I also remember vividly his tales of cures practiced by "the old folks." Recently, I came across a whole passel of these old practices in an article titled, "Some Common Superstitions of West Virginia Pioneers," by C. W. Swiger, *The West Virginia Review*, Vol. III, No. XI, August 1926.

Apparently, our ancestors spent a lot of time pondering the problem of warts and the removal of same. Toads must have been plentiful back then, since one common belief held that you could get warts from handling toads. Fortunately, if you'd been toad wrangling and warts commenced popping up, you had your choice of sure-fire cures.

Steal a dishcloth from the house and slip out without looking in any direction but straight ahead. Walk a straight line until you came to a tree or rock. Hang the rag on a limb of the tree or bury it under the rock, and as the rag decayed, your wart would fade away.

If you were in a hurry to be rid of your unsightly bump, you could mix breadcrumbs with blood from the wart and feed the crumbs to a chicken. Presto, the wart would be gone.

If you were afraid of what Ma might do if she caught you making off with her best dishrag or messing with her chickens, you might search the fields and forests for a weathered bone to rub over the wart for immediate removal.

Alternatively, you could rub a copper coin over the wart and throw the coin away. When someone found it and picked it up, the wart would leave you and transfer to that person. So much for "Find a penny, pick it up, and all the day you'll have good luck."

Toothaches were a bigger problem than warts, and various cures were avowed to bring relief. You might try picking the afflicted tooth and the gums with a splinter from a tree that had been struck by lightning, but there was a price: The tooth would immediately begin to decay.

Another cure called for someone to place a finger over the aching jaw and rub it around three times, repeating the suffering person's name each time. The middle name could not be omitted. The procedure ended with the incantation, "Christ died in pain/Tooth remain," then repeating three times "In the name of the Father and of the Son and of the Holy Ghost, amen."

Christian symbolism frequently appeared in these cures. Folklorists say slaves and their descendants often mixed African folktales with Christian allegories, but the Celts and Angles who settled the Appalachians did much the same, mingling their cultures' ancient beliefs with the newer teachings of Christianity.

A method of stopping a nosebleed, for instance, required chanting two or three times, "Under me, dot-spot-dash, 5, 4, 3, 2, 1/(name in full)/Blood be stopped." However, the chant could be replaced by repeating a Bible verse instead.

More serious illnesses called for more serious measures. For instance, drinking strained sheep manure was considered a cure for mumps.

Some people with tuberculosis reportedly wore around their waist a live rattlesnake from which the fangs had been removed, believing it could draw the "poison" from the lungs. How one attached a live rattlesnake to one's waist is not in the record at hand, and the kid here ain't about to research it.

Most of these "cures" faded when doctors, dentists and pharmaceuticals became more readily available. As health insurance becomes increasingly unaffordable, we may see a new generation of folk cures emerge. Stay tuned.

In the meantime, enjoy Father's Day and don't handle too many toads.

Dr. James Edmund Reeves and the West Virginia Medical Association

July 25, 2010

O n June 9, 1936, during a meeting in Fairmont, the West Virginia State Medical Association took time to visit Rivesville in order to dedicate a ten-ton boulder.

The rock, which had been found in the Canaan Valley, sat on a pedestal of sorts on Mill Street in Rivesville, with a bronze tablet attached to its face to honor the physicians who had founded the state medical association just four years after West Virginia officially became a state, according to *The Founders of The Medical Society of West Virginia*, compiled by the Auxiliary to the West Virginia State Medical Association, April 1936.

On February 28, 1867, sixteen doctors had signed a circular inviting other medical professionals to join in forming the association.

The organization was to serve, "As a means of elevating the standard of Practical Medicine and Surgery in West Virginia — and to render quackery odious," they wrote.

By joining together to share information and techniques, physicians could improve their skills. Furthermore, the circular stated that the state's inhabitants "must be taught the laws of Hygiene, and be able to mark the difference between the true and false — the intelligent physician and the murderous pretender."

The meeting to establish a "State Medical Society" was set for April 10 in Fairmont, so that West Virginia could be represented by a professional organization at the American Medical Association meeting in Cincinnati the following month.

Of the sixteen physicians who signed the invitation, eight came from Wheeling and a pair from Triadelphia. The rest were from the North Central area: J. W. Ramsey, J. M. Blackford, and J. M. Bowcock of Clarksburg; D. S. Pinnell from Buckhannon; Thomas Kennedy from Grafton; H. W. Brock of Morgantown; and from Fairmont James Edmund Reeves, the primary mover and shaker in creating the organization.

The *Journal of the American Medical Association*, Vol. 105, No. 2, July 13, 1935, credits Reeves with founding the town of Rivesville, but that is incorrect. The town was laid out as Pleasantville in 1776, according to information provided by JoAnn Lough from her late father's Marion County history, *Now and Long Ago*.

Around the time of the Civil War, Dr. Reeves assisted his sister, Ann (Anna), in her campaign to improve community health. She set up sanitary organizations known as Mother's Day Clubs. Anna's daughter, Anna Jarvis — Reeves' niece — would become famous as the founder of Mothers Day.

The doctor, born in Culpepper, Virginia, in 1829, did more than establish the state's medical society.

Assisted by Judge James H. Ferguson, a member of the West Virginia legislature, he drafted a bill to create a state board of health, according to *West Virginia Medical Journal*, Vol. 10. Reeves' bill passed on March 8, 1881. He served as the board's president until resigning in 1885.

He also started publication of a monthly medical journal in December 1875. Titled *West Virginia Medical Student*, it is believed to be the first attempt at medical journalism in the state.

He authored a pamphlet, "How to Work with the Baush & Lomb Optical Co.'s Microtome and a Method of Demonstrating the Tubercle Bacillus." Baush & Lomb proudly touted the fact this renowned physician had praised their product, a device for making very thin slices for examination under a microscope, in *The Carolina Medical Journal*, Vol. 19–20.

He was elected president of the American Public Health Association, according to *The History and Government of West Virginia*, by Richard Ellsworth Fast and Hu Maxwell (The Acme Publishing Co., 1901). He remained active in that organization until his death.

In 1887, the aforementioned edition of *The Carolina Medical Journal* stated he was about to relocate his practice from Wheeling to Chattanooga, Tennessee.

"We trust that the more southerly climate will prove beneficial to him and the partner of his toils," *TCMJ* wrote.

The British Medical Journal, February 1, 1896, reported his death, identifying him as the author of *Manual of Microscopy for Students, Physicians and Surgeons*.

The First Woman to Graduate West Virginia University's Medical School Made a Lasting Reputation

June 24, 2001

"I think there is a great deal of ungenerous sentiment on the part of men, so much as to be astonishing and incomprehensible, considering the strong sense of superiority which exists in the male bosom from the age of two up."

So began an article by a Mrs. Oliphant in *Fraser's Magazine*, which was reprinted in the *Wheeling Intelligencer*, June 8, 1880. The writer wasn't merely taking potshots at males; she was leveling her Oliphant gun on the men of the medical profession for their resistance to women being trained as doctors.

"The doctors, a most liberal and highly educated profession, have shown themselves in this particular not more enlightened than the watch makers, who have also resisted the entrance of women into their trade with violence, " she continued.

In truth, it was eighteen years after Mme. Oliphant's article appeared before West Virginia University permitted women into the medical school, and male students hadn't become any more enlightened with the passage of time. The thirty-three males in the med department took every opportunity to embarrass and harass the few females until the women dropped out of the program. All but one.

Phoebia Gean Moore grew up near Mannington with all the stubbornness and humor her Scot-Irish ancestry could bestow upon her. She was raised on a farm and wasn't put off by whatever dirty jobs, dirty tricks or dirty jokes her male colleagues cared to throw at her. Eventually she won their admiration and they became her friends, she claimed.

After graduating West Virginia University in 1901, she finished her studies at Bennett Medical College in Chicago, then returned to Mannington and hung out her shingle as the town's first woman doctor. A local male physician thought, "(I)t is very noble, but she won't last long."

Let us hope he was better at diagnosing disease than he was at understanding Dr. P. G. Moore. Absolutely nothing deterred her from pursuing her calling—not the prejudice of men, the distrust of women, the miserable roads she had to traverse, nor West Virginia's unpredictable weather. Gradually, patients began to trickle in. Before long, doctors from other counties were recommending her to their women patients, who traveled to Mannington for treatment by this Appalachian version of Dr. Quinn, Medicine Woman.

Generally, however, it was Dr. Moore who did the traveling—on horseback, in a buggy and finally in a Model-T Ford. By 1930, she said, "I've worn out five Fords and have had two other makes of cars since."

During the flu pandemic of 1918, she visited so many patients she had to hire someone to drive her car so she could sleep while traveling from house to house. She was among the physicians who treated casualties of June 1944's killer tornado.

Dr. Moore was part of the staff at the annual Farm Women's Camp held at Jackson's Mills. The farmwomen looked at her curiously, but no one came to see her. One night she approached a group of them and asked, "How many of you can dance the Virginia Reel?" She got them dancing, and soon they were coming by her office for exams. She diagnosed two women with cancer, one of whom embraced her the following summer, shouting, "You saved my life!"

In her final years, Dr. Moore's friends asked what sort of gift they could bestow on her. She responded, "the establishment of a Premature Baby Room in the Fairmont General Hospital." It was made so, and a plaque with her name (albeit misspelled) was placed on the room's door. When Fairmont General dedicated its new annex in April 1953, she cut the ribbon. A few days later, she was admitted to the same hospital as a patient; she died there June 4, 1953.

Information for today's column comes from "Phoebia G. Moore, M. D., First Woman to Study Medicine at West Virginia University," by Arthur C. Prichard, *Goldenseal*, October–December 1979.

GRAND, GLOOMY WESTON STATE HOSPITAL A MONUMENT TO POLITICAL PATRONAGE?

April 5, 1998

T he old Weston State Mental Hospital, as it was generally known, stands vacant now. Dry sycamore leaves cluster
around its iron fence. On a recent day when clouds skirmished with
the sun for possession of the sky, the stately old building changed
its personality minute by minute, like many of the patients who
spent their lives inside its walls.

Under the clouds, the main building glowered, its bricks dull
gray-brown behind the dark evergreens standing sentinel at every
corner. Quasimodo would have felt at home swinging down from
its clock tower.

Then sunlight glinted off the arches above its windows, the
bricks became golden, and the two-tenths-mile-long building
transformed into an aging Southern belle, her poise and grandeur
still shining through her wrinkles.

This aging lady's birth dates back to the 1850s when commis-
sioners from the state of Virginia selected it from three possible
sites to build the Trans-Alleghany Lunatic Asylum.

Weston's geographic location may have influenced the choice, but the greatest influence probably came from the political power of Lewis County, a Democratic island in a Whig sea. Edward Conrad Smith, in *A History of Lewis County, West Virginia* (self published, 1920), said, "Every measure concerning (the western counties) was referred to the delegates from Lewis."

These Democrat politicos had already managed to get the Staunton-Parkersburg Turnpike rerouted to go through Weston. With one of their members, Jonathan M. Bennett, serving as First Auditor of Virginia under Governor Henry A. Wise, securing the lunatic asylum and all the construction money that went with it wasn't even a challenge.

Seventy acres of flat land, mostly within Weston, were purchased for $1,500 from land speculator Minter Bailey, who coincidentally was president of the board of directors charged with buying the land and constructing buildings. Another 199 hilly acres to the west were added for $9,809.12, leaving the board $15,000 to start work on the buildings. The General Assembly appropriated $50,000, and in the spring of 1861 construction was underway.

Then some fellows down in Charleston, South Carolina, thought it would be fun to lob a few shells at Fort Sumter and discovered Abraham Lincoln had no sense of humor where his forts were concerned.

Virginia's secession convention decided the state really did want to secede from the Union after all and ordered the asylum's construction funds be returned for use in defending the Old Dominion. Those funds were already on their way to Wheeling, however, where all government buildings had already been seized "in the name of Abraham Lincoln to whom they belong."

Construction stalled. The fine stone quarried and hauled from Mount Clare sat waiting until work resumed the next year with $40,000 appropriated by the Restored Government of Virginia.

At that point, the embryonic state had no statehouse, university or other institution except for this partially completed lunatic asylum on the banks of the West Fork River. In Old Virginia, disgruntled Johnny Rebs probably figured that was most appropriate for their dissenting western brethren.

The first West Virginia legislature set aside enough funds to at least make the institution habitable. They also decided "lunatic asylum" was too politically incorrect even for 1863 and renamed it the West Virginia Hospital for the Insane.

The first nine patients entered in October 1864. Four years later, the building was still only capable of housing 40; most of those judged insane languished in jails. In 1870, the state finally ponied up $110,000 for buildings, including a separate brick structure for colored patients.

A quarry was opened on the riverbank to expedite building, and a steady stream of craftsmen flowed into Weston. While neighboring counties struggled in a postwar economy Lewis thrived, thanks to construction money, a significant hospital payroll and a demand for farm goods. Saw mill blades whined through thousands of feet of timber purchased from the surrounding area.

When the hospital started its own farm, it brought improved agricultural techniques that spread throughout the county.

Whatever machinations the old Democrats pulled off in the 1850s had a belated payoff, but the benefits would be felt in Lewis County for decades to come. The mental hospital was one of the greatest pieces of political patronage in the state during the nineteenth century.

The old institution closed in 1994. Its interior had often been a dark, sad place filled with the sound of shuffling feet and sights right out of *One Flew Over the Cuckoo's Nest*.

But it was also a place for those who had nowhere else to go.

Little wonder its personality seems to flicker from gloom to grace on days when clouds and sun battle for the sky.

Addendum

A relative was confined to Weston State Mental Hospital for a time, and I visited there once or twice with my parents when I was a young child. My statement about scenes "right out of *One Flew Over the Cuckoo's Nest*" is based on my impressions from those visits.

IDEOLOGICAL CLASH DIVIDED MARSHALL UNIVERSITY AND HUNTINGTON

April 4, 2004

Pundits and pollsters say America is a nation increasingly polarized along ideological lines. Truly, we are more confrontational now than at any time since the cultural, political and social upheavals of the 1960s.

That decade saw many clashes between liberals and conservatives, children and parents. One of the most bitter in West Virginia occurred when Students for a Democratic Society (SDS) organized on the Marshall University campus down in Huntington.

Born out of an ideal of participatory democracy, SDS became "the most visible New Left organization emerging from a disaffected white middle class … It educated its supporters in protest tactics and nurtured a radical analysis of liberal capitalism," according to "A Struggle for Recognition: Marshal University Students for a Democratic Society and the Red Scare in Huntington, 1965– 1969," by John Hennen, *West Virginia History*, Vol. 52, 1993.

Trouble brewed as soon as SDS petitioned for formal recognition as a student organization at Marshall in September 1965.

One member of the Student Senate, a Thai student, warned "the Marshall SDS would soon be controlled by communists who would twist the minds of students," according to Hennen.

Marshall's generally conservative student body embraced the traditional view of education as a means to a better life for themselves, rather than the emerging Leftist view of colleges as agents for social change. In 1965, the campus approved a referendum supporting America's military action in Vietnam 1,352 to 187.

(The referendum was attached to the Homecoming Queen ballot. Wonder if this was the inspiration for Cindi Lauper's song "The Homecoming Queen's Got a Gun"?)

Regardless of opposition, a local SDS chapter, independent of the national organization, was founded October 31, 1968. Its mission statement declared it "maintains a *vision* of a democratic society, where at all levels the people have control of the decisions which affect them ... It feels the *urgency* to put forth a radical, democratic program counterposed to authoritarian movements both of Communism and the domestic Right." (Italics are in the original statement.)

Still, the radical, sometimes violent reputation of the national SDS gave many Huntington citizens the heebie-jeebies. Staunch off-campus opposition organized under the leadership of several local ministers and citizen activists. They began a letter-writing campaign to college officials and the *Huntington Herald-Dispatch* arguing against recognition of the SDS. Before long, they expanded their campaign to oppose any faculty member whose views they found suspect.

An unexpected result of their efforts was increased campus support for SDS; students didn't cotton to townies interfering in campus affairs.

Caught smack in the middle of this impassioned, name-calling, town-and-gown catfight was Marshall's new president, Dr. Roland H. Nelson. He had the misfortune to succeed Dr. Stewart Smith, a very popular president who had served for over 20 years.

Stewart had been warm and ebullient, skilled in public relations. Nelson's public persona was clinical, focused on his vision of Marshall as a "Metroversity ... a major society force in its region; a brokerage house for ideas ... closely tied to the development of the region."

His vision was the one thing the SDS and their conservative opponents agreed on. They hated it.

SDS saw the Metroversity as "a training school for corporate interests" that "would accelerate and expand the military-industrial corporate influence over academia." Conservatives felt it departed from their traditional view of education as a means of "molding good, obedient citizens," according to Hennen.

Ultimately, Dr. Nelson officially recognized the SDS, based on Constitutional freedom of assembly and expression. This decision and his controversial vision undermined Nelson, who served only one year as president before resigning.

Marshall's SDS chapter dissolved in the early 1970s. Its confrontations with conservative townspeople and students were often unpleasant but devoid of the injurious violence that marked similar encounters elsewhere in America.

Today, we're back to ideological confrontations and name-calling in place of reasoned discussions. Sigh. You know you're getting old when the evening news sounds like a rerun.

Jazz: 'Dividing the Entire Music World of Clarksburg'

October 6, 2013

A world-famous dancer coming to perform at Clarksburg's opera house unintentionally started a feud when she used a four-letter word: "jazz."

On November 15, 1921, the *Telegram* printed a letter from Clarence C. Arms, supervisor of music for Clarksburg public schools. He complained about an article printed the previous evening with "statements regarding so-called 'jazz' music" made by Lada, the renowned interpretive dancer, and he begged to dispute them, "in the interest of better music for the masses."

Lada had said jazz music "creeps into the souls of humans, even against their own will." She meant it as praise, but to Arms it was "a confession and acknowledgement of the dangerous and sensuous qualities of that class of so-called music." He regarded jazz rhythms as barbaric, and he saw no future for the music.

"Regardless of the desperate last stand the music publishers are making to perpetuate this insidious and crude form of barbaric rhythm with its weird and unearthly melody, it is fast disappearing because the thinking public regards it as a serious menace to our social organization, especially the younger generation."

A *Telegram* reporter showed a copy of the letter to Lada in her dressing room at the opera house a few days later, and the newspaper printed her reaction on November 18.

With "scorn and a snatch of laughter," she said, "Jazz music dangerous? Poof! Upon the jazz rhythms rests the foundation of future American music." Professor Arms' arguments were "absurd."

If the professor thought she was defending jazz dancing he was wrong, she said. "People of any culture do not discuss jazz dancing. But jazz music — ah, that is a different matter!"

All Americans should champion this new music, she declared. "Upon jazz music and the rhythms of jazz music rest the very foundation of the future development of music in America.

"Until recently, all American music was an imitation of that of foreign schools and now comes this wonderful new music, this wonderful new rhythm … The rhythms of jazz music go way down into the very soil. They are … wonderfully, intrinsically American. They go back to the old Indian rhythms, the old negro rhythms … It gets into the very soul of people, grips them, gets down into the deeply-buried American soul."

Lada knew a thing or two about European and American music. Born Emily Schupp in Duluth, Minn., the child of a German father and Hungarian mother, at age twenty-five she accepted a position as a dancer touring the United States with the Russian Symphony Orchestra. For ten years she toured America and Europe, according to *Forgotten Duluthians* by David Ouse, and became enamored of folk music, both European and American.

She took the stage name Lada from a work written for her by Russian composer Reinhold Moritzevich Glière, according to *The Rhinebeck* (NY) *Gazette*, December 6, 1919. That article quoted a review that said, "One of the first among living dancers to realize the truth of … (the) lack of concordance between motion and music in all the ancient and new schools and to devise, intuitively, a method of her own in expressing only the music."

Her fame and accolades meant nothing to Prof. Arms. In a November 20 *Telegram* article he declared, "in the minds of the great majority of the people of this city, (jazz is) a pernicious parisite (sic) that is getting a firm hold on its victims."

He claimed to have learned of a young person of Clarksburg whom "the demon of 'jazz'" had started on a downward path.

The *Telegram* noted the controversy was "dividing the entire music world of Clarksburg into two factions: One supporting jazz and the other consigning it to the crimes of civilization … the whole town seemed about to be forced to divide itself over the question."

Eventually, the controversy over music died down—until rock 'n' roll came along in the Fifties.

THE GREAT COMIC BOOK BURNING AT SPENCER, 1948

October 21, 2012

S peak of burning leaves in autumn, and memories fill our nostrils with that sweet, smoky scent. Sixty-four years ago this week, smoke from burning a different kind of leaves rose from the town of Spencer and spread across America. To some, that smoke carried the sweet smell of morality; to others, it was the stench of fascism.

On Monday afternoon, October 28, 1948, 600 students at the Spencer Elementary School gathered around a 6-foot-high pile of over 2,000 comic books. Led by thirteen-year-old David Mace, they pledged to burn all such books in their possession and "to TRY not to read any more." Then, they consigned Superman, Dick Tracy and others in the pile to flames.

Young Mace, whose parents operated a small, family-style restaurant called the Glass Door, had been recruited by one of his teachers, Mabel Riddle, to organize the book burning. Years later, in an interview with David Hajdu, who was writing *The Ten-Cent Plague: The Great Comic Book Scare and How It Changed America* (Farrar, Straus and Giroux, 2008), Mace said he'd read comics and thought nothing of it until Mrs. Riddle explained to him the "evil effect on the minds of young children" these books had.

The *Roane County Reporter* wrote about the bonfire on October 28. Perhaps not coincidentally, directly below that story was one headlined, "Gideons Distribute 1300 Testaments to County Pupils."

With the threats of Nazi Germany and Imperial Japan defeated, America's concerns had turned to moral instruction for the young generation. A large ad in *The Nicholas Chronicle*, November 4, 1948, paid for by ten local businesses warned, "Without religious training Teddie (the cherubic-faced little boy pictured in the ad) might some day go out of this door, and no longer be the same fine son of which his mother is so proud."

That same day, the *Roane County Reporter* announced the comic-book burning had attracted attention across the nation and printed some of the letters of support that had been received.

The Spencer school wasn't the first to burn comics; a couple of Catholic schools had done so three years earlier but drew little attention.

Comic books were extremely popular—between 80 and 100 million were sold in June 1948, according to *Ten-Cent Plague*—but social critics decried some comics' over-the-top depictions of bloodletting and acts of depravity. Crime and horror comics were especially targeted; even some artists who worked in comics said later that some of those had gone too far. Critics also decried scantily clad Wonder Woman, said Betty and Veronica were too well endowed, and called Superman a fascist operating outside the law.

Not everyone agreed with burning comic books. The *Charleston Daily Mail* was among the first to point out that the memory of Nazis burning books in Germany was still too recent for Americans to be comfortable with the notion.

Six years after the bonfire in Spencer, the comics industry created a trade group and adopted the Comics Code of what would be acceptable. The *Exponent* praised their efforts on September 30, 1954, but noted the struggle still continued between two social extremes, those who feared the Hitler-like book burnings and those who feared "a contagion from poisonous words which would fill the nation with a soul-sick and misled citizenry."

The Comics Code died last year, after a quarter-century of declining impact. American comics had grown up and taken on adult themes. Art Spielgelman's graphic novel *Maus: A Survivor's Tale* won a Pulitzer Prize in 1992 for its depiction of how incarceration in Auschwitz forever affected Spielgelman's father.

In 2000–1, issues 151–7 of the adult horror series *Hellblazer* — a series that would give comics reformers of the 1940s and '50s apoplexy — were set in West Virginia and contained some of the most vile stereotyping I've seen. Each issue's cover used a state road map as background; Spencer can be seen at center left. The storyline was titled, "Good Intentions." Lingering bitterness, perhaps?

A West Virginia University Professor and W. J. Bryan Tried To Make Monkeys of Each Other

December 17, 2000

Given the letters that have been appearing in this newspaper over the issue of teaching creationism and/or evolution, a reader asked me if Clarksburg had any reaction to the Scopes "Monkey Trial" of 1925. I don't know, but the prosecutor in that trial, William Jennings Bryan, and a West Virginia University professor certainly tried to make monkeys out of each other over the evolution issue.

The story of their protracted debate is taken from Morgantown's *The New Dominion* newspaper, June 3 and 5, 1922; *The New York Times*, June 4, 5 and 13; *Bryan*, by M. R. Werner (Harcourt, Brace & Co., 1929), and *Defender of the Faith William Jennings Bryan: The Last Decade 1915-1925* (Oxford University Press, 1965), by Lawrence W. Levine.

In the 1920s young adults were less willing to dogmatically accept the social order and religious beliefs their elders clung to. They had been disillusioned by World War I, shocked by millions of influenza deaths, and exposed to recent scientific discoveries and theories that questioned the old order. In response, a fundamentalist Christian movement, primarily based in rural America, sought to win these "lost souls" back into the fold.

Fundamentalists saw the teaching of the new scientific theories as a major cause of youth's disenchantment with traditional religious beliefs. In particular, they were aghast over Charles Darwin's theory of evolution, which held that humanity slowly developed from more primitive life forms rather than springing forth fully developed in the image and likeness of God, as taught by the Bible.

Among those raging against the teaching of evolution in public institutions was Bryan, a masterful orator who had twice run unsuccessfully as the Democratic candidate for president. Known as "The Great Commoner" for his advocacy of laws that favored miners, Southern farmers and other "common people," Bryan also believed the majority should rule in all things. That helps explain his opposition to an anti-lynching law, as well as his opposition to the teaching of evolution.

Speaking in West Virginia in 1922, he offered $100 to any college professor who could show the Bible and the theory of evolution were in harmony. West Virginia University Professor R. C. Spangler took him up on it.

Peeved, Bryan sent Spangler the $100, but demanded to know if Spangler believed in the miracles described in the Bible, the virgin birth and resurrection of Christ, and Christ's claim to power as described in the Book of Matthew. When Spangler wrote that he believed in the Bible, but didn't answer the questions to Bryan's satisfaction, Bryan accused him of "cowardly evasion," then later apologized for the statement. He claimed his $100 was well spent, for it had "silenced an evolutionist in the classroom."

No, it didn't, Spangler shot back.

Bryan asked the professor if he felt he was personally descended from an ape. Not an ape of today, Spangler responded. So what animal would you prefer to have descended from? Bryan asked.

Okay, Bucko, here's my family tree, Spangler wrote, or words to that effect. He traced his own ancestry from its protozoan beginnings through several grades of animal life, an ape-man, and finally to modern man with a fully developed brain.

"Your ancestry was just the same as mine," he wrote, and your antecedents include not just apes but "the skunk, the lizard, the turtle and venomous snakes." He pointed out that at one time the human embryo has a tail longer than its legs and added, "I assure you that your embryological development was the same, except for this one point — I cannot say, I do not know, whether your tail degenerated before birth or was amputated after birth."

Mee-ooowww! Apparently, there was some cat ancestry in both men as well.

The following year, Bryan told the West Virginia legislature, "The hand that writes the pay check rules the schools."

The burning issue died down during the Depression, but continued smoldering for decades before blazing up again with the Creationist movement of the 1980s.

PIONEERS

RELIGION

WEATHER

SPORTS

MOUNTAIN MELTING POT

FATHERS' RECREATIONAL ACTIVITIES HAVE CHANGED

June 17, 2007

Recently, I was talking with two of my brothers, Howard and Clinton, about our father, Howard Harold. We couldn't recall ever hearing him talk about playing sports when he was growing up, except for a form of kickball. That's not surprising since as a boy he lived up Brushy Fork and later near the head of Goke Hollow. There just wasn't much opportunity even for sandlot baseball.

My brothers did recall he once joined them to take a couple of swings at a softball, and he drove it into the next county.

What they remembered most was his love of hunting. He traipsed Harrison County's hills and hollows with shotgun and animal traps, and the hides of bobcats, muskrats, 'coons, skunks and other critters covered an entire wall.

He also loved to ride "unbreakable" horses, once walking 10 miles to try one that he'd heard couldn't be ridden, according to a family story

While I remember hunting with him, I can't recall him trapping or breaking horses, but then I came along late in my parents' lives. They probably wanted to name me R. U. Kidding.

Thinking about what constituted entertainment for my father, I realized that in the time when he was growing up—he would have been ninety-nine two weeks ago—most "play" was a form of training for survival.

Learning how to identify animal tracks and which plants were edible in the forest, knowing how to trail a deer or spot a squirrel's den was play for a boy, but it put food on the table, too. A man could earn a dollar taming horses or selling hides when money was scarce.

Others have made similar observations about our ancestors' diversions. Gibson Lamb Cranmer, in *History of Wheeling City and Ohio County, West Virginia and Representative Citizens* (Biographical Publishing, 1902), quoted the chronicler of pioneer life Joseph Doddridge and added some thoughts of his own on the subject.

In pioneer times, boys (and many girls) learned to mimic the sounds of birds and beasts. It was, Doddridge said, "a very necessary part of education … The imitations of the gobbling and other sounds of wild turkeys often brought those keen-eyed and ever watchful tenants of the forest within the reach of the rifle."

Also, during wars between white settlers and the native tribes, both groups imitated owl hoots, wolf howls and the like to communicate. That sometimes caused sounds made by the real animals to be a trifle disconcerting.

"I have often witnessed the consternation of a whole neighborhood in consequence of a few screeches of owls," Doddridge wrote.

Cranmer, carrying on with Doddridge's theme about practical entertainment said, "Throwing the tomahawk was another boyish sport in which many acquired considerable skill."

A tomahawk made a given number of turns over a given distance, based on the length of its handle. Practice taught youngsters how to eyeball the distance to a target in order to strike it with a thrown tomahawk's sharpened edge.

Running, jumping, and wrestling conditioned the lads and prepared them for both options in any "fight or flight" situation in which they found themselves.

At age twelve or thirteen, a boy was given a small rifle and shot pouch and assigned a porthole of the local fort or station that was his to defend in case of attack, according to Cranmer.

We haven't had to make playtime into survival training for a long time now. We use plastic, not lead, to put food on the table and clothes on our backs today. Hand-eye coordination comes from playing video games, not throwing tomahawks. Running, jumping and wrestling are organized team sports. Perhaps the greatest survival skills modern fathers (and mothers) pass down to their children are defensive driving tactics.

But I'm glad I had a taste of older times growing up, roaming the hills with Dad and our shotguns. I never could throw a tomahawk worth spit, though.

CALHOUN COUNTY CLAIMS ITS OWN MIKE FINK LEGEND

February 3, 2013

I first heard the name Mike Fink in the "Davy Crockett" episodes that ran on Walt Disney's television program, when I was barely high enough to see the top of the kitchen table. The character of Fink appeared in the last two of the five episodes. He was the toughest keelboat man on the Mississippi, half horse, half alligator, and the rest snapping turtle. He claimed he could out-run, out-shoot, out-fight, and out-drink any man. A larger than life character by any measure, he fascinated me.

Imagine my surprise years later when I found out he had actually lived and had indeed lived a larger-than-life existence.

I've never quite gotten over my Fink fascination, so I was thrilled when I came across an article titled "Mike Fink Story" in *History of Calhoun County West Virginia 1989* (Calhoun County Historical and Genealogical Society). The excitement lasted just long enough to read the article's six paragraphs and determine this was a different Mike Fink.

This one might not have been half horse, half alligator, but he does have a legend of his own. The article in *History of Calhoun*

County—a reprint of one written by W. W. Bailey in the 1960s for *The Calhoun Chronicle*—laid out the story that has been passed down since pioneer times.

No one recorded from whence this Mike Fink had come to the western Virginia mountains in the years following the American Revolution. Like the Greek goddess Venus who emerged from the sea a fully grown woman, Fink first appears, full grown, along a little stream in what is now Calhoun County one day in 1780. Nothing is known of him prior to that time.

He and Adam O'Brien and another hardy pioneer whose name has been lost to history were sitting near a little stream, watching a deer lick and hoping some venison on the hoof would show up. What showed up instead were some chaps from one of the indigenous tribes, and they did not appreciate these pale-skinned Johnny-come-latelys poaching their game.

Now, Mike Fink the keelboat man likely would have stood his ground and whipped the Indians with one hand while shooting a ten-point buck with the other. Or at least that's how the story would have come down to us.

Instead, these three white men took off running upstream. Fink was shot in the foot but kept up with his companions until they reached a low gap between the West Fork River and Beech Fork Creek, near present-day Minnora. By then, blood loss had weakened Fink. He could run no farther.

His friends left him at the gap while they sought help from some men living on the West Fork. When they returned, it was too late. Mike Fink was dead, but he hadn't gone gentle into that good night—an Indian lay dead alongside him. The rescue party buried them both at the gap.

The incident hardly seems to stand out from similar tales of confrontations between pioneers pushing westward and the people who were already there, but it seems to have occupied a special place in the memories of the early settlers, who passed along the story to subsequent generations.

The stream along which the men had run was named Fink Creek in honor of the late pioneer. Today, you can read the Grave of Mike Fink historical marker along Rt. 16; its text begins, "One mile west in the low gap are the graves of Mike Fink and an Indian."

A photograph on the HurHerald Website, taken in May 2011, shows a low stone with "Mike Fink Cemetery" carved into it. It marks one of two Fink cemeteries in the area. The accompanying article by Bob Weaver says Mike Fink's burial area has been "recently resurrected through the efforts of Emma Stalnaker Deel."

As for Mike Fink the keelboat man, no one knows where his bones lie.

CONFLICTING STORIES OF PRESTON COUNTY'S DUNKARD MASSACRE

October 24, 2010

F inding disagreement among historical accounts regarding any given event isn't unusual; in fact, it's the norm. Not often, however, are there such radically different accounts as those that surround the family who were the first white settlers in what is now Preston County.

The first version comes from *History of Preston County (West Virginia)*, by S. T. Wiley (The Journal Printing House, 1882; 1968 reprint by McClain Printing), and is found in a number of other sources as well.

In this one, Dr. Thomas Eckarly and two of his brothers, "whose names have not been preserved," according to Wiley, journeyed into the unsettled wilds of the future Preston County in 1755 or '56.

They were members of a German Baptist movement that originated in 1708. Its members are often called Dunkards because they use three immersions during baptism. Opposition to all war is among their chief tenets.

In this version of the story, the three men left eastern Pennsylvania to avoid military service. What would be known as the French and Indian War had begun, and they did not want to be impressed into the military in violation of their religious beliefs.

After camping on a creek ten miles south of the future site of Morgantown—probably Cobun Creek—they settled on bottomland along the Cheat River. It was far enough from white settlement to offer them the seclusion they sought, and they remained for two or three years, until their salt and ammunition were nearly gone.

Thomas, the doctor, took a pack of furs to trade for necessities in the eastern settlements; some sources say he took poultry, although that seems less likely. At Fort Pleasant on the South Branch of the Potomac he was placed under arrest.

The Dunkards were known to have favorable relations with the Indian tribes, an outgrowth of their pacifist religious beliefs. The commander of the fort feared Thomas Eckarly was a spy.

Eventually, he was permitted to return, under armed guard, to his camp on Cheat River. Any question about him being a spy for the Indians ended when the group arrived at the Eckarly camp: the cabin was nothing but ashes, the crops were destroyed, and his brothers' mutilated bodies lay decomposing in the yard. The doctor returned with the guard to the fort.

Version two of the brothers' story can be found at www.polsci.wvu.edu/wv/Preston/prehistory.html.

This one says the brothers' name was Eckerlin, the doctor's name was Samuel, not Thomas, and they departed Pennsylvania in 1751 or 1752, before the war began. The other brothers were probably Gabriel and Israel, and the trio left their church at Ephrata near Philadelphia after a falling-out with church leaders. Yet another variation says they left after stealing gold and precious stones from the church.

Instead of three men heading into the wilderness alone, several families who shared their faith came with them, which would seem to support the story of a disagreement with church leaders.

All versions agree that Samuel or Thomas went east to trade for necessities and was arrested at Fort Pleasant. However, the story that says other families were present at the Cheat River settlement relates that when he returned there under guard, twenty-seven of the thirty inhabitants had been killed and the entire settlement destroyed.

The three survivors had been carried off to Fort Duquesne, the forerunner of Pittsburgh. They included the two brothers who were murdered in the other version. These brothers were later taken to French Quebec and disappear from history.

The third survivor, an indentured servant named Baltzer Shilling, was taken to an Indian village on the Sandusky River as a slave. He escaped, reunited with Samuel/Thomas and told the story of what had happened. He said some fifty native tribesmen led by a French priest fell upon the settlement.

So there you have the two widely divergent tales. As I said, historical disagreement is normal, but this is a rather extreme case.

Few Western Virginians Toasted the Whiskey Rebellion of 1794

April 11, 1999

H ere's a toast to the Whiskey Rebellion. Cheers!

When the original 13 colonies won independence from Great Britain in 1783, they initially tried to operate as so many sovereign nations, loosely joined by the Articles of Confederation. That proved to be about as effective as the average committee, and by the end of 1791 they had ratified a new constitution, merging as the United States of America.

This raised some thorny questions, especially where money was concerned. Each state had accrued debts during the War for Independence. Alexander Hamilton, the secretary of the treasury under George Washington and the dominant figure of that administration, believed the new federal government should assume the war debts of the individual states.

Virginia balked. Her debts weren't nearly as great as those of other colonies, such as Massachusetts, the state she was most seriously contending with for control of hearts and minds in the new republic.

Hamilton cut a deal with Thomas Jefferson: A new national capital would be located in the South instead of New York or

Philadelphia. In exchange, Virginia supported the assumption bill, making all states equally responsible for the war debt.

The next question was where to get the money from. Then, as now, the answer was obvious: Glory, hallelujah, let us pass a sin tax! Slap a tariff on the whiskey makers, boys, to — ahem — "float" the assumption debt.

A whiskey tax was no small matter. Ads in old newspapers make it clear much of the frontier economy was booze-based. Cash money was hard to come by, so every business welcomed whiskey in trade for other goods, whether it was Despard's mercantile or the *Clarksburg Independent Virginian* newspaper. Sour mash production was one of the most important markets for grain farmers, who proliferated in western Pennsylvania, and neither they nor the myriad distilleries took kindly to federal fingers reaching into their purses.

In 1794, the Whiskey Rebellion broke out, with Pittsburgh at its nucleus. Tax collectors were bullied, beaten, tarred and feathered. On more than one occasion, the insurgents came south of the state line to stir up support among Virginians.

In August, it was reported to the Supervisor of Revenue at Richmond "That the collector at Morgantown had been obliged to fly his home, and that the people of Randolph and Harrison Counties are temperate on this business and that the affair at Morgantown was the result of a rabble who have nothing to lose."

(No, students from West Virginia University were not responsible. That august center of revelry had not yet been established.)

Not to worry, Benjamin Wilson wrote from Clarksburg to Governor "Light Horse Harry" Lee on September 2. "I believe there are but few in the Counties of Harrison, Monongalia and Randolph who will dare to appear in arms, when the standard of the United

States is displayed at the head of our Federal Army."

Clarksburg's George Jackson concurred, writing "there appears to be no disposition in our part of the State, to use violence against the Government."

President Washington determined to nip this rebellion in the bud. (No, not the Budweiser; that didn't exist yet, either.) He called for 15,000 troops, with good old Light Horse Harry at their head to squelch the uprisings in Pennsylvania, New Jersey, Maryland and Virginia.

It was a bloodless effort. Several rebel leaders were arrested, the malcontents called off their revolt, and the troops were sent home by November. History does not record whether or not those troops had a drink to celebrate their victory.

Coincidentally, 65 years later Lee's son, Robert Edward, would lead a military force to put down another rebellion in the area, John Brown's attempted slave revolt at Harpers Ferry. Another three years would see that son as one of the most prominent figures opposing federal armies in the War of the Rebellion.

MISSIONARY WORK IN CHINA PUT JULIA BONAFIELD IN DANGER

April 4, 2010

Today being Easter, it seems an appropriate time to tell the story of a West Virginia woman whose service to her Christian faith put her in mortal danger.

Julia Bonafield was from Tunnelton in Preston County, but in 1888, she arrived in Foochow (Fuzhou), China, according to the 1898 report of the Woman's Foreign Missionary Society of the Methodist Episcopal Church. She would spend much of her life in that town near the East China Sea, a missionary teaching at a girls' school,

In 1909, *Woman's Missionary Friend*, Volumes 41–42, reported, "Julia Bonafield, returning for her twenty-first year of work in China, was enthusiastically received not only by her girls but by all; and while there were many open doors it was decided that 'Miss Bonafield belongs to Foochow, and Foochow belongs to Miss Bonafield.'"

One story about her relationship with Foochow's women, found in the 1919 report of the Women's Foreign Missionary Society, says that at one time a young, Christian widow learned her uncle "was trying to sell her, in accordance with Chinese custom, and fled to Miss Bonafield, the loved teacher of her brief, happy, school days.

"Miss Bonafield found that embroidery was the only thing that she could do well, and she was set to work earning her living. Other women, young and old, came begging for like help and thus the Industrial School began."

Word of the school reached another American, a Jean Adams, who was looking for ways to be of service to others.

"She appealed to Miss Bonafield for the particular place (the Industrial School) and Miss Bonafield, already overburdened with her large high school, gladly turned over to her this company of destitute widows."

Not all of Julia's years were spent in China. The 1896 edition of the *Woman's Foreign Ministry*, Vol. 27, lists her as a "Missionary at Home" in Tunnelton.

Woman's Missionary Friend, Vol. 39–40, 1907, stated she was one of "two faithful workers" the Cincinnati branch welcomed home "for much needed rest."

That edition also announced, "Miss Julia Bonafield, Standard Bearer missionary of the West Virginia Conference, has spent the summer at Mountain Lake Park" in Maryland, where summer conferences were held for young people.

Serving in a foreign country was often a dicey proposition, and the missionary teacher from West Virginia found herself swept up in global events when she was nearing her fifty year of service in China.

In July 1937, a minor skirmish between soldiers of Japan's Kwuntang Army, which had occupied provinces in northern China six years earlier, and those of the Nationalist Chinese Army near the Marco Polo Bridge escalated into open warfare. Imperial Japan hurriedly sent more troops and invaded China.

Julia Bonafield was reportedly in Shanghai when the Japanese Army occupied that city. Made prisoner by the occupying forces, she survived on three pounds of cracked wheat she was permitted to purchase from the Red Cross each month. For several years, she and other American missionaries remained in captivity with death as a constant threat.

In 1943, they were put aboard a Japanese transport and spent a month crossing and re-crossing the equator before the ship landed at a Portuguese port. There, they were put aboard the *Gripsholm*. It reached America on September 19, 1943, according to a biography of one of the other missionaries aboard, Pearl Pauline Caldwell of Pontotoc, Miss., that is on A Mission-Driven Life Web site.

Julia Bonafield returned home to West Virginia. On June 7, 1944, in a speech before Fairmont's Rotary Club she talked about evidence she had personally gathered regarding the atrocities of the "Rape of Nanking," a six-week reign of terror that began in December 1937; as many as 300,000 Chinese civilians and soldiers were killed. She also told of "how the missionaries were subjected to indignities and indecencies."

She kept her audience "spellbound," according to the *Fairmont West Virginian* of June 8.

PERSECUTION BROUGHT QUAKERS TO WESTERN VIRGINIA

February 19, 2006

Y ou know, it's hard to imagine a group less likely to inspire violent reactions than the Religious Society of Friends, more commonly known as Quakers. Nonviolence is a basic tenet of their beliefs. Who would get angry with them?

For starters, most of Europe and colonial America did during the seventeenth and eighteenth centuries. Even today, the Friends' creed of nonviolence makes them targets of ridicule in wartime, but reaction against them once included imprisonment and death. This persecution was largely responsible for their arrival in Jefferson County, in what is now our eastern panhandle.

The Friends date their origin to 1652 when George Fox, a charismatic shoemaker-cum-preacher spread throughout England's north country his doctrine called Inner Light, "the illumination of God within each soul which could guide humans on the path of righteousness."

He taught "the risen Christ was present and available to everyone as a teacher and that through inner baptisms and inner communion it was possible for men and women to rid themselves of the burden of sin and become as Adam and Eve had been before the fall," according to The Foundation for Religious Freedom's Web site.

Furthermore, Fox "refused to take off his hat to authorities, or in fact to recognize anyone's authority over him; objected to all priests and steeple houses; believed that the sacraments must be inward not outward."

Those kinds of teachings were just bound to get his followers in trouble with the Powers That Be, i.e., royalty and state-endorsed religions.

The Friends' inclination to break up other religious groups' worship services didn't increase their popularity any, either.

Within four years, two Friends had arrived in Massachusetts and one in Virginia.

The Massachusetts Bay Colony had been founded by the Puritans, who came to these shores seeking religious freedom and proceeded to deny it to everyone who came afterward.

Anti-Quaker laws were passed. ("Quaker" was a derisive nickname based on Fox's admonition to "tremble at the name of the Lord.") Friends were suspected of witchcraft and were deported. Members of the Society were flogged, imprisoned, even hanged in New England and New York.

Relief came when William Penn, a convert to Fox's Inner Light doctrine, established the Pennsylvania colony as a safe haven from religious persecution. But the good times never last, do they?

During the Revolutionary War, Friends in Philadelphia were accused of spying for the English king. Numerous documents chronicling this curious turn of events are on the Christian History Institute's Web site.

These accounts tell how a group of Friends were forcibly loaded onto wagons and exiled to Winchester. Members of their society had established a colony there around 1726 to put distance between themselves and the authorities at Williamsburg. Persecution existed in Virginia, though not as severe as in New England.

Some of the Philadelphia exiles later took up residence in Jefferson County, north of Winchester. Israel Pemberton, whose name appears among those banished from the City of Brotherly Love, later sold his Jefferson County farm to a relative of George Washington.

A few Friends had already settled in the county before the war. Robert Worthington and his wife were probably the first, arriving around 1729, according to "The Friends or Quaker Element in Jefferson," by Carrie B. Wilson, *Magazine of the Jefferson County Historical Society*, Vol. V, December 1939.

Some fifty years after the first arrivals and a decade after the Philadelphia banishment, Jefferson County had groups of Friends at Hopewell and Bullskin (Berkeley). They decided in 1785 that the two groups should meet together on the first and fourth days of the week.

A meetinghouse was established between the forks of Bullskin Run but fell into disuse in the nineteenth century. The road beside it was still known as Quaker Road long after the building was gone.

Additional information came from "The Bullskin Run," by W. F. Alexander, *Magazine of the Jefferson County Historical Society*, Vol. II, December 1936.

Church, State, and the Great Revival

October 1, 2006. This column was inspired by furor over a painting of Jesus that had been donated to Bridgeport High School many years before. A request by non-Christian parents had been made to remove it because it sent the signal that the school, and hence the local government, favored one religion over all others. This wasn't the first time the school had been asked by Jewish students and parents to remove the painting, a request that was always rejected. The debate became moot not long after I wrote this column; someone or someones took the painting when the school was closed; as far as I know it has never been found.

Well, the clamor over a painting of Jesus in Bridgeport's school has drawn Harrison County into the national debate over religion and government.

Whenever protests arise that a display of Christian symbols on government-owned property constitutes support of a religion by the state, we hear both sides arguing about what our Founding Fathers intended. Things aren't quite that simple.

In 1776, the Hanover Synod of the Presbyterian Church told Virginia's General Assembly there was no argument for establishing Christianity as a state religion that could not also be made "with equal propriety" for establishing Islam. They wanted no religion or sect, including their own, favored by the state, according to *American Christianity: An Historical Interpretation with Representative Documents*, by H. Shelton Smith, *et al* (Charles Scribner's Sons, 1960).

In 1797, the Senate sent a placating message to the bashaw of Tripoli assuring him our country was "not, in any sense, founded on the Christian religion."

Ah, but change was coming, a hint of which appeared in Clarksburg's *The Independent Virginian* newspaper, August 19, 1820, to wit:

"A Camp meeting will be held on the land of James Arnold, esq. on Elk creek, about seven miles from this town ... It is supposed it will continue four days."

Christian revivals, or camp meetings, were sweeping across Kentucky, Tennessee and, obviously, Western Virginia. This came to be called the Great Revival or Second Great Awakening. (The first Great Awakening peaked about 1740.)

Religious intensity marked these events. In 1801, a Kentucky girl fell down in a spasm of religious ecstasy. Her arm and hand stiffened, her body turned cold, and she lost her voice for two hours. Three weeks later she remained "in a state of despare" (sic), according to a contemporary account reprinted in *American Reformers 1815-1860*, by Ronald G. Walters (Hill and Wang, 1978).

Such "manifestations of the spirit," common at these revivals, repulsed some Christians while reinforcing others' faith.

"What counted to believers more than creeds and doctrines was whether a church was for or against revivals," Walters wrote, "and far more people belonged to revivalist than to non-revivalist churches."

Baptists, Methodists and Presbyterians were the primary supporters, he wrote.

Many people believed the millennium, the thousand-year reign of a returned Christ prophesied in Revelations 20:1-5, was near, and they believed God had given the young United States a mission to create heaven on earth.

Thus, religious evangelism inherent in revivals soon merged with social evangelism, such as opposing alcohol and slavery and supporting reform in prisons and mental asylums.

"In some guise or another, evangelical Protestantism was the religion of most Americans," Walters wrote.

This gave the nation a social bond and a shared moral code. It encouraged a sense of patriotic nationalism that linked God and Country in the public mind; Americans were called on to fulfill our nation's "Manifest Destiny" under Protestant ideals. Non-Protestants had to be converted or repressed.

During the Mexican War, 1846–8, all American soldiers, regardless of personal beliefs, were required to attend Protestant services.

American Indian children, placed in institutions to assimilate them into white culture, were punished for practicing their traditional spiritual beliefs.

Nineteenth century America saw anti-Catholic riots, and Catholicism was considered a political liability until 1960 when John F. Kennedy won the Democratic primary in predominantly Protestant West Virginia.

A woman's magazine, *She*, in November 1942, carried an anonymously authored article, "I Am a Jewess," which told how Jews at that time were barred from many colleges, professions, organizations, vacation resorts and sometimes even from volunteer work to support America's war effort.

A nation that guarantees all citizens freedom of religious choice but which has a long heritage of evangelism faces a nearly impossible balancing act. For most of our history, we largely ignored that balance, which makes finding it now even harder.

Maybe the only solution lies in that most difficult of all admonitions: Treat others the way you want to be treated.

Shape-Note Singing Helped Worshippers Make 'A Joyful Noise'

April 8, 2012

Happy Easter. In earlier times, descriptions of Christmas observances often found their way into newspapers, diaries and letters, but until the late nineteenth or early twentieth century not much fuss was made over Easter. Even then, most accounts simply tell what services were planned at churches or provide excerpts from sermons.

Regardless, we know church-going was a big part of our ancestors' lives, providing both spiritual affirmation and social opportunities. The singing of hymns fits into both categories and fulfills the Biblical injunction to "make a joyful noise unto the Lord."

But in pioneer times, when even instruction in readin', writin' and 'rithmatic could be hard to come by, formal musical education was the realm of the privileged.

Then, at the dawn of the nineteenth century, a solution appeared. "The Easy Instructor: A New Method of Teaching Sacred Harmony," was published in Philadelphia in 1801. Today, we are used to seeing whole, half, fourth, and other notes placed on an eight-note musical scale to indicate whether a syllable should be sung bass, soprano or somewhere in between. The shaped-note method uses geometric shapes to convey similar information.

The Shenandoah Valley was among the first areas outside of cities to widely and rapidly embrace shape-note music, and it remained popular with "play by ear" musicians throughout the southern Appalachians for generations.

The shaped-note system evolved from *solfeggio*, an Italian concept that assigns a syllable to each note. The syllables were Italian words: fa-sol-la-fa-sol-la-mi-fa. Eventually, those became the do-re-mi-fa-so-la-ti-do of today.

In shape notes, fa is represented by a right triangle, sol (so) is a circle, la is square, and mi gets a diamond shape. Thus, an eight-note scale was reduced to four, making it easier to learn. Singers only need to identify the shape of the note, not what line of the musical scale it appears on.

In 1846, a book called *Christian Minstrel* added three shapes, allowing shape-note singing to utilize the diatonic scale of five full notes and two half notes.

Itinerate singing masters spread shape-note singing across the South, where it was quickly adopted in the frontier camp revivals of the Great Awakening. Some of the teachers came up with their own simple shapes.

The singing instructors also sold shape-note songbooks, and publishers competed fiercely in this market. Some of them tried to patent shaped notes, which is why the term "patent note" is also applied to shape notes.

In 1835, a deacon and song leader of the First Baptist Church of Spartanburg, South Carolina, named William Walker published the first of five editions of "The Southern Harmony." His books were so popular in Dixie that he has been called "The most famous Baptist musician of the pre–Civil War South."

Walker relied upon the four-note system until devising his own seven-shape system, which first appeared in his 1867 songbook, *The Christian Harmony*. In his system, both do notes are a trapezoid, re is a crescent moon, mi a diamond, fa a right triangle, so an oval, la a square, and ti is a triangle on its side.

One ponders how confusing it may have been for singers and musicians who had learned one set of shapes to adapt to new ones.

Walker's wife's brother-in-law B. F. White was the primary compiler of what would become the most famous shape-note songbook, *The Sacred Harp*. Published in 1844, versions of it are still used today among practitioners of the shape-note style. Tradition and interest in cultural heritage keep it alive.

Information for today's column comes from "Shape-note Singing," by H. G. Young III, *The West Virginia Encyclopedia*, edited by Ken Sullivan (West Virginia Humanities Council, 2006); "A history of shaped notes," by Michael Beadle, MountainGrownMusic. org; "A Shape-Note Singing Lesson," from "Smithsonian in Your Classroom," October 2000; and *"I Will Sing the Wondrous Story": A History of Baptist Hymnody in North America*, by David W. Music and Paul A. Richardson (Mercer University Press, 2008).

1950 Thanksgiving Weekend Blizzard Broke All Records

November 23, 2003

West Virginians who experienced the Thanksgiving weekend blizzard of 1950 aren't likely to ever forget it, though they might prefer to.

Say what you will about the year 1950, it was up front about its nasty intentions, weather-wise. Before the new year was a week old — still a babe tottering in diapers, so to speak — it smacked Memphis, Tennessee, with that city's worst ice storm in 17 years. In February, it sent tornadoes writhing across Arkansas and Louisiana, killing 31 people and injuring 200. Other lethal twisters struck in Texas and elsewhere as the months went by.

Summer brought killing floods to West Virginia. A June 24 cloudburst sent rivers roaring out of their banks. Weston suffered the worst flooding in its history when the river there crested at 25 feet, 5 inches, causing $2 million in damages. In Doddridge County, as many as 33 people were killed (Accounts differ on the number of fatalities.) amidst extensive property damage.

In September, a hurricane hit Florida at Key West and continued up the interior of the state, but it was just a harbinger of what was around the bend. The following month, another hurricane came ashore, striking Miami and causing $19 million in damage, a hefty figure at the time.

One would think all this weather-inflicted damage would have exhausted 1950's bag of tricks, but the old curmudgeon was far from finished. It was out to make the record books and it did, spoiling the Thanksgiving holidays on two coasts.

In mid-November, 16,000 Californians fled their homes when floods swept through the Golden State. Thousands spent Thanksgiving in Red Cross shelters.

Meanwhile, just before the holiday, a cold wave sweeping out of Canada crossed the Midwest. It got into a squabble with warm, moist air over Dixie, forming a low-pressure area over North Carolina before moving on to destroy Florida's fruit crops.

The low-pressure area brewed a storm that swept north out of Carolina the day after Thanksgiving. Stretching from the Atlantic seaboard to the middle of Ohio, it hit the Appalachians with a blinding blizzard and flooded New York and New Jersey. Winds averaged 60 miles an hour, with gusts up to 100 mph.

Simply put, it was the worst storm of its kind on record up to that time, according to the National Weather Bureau.

Ninety people died from winds, snow and flooding in the afflicted area. Some 5,000 were left homeless. Damages were estimated at $100 million, according to *The New York Times*, December 5. Pennsylvania, where 40 people died, called out armed National Guardsmen to prevent traffic from entering Pittsburgh's snow-clogged streets.

In West Virginia, nineteen people perished in the worst winter weather in fifteen years. The greatest problem was near-zero temperatures and snow that fell in copious amounts over a short time period. Lumberport got a mention on the front page of *The New York Times*, November 26, for receiving forty-two inches, the most snowfall of any town in the storm's path. (As snow continued to fall, Pickens got fifty-seven inches, Fairmont forty-six, Weston forty-five and Clarksburg thirty-eight inches, the National Weather Service reported.)

Bus schedules were canceled. Trains ran as much as nine hours behind time. Air service in the Mountain State was suspended.

Three prisoners in the Fayette County jail refused to leave although their sentences were up, and they were permitted to remain in their cells.

Parkersburg was the hardest hit, according to the *Times* of November 27. There, road equipment disappeared into drifts more than three feet deep.

It wasn't over yet.

Snow continued to fall. Then rain moved in, sending rivers rampaging. Wheeling's residents braced for their worst flood since 1945 as the Ohio was predicted to rise five to nine feet above flood stage from East Liverpool to Cincinnati.

Rain, snow and cold continued off and on throughout December. When 1950 finally shuffled off the stage, no one was sorry to see it go.

The Red Cross in West Virginia's Flood of 1936

May 22, 2011

W e're not even through with spring and already 2011 is like-ly to be known as the Year of Nature's Wrath in America. Between record-breaking snowfalls, tornados and floods, the coun-try has already suffered five weather-related disasters that have caused in excess of a billion dollars each, according to a recent *USA Today* story.

Thus far, West Virginia hasn't been among the hardest-hit states, but as I listened to appeals for donations to the Red Cross for the people of Alabama, Tennessee, Louisiana and elsewhere, I remembered reading about those same appeals for aid to our state following the disastrous flood of 1936.

The *Wetzel Democrat* summed up the situation a few months after those spring floods, in its November 5, 1936, edition. The *Democrat* said, "literally hundreds of thousands of persons in West Virginia, Ohio and Pennsylvania, regardless of position or wealth were entirely dependent upon the Red Cross and other relief agen-cies for food and shelter in scores of cities and towns affected.

"In New Martinsville and in the scores of other cities and towns swept by raging rivers, the Red Cross established hundreds of relief stations where food, clothing and other shelter were available to those forced to flee from their homes. Records show that in West Virginia alone more than 26,000 persons received assistance."

In Wetzel County, Red Cross expenditures for the year totaled $3,353.05, "most of which was used for disaster relief in the spring flood of 1936. Of approximately 450 families which made application for assistance, 360 families were aided."

(The story of that "flood of the century," as it was called in 1936, and of the one that surpassed it in fury the following year were the subject of two "Once, Long Ago" columns in May 2010.)

The *Wetzel Democrat*'s November 5 article recapping the previous spring's relief efforts, published six days before the Red Cross was to kick off its annual "roll call" drive in the county, went on to describe the charitable organization's other activities within the state during the preceding months, though those were "far overshadowed by these flood relief operations."

Over 5,500 current or former members of the military were given some form of assistance in West Virginia that year. Red Cross first-aid classes graduated 3,829 men, women and children, "an increase of approximately 1,200 over certificates awarded the previous year."

Additionally, public health nurses wearing white uniforms with a red cross on their caps provided treatment to more than 11,750 people within the state.

The organization was making a special effort to reduce the number of home and farm accidents in the state, "the leading cause of accidental deaths and injuries", according to the *Democrat*—a situation that is still true 75 years later.

To deal with on-the-road accidents and other emergencies, 37 highway emergency first-aid stations were already in operation and 54 more were scheduled to open shortly. In the days before LifeFlight helicopters and the growth in ambulance services, the ability to provide first-aid assistance from these stations sometimes meant the difference between life and death along West Virginia's twisting roads.

A September 6, 1941, notice in *The Welch Daily News* hinted at another crisis then challenging the Red Cross, one that would soon envelop the state and the nation:

"All individuals in Welch having Red Cross knitting needles not in use at present will please return them to the production room in the World War Memorial building at their very earliest convenience.

"With the exception of Toddler Pack Garments it is necessary that all finished garments be turned in as soon as possible as a shipment will be made soon to complete the past quota, in order to allow work to go forward on the new quota."

Volunteers were knitting warm clothing for war refugees from Europe and China. Very soon, those volunteers would be knitting for American troops as the United States was pulled into World War II.

Two Killer Tornadoes Ripped Through Harrison County In The 1940s

July 18, 1999

T wo killer tornadoes in the same part of West Virginia, less than five years apart is a remarkable occurrence to say the least. This isn't exactly the Texas Panhandle where counting twisters is how you keep the kids entertained on a Sunday drive. The Mountain State gets about a half-dozen tornadoes every year, but most are in rural areas and cause little damage.

The funnel cloud that smashed Shinnston on June 23, 1944, is infamous. Dorothy Davis called it "The greatest natural disaster in the history of the state" in her *History of Harrison County* (American Association of University Women, 1970). Numerous articles and at least one book have been written about it.

Less well-known is the storm that hop-scotched through three counties four years later.

May 2, 1948, was a Sunday. No evening services had been scheduled at Big Isaac, a small Doddridge County community near the Harrison County line a few miles south of Salem. That turned out to be very fortunate for the congregation.

Clouds began to swirl a couple miles south of town around 8:30–9:00 p.m. A roaring funnel ripped through Big Isaac, turning a church and a school to splinters. If worship services had been going on at the church, "it is believed everyone in the building would have been killed," according to an account in the *West Union Record* of May 6.

Apparently the twister had an appetite for places of worship.

It skipped northeast over the hills to Mount Clare, where it chewed up a Methodist church and regurgitated a Sunday school banner from the devastated sanctuary in Big Isaac.

Francis Frazier, now a resident of Stonewood, was a 10-year old boy in Mount Clare when the storm hit. That evening he was sitting with friends on a bridge behind two stores, he recalled. (Frazier said the bridge is no longer there.)

The sky was red. So much for "Red sky at night, sailor's delight."

Then rain came in a heavy downpour, followed by an absolute, eerie silence. The evening turned black.

A bus arrived, Frazier said, moments before the twister struck. Roaring winds carried the bus down the street.

The freaky funnel picked up several of the boys, spun them around and dropped them in the road, unhurt, he said. It destroyed the Hutchinson Coal Company store and the company's meathouse, according to Davis's account.

The *Record*'s story said chairs, dressers, baby beds, highchairs, refrigerators and broken dolls littered the streets. "People scrambled through splintered wood and crumbled metal carrying their children and hunting for possessions."

The evening was still young, and so was the storm. It hit Quiet Dell next, then went after the Hupp Hill area near West Milford. There, it changed from destructive to deadly.

Thirty-three year old Raymond Aylor of Lewis County was driving to Weston. The twister seized his car, killing him, his wife Pearl Hitt Aylor, their five-year old son Raymond, Jr., and Henry Moore, age 74.

The only family member to survive was three-year old Arthur Aylor, who was found buried in the mud, according to the *Record*.

The tornado swept on into Barbour County before pulling back into the clouds. Seventy-five people were treated for injuries and 120 buildings destroyed or damaged.

As I was preparing this story, I got an anecdote from an unexpected source: my brother, Clinton Swick, who now lives near Wichita, Kansas. He said he remembered the event.

Clinton was six. The family lived in a frame house with no basement on the banks of Elk Creek when the storm roared through nearby Quiet Dell. Clinton asked Dad, "What are we going to do if the tornado comes here?"

With perfect stoicism, Dad replied, "I guess we'll wait for it."

EASTER SERVICES ENDED IN TRAGEDY AT WELLSBURG

March 27, 2005

E aster, highest holy day of the Christian religion, is a time of rejoicing among the faithful, but the day's joy once turned to mourning in Brooke County.

Easter Sunday, March 30, 1902, started out under sunny skies across northern West Virginia, according to accounts in Wheeling's *The Intelligencer* on March 31 and April 1.

In Wheeling an unprecedented number of flowers blossomed in nearly every window in town. White Easter lilies predominated, of course, but azaleas and hyacinth spread their colors across the city as well.

Even the poorest family managed to buy a potted plant, and lovesick swains spent a half-week's salary to give corsages to their ladies, *The Intelligencer* observed.

Church services were widely attended across the state. Perhaps worshippers were asked to pray for those who were under siege by harsh weather from North Dakota to Alabama.

The *New York Times* reported that morning that Middle Tennessee was enduring its worst floods in over a decade, destroying property from the small town of Murfreesboro to the tiny hamlet of Bell Buckle. Harriman, in East Tennessee, virtually washed away. Eastern Kentucky was afloat after three days and nights of rainfall.

But clear skies over West Virginia promised a bright day for church services and Easter parades. As the morning progressed, clouds and sun began a game of tag across the heavens. High winds "caused the plumes and feathers on the hats and skirts to fly and wave in such a manner as to give the wearers no end of trouble," *The Intelligencer* reported.

About 11 a.m., when many church services were ending, a storm broke over most of the northern part of the state, raging with wind and rain for 30–45 minutes. Churchgoers elected to remain in their pews a while longer in Wheeling, Mannington, Fairmont and other communities.

Then the storm was gone. By afternoon, Morgantown was able to hold its annual parade, and thousands strolled through South Park. Evening services went ahead as scheduled nearly everywhere. For most folks around the state, the nasty weather merely soaked Spring outfits and delayed Sunday dinner.

Not so in Brooke County.

About four miles east of Wellsburg, the faithful had gathered for Easter services at the Franklin Methodist Church. It was a venerable brick building, erected in 1852 to replace the original 1832 log cabin where the church began, according to *A History of Brooke County*, by Nancy Lee Caldwell (Brooke County Historical Society, 1975). Caldwell wrote that it had two front doors and divided pews — one side for women, one for men, although I suspect the practice of segregated seating had ended by 1902.

Rev. Allshouse (I could not find an account that included his first name) was just at the conclusion of his sermon on the Resurrection when the gable end of the church blew in. Falling timbers and debris flew around him, causing serious injury to his head.

Panic-stricken worshippers fled the building, but some were still inside when a gale lifted the roof off, then dropped it back on top of them.

Friends, families, neighbors scrambled to help the fallen. Most injuries were not serious, but Melvin Harvey had a broken arm and gashes on his head. Russell Gist also had head and body wounds.

Estella Brady, just 16, was not so lucky. She had been killed instantly. Rescuers lifted 10-year-old Robert Gist from the wreckage and carried him to his home, but he died en route.

There had been no tornadic funnel, according to the Weather Bureau office at Pittsburgh. Although cyclonic conditions existed, winds in the storm generally only reached thirty-five miles an hour, with some fifty to sixty mph gales.

Churches across Eastern Ohio, West Virginia and Pennsylvania seemed to be targeted by the tempest, probably because of steeples and higher silhouettes that caught the winds. Eleven were damaged around Pittsburgh alone.

In Wellsburg, a day that began in joy ended in mourning.

CALLS FOR STRICTER GAME LAWS IN THE 1890S

November 17, 2013

As hunting season came to a close in February 1893, some West Virginians were concerned that game would soon be gone from the forests and the rivers. On February 7, Wheeling's *Intelligencer* ran a letter from a subscriber in St. George, the county seat of Tucker County at the time. The letter began, "I think the game laws of this state should be revised in some parts, and let the rest be as at present."

He was primarily concerned with practices he felt were decimating the fish population, starting with seining. For the uninitiated, a seine, as defined by *Webster's New Encyclopedia Dictionary*, is "a net with sinkers on one edge and floats on the other that is hung vertically in the water and used to enclose fish when its ends are pulled together or are drawn ashore."

The letter-writer claimed to have seen "as many as 400 fish seined after night in one draw."

Dynamiting—tossing dynamite into the water and gathering up fish the explosion left floating on the surface—and using firearms to shoot spawning fish killed thousands more, he said.

The hunting laws were strict enough if enforced, he reckoned, but "everybody is everybody's friend in the country," so nobody was going to turn in a neighbor for breaking the game laws. Furthermore, he had noticed hunters from out of state were killing more even game than locals did. The state needed to limit how many squirrels or other game could be taken, as other states had done. If something didn't change, he speculated, there would be no game to hunt in just a few years.

A week later, one O.P. Hoff from Hall in Barbour County, near the present-day Audra State Park, weighed in. His letter appeared in the *Intelligencer* February 15, 1893. Apparently, a group of Wheeling sportsmen had put forth a bill for the protection of game, and Hoff supported it.

He hoped the legislature would not adjourn "without enacting some law that will protect the game of this state from the present rate of destruction." Something needed to be done to increase enforcement of the present law.

"By all means the buying and shipping of game out of state should be stopped. It would certainly be better to stop the shipments by law than by the annihilation of the game."

Both letter-writers supported a bounty on natural predators like foxes, hawks and owls. Predators' role in the ecosystem wasn't understood at the time.

West Virginia passed its first game laws surprisingly early, in 1869. Killing game was prohibited between February 14 and September 15 of each year, and some birds were protected year-round, according to "Game Laws" by Skip Johnson in *The West Virginia Encyclopedia*, edited by Ken Sullivan (West Virginia Humanities Council, 2006).

Violators were to be fined not less than $5 or more than $10 — a hefty sum in 1869 — and those who didn't pay could be jailed for up to 10 days. Half the fine was to be paid to the person who informed on the violator. But as one of the letters to the *Intelligencer* said, "everybody is everybody's friend in the country," and few took advantage of the incentive.

The laws were amended in 1882 to prohibit deer hunting between January 15 and September 1, and fish could only legally be taken using a hook and line. No special provisions for enforcement were made, however; the result can be seen in the dire warnings of the 1893 letters to the *Intelligencer*.

Not until 1897 did the legislature provide for a state fish and game warden, paid from the fines collected. In 1901 that was changed to a salaried position, and the warden was given authority to appoint deputy wardens. In 1899, non-resident hunters were compelled to buy a license, good only in the county where it was issued.

The Conservation Commission was created in 1933, replaced by the Department of Natural Resources in 1961.

Charleston Could Have Hosted
Jack Dempsey's First Fight

April 10, 2005

B oxing legend William Harrison "Jack" Dempsey is among the most idolized champions of the ring. If not for 30 dollars, his career would have begun in West Virginia instead of out West.

One of the most powerful and punishing men ever to wear boxing's crown, Dempsey was dubbed the "Manassa Mauler" because he was born in Manassa, Colorado. He fought his way into this world on June 24, 1895, the son of Hiram and Celia (Smoot) Dempsey.

His parents had migrated to the Rockies from their native Island Creek in Logan County, West Virginia, according to *History of Logan County West Virginia*, by G. T. Swain (Kingsport Press, 1927), and the family returned to that area when little "Jack" was five.

When he was a bit older, he found work as a "pin boy," setting up pins in a bowling alley on Logan's Main Street. He already dreamed of being a prizefighter, but at the time he was a rather awkward country boy and no one took him seriously, according to Swain. Conversations must have been interesting between him and the pin boy in the next alley, one Oza Avis, who would become sports editor at the *Logan Banner*.

Dempsey left his job of picking up ten-pins to load Number Nine coal in a mine owned by the Gay Coal & Coke Company, just a mile west of town. If life worked the way fiction does, the future strongman would have awed his fellow miners with the amount of black gold he shoveled into cars each day, but in truth he didn't break any records, as Swain graciously describes Dempsey's mining experience.

Regardless, working with pick and shovel day after day started building the whipcord muscles that would become world-famous.

As fate would have it, West Virginia's champion prizefighter, Pat Canepa, was also from Logan County. Young Dempsey, anxious to trade the shaft for the ring, decided if no one else would give him a chance to prove what he could do, he'd make his own opportunity.

He challenged Canepa to a match. The prizefighter took him up on it, and a bout was scheduled in Charleston.

Dempsey arrived in the fair city on the Kanawha with most of the clothing he owned packed in a pasteboard suitcase. That's when Canepa and his manager demanded the young hopeful post $30 up front, which would be forfeited if he got cold feet and didn't show for the match.

He didn't have $30 or any way to raise it. Heck, he didn't even have money for rent on his hotel room. Thus it was the match was canceled, and the hotel manager seized the pasteboard suitcase for nonpayment. The manager held onto it, and a few years hence had a real conversation piece.

Dempsey, the story goes, spent his bottom dollar on a pint of booze and hopped a westbound freight. By 1918, he was clobbering opponent after opponent in the first round. On July 4, 1919, the 190-pound Dempsey knocked 260-pound Jess Willard to the canvas seven times in the first round en route to victory and the national heavyweight championship.

He went on to fight in the first boxing championship ever broadcast, which was also the first to draw a million-dollar gate, a four-rounder in which he pummeled handsome Frenchman Georges Carpentier.

In my oddities collection is a twenty-four page booklet my father gave me, "The All Time Heavyweight Tournament & Championship" (Kirsh Publishing, 1967). It's a souvenir of a national promotion in which 100 sports writers selected the 16 greatest boxers of all time. The savage sixteen then "fought" each other in computerized match-ups that were broadcast locally over WHAR, sponsored by Hope Natural Gas and The Workingman's Store, according to the booklet. I don't know who won, but Dempsey was the top-rated of the sixteen fighters.

If not for $30, maybe the Manassa Mauler would be known as the Logan Lambaster. Or maybe not.

When the Mountaineers Played a Real Stinker

October 3, 1999

Well, West Virginia University's football team isn't having one of its greatest years, is it?

Put down the pitchforks, sports fans; this is not going to be a Mountaineer-bashing column. Nay, we shall leave that to sports analysts, bookies and Monday-morning quarterbacks. Let us turn a deaf 'eer to complaints about the present team.

Let me tell you about a West Virginia University game that really stunk up the stadium.

Pour another cup of coffee to fortify yourself for this tangled tale of broken contracts, seized equipment and other unpleasant surprises. This one comes from *Hail West Virginians!* by Kent Kessler (self-published, 1959).

The year was nineteen-ought-five and Teddy Roosevelt was speaking softly while carrying a big stick in the White House, although that didn't have a thing to do with what happened in Morgantown.

The year started off with California Normal (Now there's a phrase you'll never see again.) sneaking in spies to steal the

Mountaineers' plays. The perfidious plot was discovered while the game was in play. West Virginia University changed its signals and sent California whimpering home with its tail between its legs after enduring its second loss to the Morgantown maulers in one season.

"We are indignant that West Virginia plays such crooks," a sportswriter thundered. "We should be more careful in scheduling games."

Morgantown needed to be more careful after winning games, too. A few celebrating lads commandeered a streetcar during the victory celebration.

The rest of the season went whippingly—West Virginia University whipped Westminster 15-0, Ohio University 28-0, Bethany (twice) 46-0 and 24-0, Marietta 17-6 and lost to Penn State 6-0. The only game left on the schedule was against the Kentucky Wildcats.

Trouble was, the Kentuckians had changed their minds about making the trip to Morgantown. They reneged on their agreement to play. Furthermore, they refused to pay the $225 forfeit fee assessed for such actions.

These are the times that try men's souls. Fortunately, West Virginia University team manager John Prichard was a man with a plan. He hied himself down to Huntington where the 'Cats were playing Marshall and had all their equipment attached.

Pay or play, boys.

Grudgingly, the University of Kentucky agreed to accept a $300 guarantee in return for making an appearance in Morgantown.

Fine and dandy. The game was on, the fans were waiting in breathless anticipation.

Somebody forgot to tell the groundskeeper, who thought the season was over.

A diligent chap he was. Prompt in carrying out his duties, he wasn't about to let any grass grow under his feet. Well, actually, he was *trying* to get grass to grow under his feet.

He had covered the entire playing field with manure.

To exacerbate the situation, on game day the rain fell in buckets. Who says God doesn't have a sense of the absurd?

Fifty freshmen were sent out with rakes to remove the fertilizer. Ever raked manure in the rain? Nothing smells quite like it, except maybe Newark in August.

The Kentuckians were not amused, but they had learned a deal is a deal. Up and down the field the players ran, stirring the manure like an eggbeater. The conditions didn't seem to bother the Mountaineers much; they made a long run following a kickoff, some forty-yard gainers, and one carry that went fifty yards.

The captain later claimed his players didn't want to get tackled.

Final score, Mountaineers 45, Mildcats 0.

Someone's got to say it, so it might as well be me. If you've ever wondered if this column is full of manure, you've got your answer.

We have a new entry in the all-time greatest sports memorabilia. I spotted an oversized button at the Book N Bean in Fairmont with a picture of artist Vincent Van Gogh, who lopped off one of his ears to prove his love for a woman. Under his portrait is the phrase, "How about them 'eers?"

When 'Bloomer Girls' Baseball Came to Clarksburg

August 14, 2011

C larksburg was all a-twitter. Like virtually every community in America at the beginning of the twentieth century, the town was nuts for baseball, and the first weekend in June 1901 promised fans something special.

The Bloomer Girls were coming to play.

Between the 1890s and 1930s, teams of women players from all over the country toured America, generally playing local men's teams or even sandlot players. They were known as Bloomer Girls, after Amelia Bloomer, who popularized Mideast-style pantaloons for women in the 1800s. The pants made playing sports much easier. Eventually, many Bloomer Girls traded them in for regular baseball uniforms, however.

The Bloomer Girls coming to Clarksburg weren't just any old team. Their pitcher, according to the *Telegram*, May 31, 1901, was Lizzie Arlington, "the leading and best lady ball pitcher in the world."

That wasn't hyperbole. Lizzie—whose real name was Elizabeth Stroud—had been coached by Jack Stivetts, pitcher for the Baltimore Orioles. He described her as "quite a hurler," with "a really good windup and delivery."

She became the first woman in history to sign a contract to play minor league ball, according to *Breaking into Baseball: Women and the National Pastime*, by Jean Hastings Ardell (Southern Illinois University, 2005).

Captain William J. Conner, well-known in both sporting and theatrical circles, signed Lizzie to a $100-a-week contract—an incredible sum for the time—hoping the novelty of a woman pitcher would draw vast crowds.

In July 1898, he put her on the mound for the Philadelphia Reserves in the ninth inning, when the team was up by five runs.

She kept the opposing Richmond club from scoring, but turnout was far below what Conner had hoped for. A *Philadelphia Inquirer* account of the game said "not over 500 were present," while the *Reading Eagle* claimed there were over 1,000, "including 200 ladies." Conner soon dropped his expensive pitcher.

When Lizzie Arlington and the New England Bloomer Girls came to the field at Kelley's Hill in Clarksburg they were playing the local men's club.

Based on a description of Lizzie in the *Reading Eagle* article, fans saw "a plump young woman with attractive face and rosy cheeks." The *Inquirer*'s description said, "In her baseball uniform, she doesn't look over five feet in height, is stockily built, has brown eyes and hair."

About 500 people turned out for the Saturday game, which the local boys won 18 to 11.

The Sunday afternoon game was called on account of jail.

In the ninth inning on Sunday, with the Clarksburg team leading, police officers arrested the Bloomer Girls for plying their profession on the Sabbath, according to the *Telegram* of June 7. The local players were okay — they were amateurs — but the New Englanders were getting paid. For the record, professional male teams got arrested here for playing on Sunday, too.

The Bloomer Girls were incarcerated and, if a description of the vermin-infested jail that appeared in the *Telegram* on June 14 is accurate, the walls were crumbling, the floor was rotten, ventilation and sanitation were lacking, and the whole structure was in danger of collapsing at any moment.

Their stay at the county bed-and-breakfast was mercifully short; later in the day, their manager paid a total of $46.80 to spring them.

The experience wasn't uncommon. Period newspapers tell of Bloomer Girl teams being arrested for playing on Sunday in Fort Worth and elsewhere, and the experience obviously didn't turn the New England team against West Virginia.

On October 4, the *Telegram* reported they'd played "a warmly contested game" against a local team at Bristol. The Bristol club's pitcher, a chap named Cunningham from Pennsboro, "pitched a good game and was closely rivaled by the petite pitcher for the Bloomers, Miss Lizzie Arlington."

Sporting events are always good for the saloon business, and that was certainly true in Bristol, where "a number of drunks were in evidence later in the evening."

FOUNDER OF BLACK HISTORY MONTH BEGAN HIS CAREER IN WEST VIRGINIA

February 15, 2004

W e are in the middle of Black History Month, an annual observance that began as a one-week affair in 1926. The man responsible for the original event, Carter G. Woodson, known as the Father of Black History, began his career as an educator in southern West Virginia.

Born December 19, 1875, near New Canton, Virginia, Woodson was the child of former slaves, James Henry and Anne Eliza Woodson, according to an article by Jacqueline Goggin in *The African-American Experience*, edited by Jack Salzman (MacMillan Library Reference USA, 1993).

Reportedly, Carter Woodson, the youngest boy among nine children, was a frail lad and his mother's favorite. She tended to shelter him and began his education herself. She had secretly learned to read and write as a child, something forbidden under Virginia's laws, according to information on the Berea College Web site. Two uncles, trained in Freedman's Bureau schools, also became his tutors.

The family moved to West Virginia in the late 1880s, where Woodson's father took a job in railroad construction and the young Woodson became a coal miner in Fayette County, according to Goggin.

In 1895, Woodson was living in Huntington, and he enrolled in Frederick Douglass High School at the age of 20. He completed the four-year course in two while also working to pay for his tuition. His first job after graduation was teaching in Winona, West Virginia, but he returned to Frederick Douglass as an instructor and later became its president.

The United States War Department hired him to teach English to Spanish-speaking students in the Philippines, a country the United States had recently acquired in the Spanish-American War. Before returning to America, Woodson traveled through Europe.

Traveling the world allowed him to observe diverse cultures firsthand and likely was a direct influence on his future work in researching and preserving African-American history. He would later state, "If a race has no history, if it has no worthwhile tradition, it becomes a negligible factor in the thought of the world, and it stands in danger of being exterminated."

He obtained bachelor's and master's degrees from the University of Chicago, in addition to his 1903 degree from Berea College in Kentucky. In 1912, he became the first and only black child of slave parents to earn a Ph. D. in the subject of history, according to Goggin — and he earned it from Harvard University, no less.

His doctoral dissertation explored the events leading to West Virginia's secession from Virginia in 1861.

Woodson went on to become dean of liberal arts at Howard University and West Virginia State College, but the work that would make him famous began in 1915 when he founded the Association for the Study of Negro Life and History (now the Association for the Study of Afro-American Life and History).

He became one of the first scholars to study slavery from the slaves' perspective. Using new sources and research methods, he and his assistants pioneered writings on African-American social history.

In addition to authoring or co-authoring 19 books, he founded *Journal of Negro History*, *Negro History Bulletin*, and Associated Publishers.

In 1926, Dr. Woodson conceived the idea of Negro History Week and chose a week in February that included the birthdays of 19th-century black author and activist Frederick Douglass and Abraham Lincoln, called The Great Emancipator.

The week was to be "a period in which the contributions of the Negro to the development of civilization would be sufficiently emphasized to impress Blacks as well as whites," according to the 1982 Annual Report of the Iowa Civil Rights Commission on National Black History Month. Woodson hoped it would improve race relations.

During the 1960s, Negro History Week became Black History Month, but Dr. Woodson did not see that happen. He died April 3, 1950.

The Journal of Negro History, January 1937, honored this former West Virginia school teacher by declaring the study of African-American history "falls into two divisions: before Woodson and after Woodson."

First Syrian-Lebanese Came to State for Economic Opportunities and to Escape Turkey

Not published previously

During West Virginia's sesquicentennial celebration in 2013 I visited the MacFarland-Hubbard House in Charleston, home to the West Virginia Humanities Council. A staff member called my attention to a fig tree growing just outside the stately old mansion.

Fig tree? In West Virginia? Not exactly native flora, but it was explained to me that there are many fig trees in the Kanawha Valley, planted by Lebanese-Syrian immigrants.

In the late nineteenth and early twentieth centuries a small wave—more of a ripple, actually—of immigrants arrived from a part of the Ottoman Empire known as Syria, which encompassed modern Syria, Lebanon, Jordan, Israel and Palestine. Many who came to West Virginia were from the Syrian Province of Lebanon, and many of the earliest arrivals were Christian. Present-day Lebanon was created by the League of Nations after World War I.

Various sources say the immigration was the result of increasing intolerance and pressure from the Ottoman government. Mark A. Sadd, in the *The West Virginia Encyclopedia*, edited by Ken Sullivan (West Virginia Humanities Council, 2006), wrote, "They came as refugees from increasingly rigid Ottoman rule, which after centuries of relative acceptance had grown hostile to Arab Christian enclaves and their special economic and cultural relationships with the empire's rivals of France and Great Britain."

An article at WheelingHeritage.org, "Familiar Face from a Far Land," written by Dominick Paul Cerrone with Alex Nagem, says virtually the same thing and notes "The first Lebanese to arrive in Wheeling in 1888 is recorded to be Roger Saad, a dry goods merchant. By 1900 Wheeling had approximately 300 Lebanese that called it home."

Hanady M. Awada, in his master's thesis "Planting the cedar tree: the history of the early Syrian-Lebanese community in Toledo, OH, 1881–1960" (University of Toledo, 2009) says "persecution was rarely the primary motive to immigrate," and cites "Back to the Mountain: Emigration, Gender, and the Middle Class in Lebanon" by Akram Fouad Khater, who calls the religious persecution motive a myth created by the immigrants to engender greater sympathy among Americans. Khater and others cited by Awada held that most Syrians did not come to the United States with the intent of remaining permanently; they came to make a few bucks and go home.

If so, they were no different than many Europeans of this same period. And, like the Europeans, many decided to stay after coming here.

Syrian-Lebanese traders had great success at the 1876 Philadelphia Centennial Exposition and the 1893 World's Fair in

Chicago, and this influenced many of their countrymen back home to choose America rather than Europe as a land of opportunity, according to Awada.

The vast majority who immigrated were single men in their teens and twenties, and in 1908 they suddenly had reasons other than financial opportunities to hop a ship bound for America's golden shores. That year a new constitution in Turkey made the previously exempt Christians eligible for conscription into the Ottoman military. Muslims had already been fleeing conscription, and now the Christians joined them. This was part of the "increasingly rigid Ottoman rule" mentioned in the *West Virginia Encyclopedia*.

Few of the earliest Lebanese-Syrian arrivals turned to West Virginia's mines or factories for employment, according to the *Encyclopedia*. Instead, "They singlemindedly continued their mercantile traditions, which date to Biblical times, and assumed a leading role in state commerce." The newcomers, both men and women, often became "pack peddlers," carrying merchandise on foot to remote communities and farms. Others opened fruit stands, green groceries, clothing, hardware and department stores in the state's prominent cities.

Eventually, some of those stores became retail chains. Fred Haddad founded Heck's discount stores, the first West Virginia-based corporation to be listed on the New York Stock Exchange, according to the *Encyclopedia*.

Today, "Mahrajan," which translates as "festival," is held in Wheeling each summer, hosted by volunteers from Our Lady of Lebanon Church, a Maronite Catholic Church founded in 1906.

West Virginia and the Chinese Exclusion Act

July 22, 2012

W est Virginia is home to many ethnic groups, but the number of Chinese Americans here has always been small—not surprising, given the distance from West Coast ports, the traditional gateways for Asian emigration. That didn't keep the state from getting swept up in the "Yellow Peril" hysteria of the late 1800s, though.

Of the 200 Chinese living east of the Mississippi at the time of the Civil War, about 60 fought for the Union. A much smaller number served the Confederacy, but one of them—Christopher Bunker, a North Carolinian in a Virginia cavalry unit—was wounded and captured at Moorefield, West Virginia He was a son of one of P. T. Barnum's famous "Siamese Twins" Chang Eng Bunker. The Engs, ethnic Chinese from what is now Thailand, had adopted the American name Bunker, according to the Asian Week Web site.

In 1868, the Burlingame Treaty between the United States and China recognized mutual free immigration and guaranteed immigrants had permanent residency rights in each other's country.

A number of Chinese had been brought to California to work the gold mines, and others laid track for the Union Pacific Railroad. But as the mines played out, white residents in the West began to view the Chinese and other foreign laborers as unwelcome competitors for jobs.

In 1880, the Angell Treaty ended free Chinese immigration and separated United States -China trade from the immigration issue.

Two years later, Congress passed the Chinese Exclusion Act of 1882, the first time that body had empowered the federal government to deport immigrants. It barred all Chinese laborers from entering the United States for ten years.

The Asian and Euro-American cultures had little in common, and anti-Chinese feelings quickly spread beyond the West Coast. Senator Eli. M. Saulsbury from Delaware believed them "incapable of being brought into assimilation in habits, customs, and manners with the people of this country."

In West Virginia, the 1880 census showed just five Chinese in the state.

In an era when most Americans viewed society through the lens of Christianity, for both good and ill, a popular phrase in America was the "heathen Chinee."

The *Preston County Journal* on November 25 of that year wrote, "the people known as Chinamen, who although dwelling in a Christian land and among enlightened people, are still heathen and bow down to idols."

Of greater concern to many editors around the state was the threat of these strange foreigners taking American jobs.

In 1892, things got worse. Congress passed the Geary Act, which required every Chinese person in America to carry a resident permit at all times; failure to do so was punishable by a year of hard labor or deportation. Additionally, they could not be witnesses in court or receive bail.

The Supreme Court upheld the Geary Law, ruling in *Fong Yue Ting v. United States*, "The right to exclude or to expel aliens ... is an inherent and inalienable right of every sovereign nation."

The April 27, 1893, *Intelligencer* said of the dozen or so Chinese living in Wheeling that only two brothers, Ho Ching Why and Ho Ching Hong, had registered; both hoped to be come naturalized citizens. An unidentified source told the paper that many of the others wanted to go home but didn't have the money, so they were hoping the United States government would ship them back.

However, then as now, Congress didn't adequately fund the laws it passed. Typically, only a few hundred immigrants were deported each year, according to the "Encyclopedia of Immigration at Immigration Online."

The "Yellow Peril" days are long gone. The Chinese Professional Association of West Virginia was founded in 2002, and West Virginia University has a Chinese Students and Scholars Association.

Among the best-known stories of Chinese-Americans' struggles with assimilation and finding acceptance is *The Star Fisher*, a book by Newberry Award–winning author Laurence Yep. Set in Clarksburg in 1927, it is based on his Chinese mother and her family's experiences there.

WHO WERE THE MINGOS AND WHERE DID THEY LIVE?

July 17, 2005

S outh of Valley Head, in the mountains near the Randolph-Pocahontas county line, are the towns of Mingo and Mingo Flats, plus Mingo Run and Mingo Knob.

The question is, did any Mingo Indians ever live there? And exactly who were the Mingo?

In 1920 those questions spawned a debate that at times showed the vituperation usually reserved for arguments about gun control or free silver.

The heated exchanges were collected in *Monument to and History of the Mingo Indians*, by William H. Cobb (1974 reprint by McClain Printing Company.)

Plans were underway to erect a monument to the indigenous people of America at the mouth of Mingo Run, near Mingo Flats. Tradition held this had once been home to a settlement of Mingo Indians.

In honor of the pending occasion, Captain William H. Cobb of Randolph County, Vice-President of the National Historical Society, was asked to pen a few comments about the Mingos and Mingo Flats.

Horror of horrors, he wrote that Mingos probably never inhabited the area.

Andrew Price, who I believe was editor of the *Pocahontas Times*, took umbrage and—forgive the expression—went on the warpath. To say there were never any Mingos at Mingo Flats was equivalent to a historian 100 years hence denying catfish ever lived in the Greenbrier River and concluding there was never any such thing as a catfish anyway, Price declared.

He produced pages of anecdotes to prove Mingos did too live at Mingo Flats and were still there as late as 1750.

Hu Maxwell, who had written a history of Randolph County, jumped in saying his research convinced him Mingos never lived in the Randolph region.

Price responded that Maxwell "prides himself on what he does not know," and renewed his previous arguments, adding that the Mingos fought alongside the French at the Battle of Point Pleasant.

That last remark cast serious doubt on the rest of his words. The French had nothing to do with that battle, fought in 1775 on the banks of the Ohio.

Maxwell was quick to point that error out. In a piece titled "Imagination Versus History," he dismantled many of Price's claims.

Adding steam to the debate was argument over who the Mingos were. Cobb said the name meant "despised, contemptible and unworthy, and that name was put on them by the Indian, not the white man."

Indeed, several sources say Mingo was a corruption of the Algonquin word *mingwe*, meaning untrustworthy or treacherous. *Indians of West Virginia, Past and Present*, edited by Frank H. Gille (Somerset Publishers, 1999), says the Lenape used the Algonquin *mingee* or *mengwe* in reference to all detached bands of Iroquois and the word Mingo came into general use among many tribes and the European settlers.

I could not find Mingo among the list of federally recognized tribes or on a list of tribes recognized by states.

Mary Ahenakew of the Resource Center of NIN (Native Information Network) sent me an excerpt from *Handbook of American Indians North of Mexico*, Part I, by Frederick Webb Hodge (Pageant Books, 1959).

It agrees Mingo came from mingwe and means stealthy or treacherous. The Delaware and affiliated tribes applied the name to Iroquois, particularly to detached Iroquois bands.

Even among the antagonistic debaters of 1920, there was general agreement the Mingo were a branch of the Iroquois who settled on the upper Ohio, where they became closer to the tribes of that region than to the rest of the Iroquois Nation. That could explain "treacherous."

The monument at Mingo Flats was erected September 25, 1920, "In Memory of the Passing of the 'Red Man'." Its inscription reads in part, "An Indian village was located near this point. According to local tradition it was frequented by the Mingo tribe and at one time was an Iroquois outpost. Mingo meaning 'foreign service'."

INDUSTRY

LABOR

TRANSPORTATION

WEST VIRGINIANS AT WAR

An 1865 Prediction About Coal's Future in West Virginia

May 23, 2004

C oal production has been so closely associated with West Virginia for so long that it seems the two have always been bound together. That's pretty close to the truth, but when a "practical geologist" in 1865 predicted the future of coal in West Virginia, he was a visionary.

The first coal discovery in our mountains occurred in 1742, made by John Peter Salley along what he named Coal River, according to an article in *The Charleston Gazette*, July 9, 1950. Not a great deal was done to extract the "black diamonds" since significant demand didn't exist until the Civil War drastically expanded railroads and manufacturing.

At the close of the war The Great Kanawha Petroleum, Coal and Lumber Co., headquartered in Schuykill County, Pennsylvania, owned some 3,000 acres in Kanawha and Boone counties, and it wanted to know about the mineral possibilities within its holdings. Toward that end, it employed practical geologist S. Harries Daddow.

The highlights of his report comprised most of the *Gazette*'s 1950 article. (Charleston mining engineer Thomas W. McGuire owned a copy, which he loaned to the *Gazette*.)

Daddow's report was more enthusiastic than a soccer granny talking about her grandchild's athletic prowess.

"The Kanawha region is still undeveloped," he wrote. "In no other portion of our country, north or south, are there more inviting prospects to labor, enterprise and capital, than is now presented in the Great Kanawha Valley."

Daddow described the Kanawha Valley's mineral resources as "unlimited," and he saw the possibility of diverting "the best portion" of the Mississippi Valley's trade there.

The region's coals were "adaptable to all requirements of the trades and manufactures. The hard and caking, with the fat and gaseous bituminous, the variable splint, and the rich and oily cannel, are all found in the same mountains, and are all accessible."

(Did you know there were so many types of coal? Personally, once I get past bituminous and anthracite, I'm pretty much at a loss. Has *Jeopardy* ever used this as a category?)

The mineral wealth, as reported by Daddow, lay in nearly horizontal seams that might not even require shafts for extraction. Lens Creek, the area of his exploration, falls about 25 feet per mile on its journey to join the Big Kanawha, "all that could be desired as a grade for a railroad" to haul out the coal, he wrote.

An appendix to the report estimated the cost per ton as follows:

Cost of mining delivered on cars, 75 cents; hauling four miles to river, 10 cents; freight by water to Cincinnati, 85 cents; expenses, agencies and so forth, 25 cents; delivered in Cincinnati, $1.95."

Would the rewards justify the investment? Well, the previous year coal had sold in Cincinnati for $5–$10 a ton, depending on quality. Not a bad little profit.

Furthermore, a railroad along Elk River to connect Charleston with Grafton and the east-west tracks of the Baltimore and Ohio had already been proposed.

All in all, geologist Daddow saw only diamonds in the Kanawha Valley coalfields. Indeed, he felt that if the prewar, slave-owning Virginians of the region "had any show of free enterprise and energy, Charleston would long ago have been a formidable rival of Pittsburgh."

History has proven his rosy predictions for the future of coal extraction in the new state were pretty much on the money. In less than twenty years, on February 4, 1882, Wheeling's *The Intelligencer* reprinted an article from the *Monongahela Republican* listing wages earned in a mine near Morgantown.

Miners were paid by the amount they dug, carried out of the mine in bushel baskets. One fellow, producing 2,192 bushels of coal over 20 days received $3.84 a day. He was on the low end. Another industrious miner earned $4.65 a day for filling 2,525 bushels in 19 days.

The state's fortunes have been largely tied to coal, for good or ill. Daddow foresaw that in 1865.

A Failure Led to an Oil Boom on the Little Kanawha

April 18, 2004

Take one failed salt well. Offer a chance to get rich quick, then get out of the way, 'cause a stampede is coming through.

That's what happened down Wirt County way between 1860–1861, when the population went from a couple dozen people to well over 1,000.

The story began in 1840, according to "First Oil Lease South of the Mason and Dixon Line," by Louis Reed, *West Virginia History*, Vol. XXV, No. 2, January 1964. A former sea captain and New York City alderman named William P. Rathbone, along with several of his family, purchased land along the Little Kanawha River. A community there was called Burning Springs. (For a few years it was named Rathbone, then changed back to Burning Springs.)

The Rathbones set about drilling two years later. They may have brought a steam engine with them, or they may have dug what was called a "spring pole well."

A flexible pole about fifteen feet long was placed on a fulcrum with the large end fastened to the ground. A drilling apparatus consisting of a blunt bit suspended on hemp rope was attached to the free end and dropped into a pipe.

A pair of stirrups adorned the pole's free end. Two men would put their feet in the stirrups and pull down, dropping the heavy bit onto dirt and rock, a process called kicking down a well, according to gorockets.org, a Titusville, Pennsylvania , Web site. When they lifted their feet, the pole sprang back and the process was repeated. And repeated. And repeated. And …

You could drill about three feet a day like that, on a well that needed to be 200–1,000 feet deep. Want to develop your leg muscles? Sell your Stairmaster and build a spring pole well in the back yard.

David and Joseph Ruffner pioneered this method of well-digging in the Big Kanawha Valley between 1806–1808, according to Samuel T. Pees at oilhistory.com.

Great efforts have never guaranteed success. Whether the Rathbones used spring pole or steam power, what they were looking for on their Wirt County land was salt. Instead they got a gusher of oil, which had little practical use in 1842. They built some mills and went to farming instead.

Then, a few years later, a means of refining kerosene from petroleum created a viable market for oil. In 1859, the world's first oil well, at Titusville, Pennsylvania , started the world's first oil boom. Some speculators remembered hearing about the Rathbone's failed salt well and headed south.

General Samuel D. Karns, who reportedly had made and lost a fortune in the California gold rush and made another in Colorado, leased the right to work the Rathbones' original salt well on February 20, 1860, from which he pumped eight or nine barrels of black gold a day.

Karns also leased a steam engine and belt from the Rathbones' mill to power his digging equipment. They got one-eighth of all the oil he produced.

One-eighth became a standard royalty in the oil industry and is still known as "the farmer's eighth," according to "Conflict and Error in the History of Oil," by Louis Reed, *West Virginia History*, Vol. XXV, No. 1, October 1964.

The Rathbones had already surveyed their land into one-acre parcels and were leasing to a few other speculators before Karns arrived. Others followed, and the Little Kanawha oil boom was on, the first "oil rush" south of the Mason-Dixon Line.

The oil lay about 300 feet below the surface, according to "Conflict and Error in the History of Oil." This accessibility contributed to the number of speculators pouring into the area.

Burning Springs became a boom town, only to die in flames when Confederate raiders torched the oil in 1863. It was later rebuilt but withered when the oil and gas played out. The sheer number of wells drilled during the boom contributed to the town's early demise as reserves quickly dried up.

SANITARY POTTERIES RAN AFOUL OF THE LAW IN 1923

July 10, 2011

Pottery manufacturing was an important industry in West Virginia by the late 1800s. By the 1920s, much of that industry was in the toilet—literally. And that led to trouble with the Sherman Antitrust Act.

The Gilded Age in the second half of the nineteenth century brought a spate of house building that created handsome Victorian mansions. If you build a mansion, you don't want to have to make the midnight dash from it to "the little shack out back" when nature calls.

The first patent for a flush toilet was filed in England by Alexander Cummings in 1775—not by a man named Thomas Crapper in the 1800s as is frequently claimed—and indoor plumbing goes back some 6,000 years. The Gilded Age's housing boom, however, brought a dramatic growth in the demand for indoor plumbing, and that created demand for what was called "sanitary pottery."

Said pottery included such things as washing basins and pitchers, toothbrush holders and shaving mugs, as well as chamber pots and slop jars. A number of American potteries switched to the sanitary pottery business.

Indoor "flushables" of the time were primarily copper-lined wooden tanks. The Eljer Company, which bought an old dinnerware plant in Cameron, West Virginia in 1907 and converted it to a sanitary pottery, is credited with being the first American company to produce a vitreous china toilet, according to victoriaplumb. com. Vitreous china is a mixed-clay ceramic material glazed with enamel, a process that dates to Ancient Egypt.

In short, sanitary pottery manufacturing and sales was a good business to be in in early twentieth century America. Apart from the Eljer Company, West Virginia was home to the Wheeling Sanitary Manufacturing Company, Broadway Pottery, Keyser Pottery, and Bowers Sanitary Pottery, according to James R. Mitchell's entry on the pottery industry in *The West Virginia Encyclopedia*, edited by Ken Sullivan (West Virginia Humanities Council, 2006).

Bowers, owned by George W. Bowers, who also owned Warwick China in Wheeling and S. Bowers Company in Wellsburg, was located in Mannington. The Mannington plant was among the largest manufacturer of toilets in the world at one time, producing up to 200,000 a day and employing 250 laborers by 1913.

West Virginia still ranked well behind Trenton, N. J., where Thomas Maddock's pottery, a nationally known manufacturer of tableware and tiles, branched into the sanitary pottery field in 1874 and was soon providing more than eighty percent of America's bathroom fixtures, according to the Trenton Web site www. capitalcentury.com.

The Trenton Pottery Association organized in 1894 to control prices and assign production levels to every pottery in the city. And there the troubles began.

By the 1920s the organization had evolved; the Sanitary Potteries Association had member companies in several states, including West Virginia. It used price fixing and the practice of selling only to selected distributors, like the original 1894 association, in order to suppress new potteries in Ohio and Indiana that were undercutting prices.

The Sherman Antitrust Act said that was a no-no. On April 20, 1923, Clarksburg's *Daily Telegram* reported that Federal Judge Van Fleet in New York had found the Sanitary Pottery Association guilty of restraint of trade, convicting twenty individuals and twenty-three companies.

"You refused to allow the American public to have a cheaper commodity when it was so urgently in need of securing your output at a reasonable cost," Van Fleet chided them.

J. E. Wright, president and general manager of Wheeling Sanitary Manufacturing, and Raymond E. Crane, vice president of Eljer, who were on the association's executive committee, were fined $5,000 each and sentenced to six months penitentiary time, and their corporations fined $3,000. Bowers Company in Mannington was hit with a $5,000 fine.

The case was overturned on appeal, but the Supreme Court upheld the original ruling in 1927, *United States v. Trenton Potteries Company*. The www.captialcentury.com article says the association's lawyer, future United States Chief Justice Charles Evan Hughes, managed to save the committee members from prison, however.

A Century of Success at Fenton Art Glass

December 11, 2005

One hundred years ago a company was formed that soon relocated to West Virginia. Today, its name is known worldwide, and its fans are legion.

Fenton Art Glass Company was founded in 1905, in an old glass factory building in Martins Ferry, Ohio, but the story actually began in 1903. Frank L. Fenton and his brother John W. started their own glass factory. Other brothers joined the venture later. Frank was a supervisor and former decorator for the Northwood glass factory in Indiana, Pennsylvania.

Initially, Frank and John bought blank glass from other manufacturers, decorated it and sold it under the Fenton name. Those manufacturers realized the Fentons were taking sales away from them, and supplies soon dried up.

Thus it was that the brothers started their own manufacturing company in Williamstown, West Virginia They turned out their first pieces there January 2, 1907, according to the Fenton Art Glass Museum's Web site.

Jacob Rosenthal was their manager. He had previously developed colors for Indiana Tumbler and Goblet, according to *The Big*

Book of Fenton Glass 1940-1970 by John Walk (Schiffer Publishing Ltd., Revised 4th Edition, 2003).

In late 1907, Fenton introduced the iridescent glass that would make it famous. Commonly called "carnival glass," it has a satiny finish with multiple colors that gleam the way oil glistens in sunlight. It's created "by a spray process on the surface of the glass before firing," according to *Standard Encyclopedia of Carnival Glass*, by Bill Edwards and Mike Carwile (Collector Books, 8th Edition, 2002).

Frank Fenton's designs were influenced by glass artists at upscale Tiffany and Steuben, but the new iridescent process allowed his company to create decorative pieces at a price the average family could afford. Fenton Art Glass got off to a running start. Then came the hurdles.

Frank, who was responsible for many of the Fenton designs, "was conservative and level-headed while John was brash and eager — a constant dreamer and the pitchman of the family," according to Edwards and Carwile.

Conflicts escalated. John sold his interest and started his own company at Millersburg, Ohio, but it went bankrupt in 1911.

Meanwhile, Fenton Art Glass did well, thanks to lucrative contracts with Woolworth's and other chains, but by the 1920s, carnival glass was falling out of favor. New lines were introduced, including Stretch Glass, a metallic-sprayed glass not far removed from carnival glass, and opaque colors like Mandarin Red and Periwinkle Blue. The company enjoyed tremendous prosperity.

Then the Great Depression of the 1930s set in. In 1933, Fenton began making mixing bowls and reamers for use with the Dormeyer Company's electric eggbeaters, but the lean Depression years nearly shut Fenton down.

Enter one L. G. Wright, who paid the company to make items using molds he bought from failed glass companies. In 1936, he asked Frank Fenton to reproduce an old Hobb's barber bottle for him to wholesale. It had a pattern of raised "bumps" across its surface.

A buyer from Wrisley Cologne happened to see the finished reproduction and asked if it could be mass-produced. Yep, it could, with a little realignment. In 1938, Wrisley began selling colognes packaged in what were called Hobnail-pattern bottles. They were an instant hit; Fenton couldn't keep up with demand. The Hobnail design is still part of Fenton Art Glass products.

The contracts for Wrisley's cologne bottles and Dormeyer's bowls saved the company during the Depression.

During the 1950s and 1960s, one glass company after another went out of business, but Fenton kept its popularity by continually making innovations to its product lines and developing creative marketing strategies. When the QVC shopping channel began on television, Fenton Art Glass saw an opportunity to reach millions of homes and became a regular feature of the program.

By the 1970s, Fenton Glass was so popular a collectors club formed. After 100 years, the West Virginia company still ships its colorful glass to stores around the world.

EARLY COAL MINING STRIKES BROUGHT A CALL TO ACTION

November 1, 2009

B ack in '63, strikes by coal miners were almost commonplace, causing a rise in coal prices that led to a call for action to prevent future strikes.

That's 1863, not 1963, and the strikes in question weren't occurring in the southern coalfields or those of the Monongahela Valley. They took place in the Northern Panhandle, and the editor of Wheeling's *Daily Intelligencer* thought enough was enough.

On September 25, 1863, the paper ran an article titled "Coal Digging as a Striking Occupation" that found the situation both curious and annoying.

"We are getting convinced that there must be something very peculiar about coal digging as an occupation," the *Intelligencer* observed. "Butchers used to be excluded from juries in life and death cases in England, because it was thought that their occupation tended to hardness of heart, ferocity of disposition and a general disregard of wholesome restraint. Their business, although a very necessary one, was not considered promotive of the necessary sympathy between man and man.

"The people of this immediate region will begin to indulge a similar suspicion in regard to coal digging as an occupation. For two years past the city has been, at short periods, visited with a coal diggers strike. If we mistake not, there has been within the period named some five or six advances in the price of coal."

The importance of coal had been increasing dramatically since the beginning of the nineteenth century. In much of the eastern United States, as in Europe, deforestation was forcing a shift from wood to coal for heating homes and businesses, particularly in larger urban areas. With increased demand comes increased prices. Remember the scene in *A Christmas Carol* in which Scrooge admonishes his clerk, Bob Cratchit, for adding coal to the fire? That was written in 1843.

In America, increased industrial demands of the Civil War exacerbated the problem, and Wheeling's war and consumer industries would have been affected by the supply-and-demand problem.

The *Intelligencer* noted that "All the occupations of the city together have not done the same amount of striking" as coal miners had done.

"The result is that coal is now held as high as eight cent per bushel in this, par excellence, coal-blessed region ... If Wheeling is not a place of cheap fuel, she has little to boast of.

"Yet the fact is proverbial that coal is dearer in Wheeling today than at other points less favorably situated ... If there is a reason the diggers in this vicinity should be perpetually on a strike we have not heard it. And if there is no good reason, this annoyance should be summarily dispensed with. The town should not be at the mercy of extortioners."

Several "plans and projects" were being considered. One involved forming a citizens' association in which each member would agree to buy a certain number of bushels of coal (Yes, it was measured in bushels then.) from any dealer who agreed to provide "say a hundred or two hundred thousand bushels at a fixed reasonable rate."

The newspaper felt if that idea came to fruition, "we may look for an end of our coal difficulties."

The entire matter was likely viewed differently by the American Miners' Association (AMA), founded in January 1861 in West Belleville, Ill., according to *United We Stand: The United Mine Workers of America 1890 – 1990*, by Maier B. Fox (1990, International Union, United Mine Workers of America).

That group, which had branches in the East, was formed when mine owners cut workers' wages, according to Fox. It enjoyed early success because of increased demand for coal plus a labor shortage, both caused by the Civil War. Of the estimated 56,000 miners in America at war's end in 1865, 22,000 were AMA members, concentrated in a few areas.

It is reasonable to assume the AMA influenced the strikes around Wheeling, leading to the price increases decried by the *Intelligencer*.

West Virginia Asked for Federal Troops to End America's First National Labor Strike

April 29, 2001

In 1877, organized labor was a contradiction in terms. Industrial, mining and transportation accidents were higher than in any other industrialized country. While stockholders grew wealthy, workers often toiled in deplorable conditions for subsistence wages. It was the era of the Golden Rule—"Them as got the gold makes the rules."

William H. Sylvis had created the National Labor Union in 1866, uniting laborers and America's various craft guilds to give workers a single, powerful bargaining voice, but it didn't last long.

The NLU boasted 300,000 members by 1873, but that year, a disastrous financial panic gripped the country, and workers scrambled to find jobs. For some odd reason, employers didn't want to hire union members. NLU membership plunged to around 50,000 within four years.

During those troubled times, railroad jobs paid more than many other occupations. When their employers declared they had to cut wages, the railroad men swallowed hard and accepted it— until the Baltimore and Ohio goofed.

In 1877, the company reported unusually good profits and congratulated its board of directors for the amount of business the road had handled the previous year, then tried to plead poor mouth to its employees. On July 11, an official bulletin announced wages for all officers and operatives would be cut ten percent on July 16. The company claimed it wouldn't take this action until all of its competitors had done so, but some already had.

The B&O's firemen were not amused. Aided by the Tradesman's Union, they went on strike the 16th. Among the first towns affected was Martinsburg in West Virginia's eastern panhandle. Passenger and mail trains could travel unmolested, but anyone who attempted to move a freight engine would be killed, the strikers declared.

Mayor A. P. Shutt's pleas to the strikers were ignored, so he ordered police to arrest the ringleaders. The police were also ignored. Railroad authorities turned to Governor H. M. Mathews, who promptly ordered out West Virginia militia under Colonel C. J. Faulkner, Jr. Problem was, the militiamen were friends and relatives of the strikers.

On July 17, telegraph wires hummed with messages between the governor and Colonel Faulker. Reading between the lines of their telegrams, it is obvious neither wanted to take the blame for any civilian casualties.

Casualties occurred as soon as Faulkner tried to get a train out of Martinsburg. He wired Mathews that one militiaman and one civilian were shot in the process. Volunteer engineers and firemen bailed out, leaving Faulker to whistle down the tracks. He so informed the governor and got the following response:

"The peace must be preserved and law abiding citizens protected. Whatever force necessary to accomplish this will be used. I can send if necessary a company in which there are no men who will be unwilling to aid in suppressing the riot and executing the law. Answer"

The militia was deployed along the track and an attempt made to turn a train around on a siding. Embarrassingly for Colonel Faulker, one of his own troops leapt onto the train to foil the effort. Bullets flew and a volunteer engineer was mortally wounded. Once again, trainmen fled from the strikers. Faulker declared he had done his duty, marched his company to the armory and dismissed them.

Mathews appealed to President Rutherford B. Hayes for federal troops on the 18th. Accordingly, Brevet Major General W. H. French arrived with 200 men to disperse the strikers. It worked. Trains were running in the panhandle by July 29, but violence in Baltimore, Philadelphia and elsewhere left over 100 dead before America's first national work stoppage ended.

Most of the information for today's column came from *Chronicles of Old Berkeley: A Narrative history of a Virginia County from Its Beginnings to 1926*, by Mabel Henshaw Gardiner and Ann Henshaw Gardiner (The Seeman Press, 1938).

Survival Needs Often Foiled Child Labor Reform

November 5, 2006

W hat is the most popular age among children? Seven? Thirteen? Five-and-a-half?

In the early part of the twentieth century, the most popular age to be was fourteen. At least, that's what State Labor Commissioner J. H. Nightingale discovered during an inspection tour of factories in the northwestern part of our state, according to *The Charleston Daily Mail*, August 14, 1914.

"I'll wager there are more children 'just fourteen' years of age working in the factories than any other age," he said. "If they're small, they're always fourteen when I ask their ages. It looks like some of them would be fifteen or fourteen and a half, but they never are that old. It's evident on the face of things that they have been instructed to give their ages in that way."

Under the state's labor laws, children younger than fourteen could not legally be employed in manufacturing, mining or most other non-agricultural jobs.

Commissioner Nightingale discovered factory owners' instructions weren't the only reason youngsters lied about their age.

Many were supporting their families, so they claimed to be fourteen to keep from being yanked away from their income, meager though it might be.

"At present I find scores of children far under the legal age limit of fourteen years who work the year around to support widowed mothers and younger brothers and sisters," Nightingale acknowledged. "If I carry out the strict provisions of the law and compel these little bread-winners to go to school, I am literally taking the food from the mouths of their loved ones, robbing them of the little clothing they have and wantonly depriving them of the often scant shelter which is theirs."

To illustrate the harsh realities widowed or abandoned women and their children faced, he cited the story of an East Wheeling boy he talked to, who admitted to being just thirteen.

"Dad was killed working on the railroad a few years ago," the lad reportedly told Nightingale. "That left mother and 'Sis' and me. 'Sis' is only nine years old, now. Mother kept up for awhile, but she took sick and died.

"They wanted to send us to a home, but 'Sis' and me cried and fought against it, until at last a good woman who lived neighbors to us agreed to give us a home. They were poor, though, so I had to go out and work to keep 'Sis' and I.

"I've been working now for over a year. Every Saturday I take home every cent I earn and give it to Mrs. Blank to help keep 'Sis' and I. 'Sis' goes to school and is going to go clear through and be a teacher. It is almost as hard for her as it is for me, 'cause we never have nothing. We don't even get to go to the movies, only when some of the fellers around here tosses me an extra nickel or a dime."

This boy's story continued and, forgive your cynical old columnist, gentle readers, but it began to sound too pat, as if it were something he had learned and rehearsed. Commissioner Nightingale took it at face value, though, and why not? Many children lived in similar situations.

The commissioner planned to ask the West Virginia Federation of Women's Clubs to work with his department to raise money and furnish shoes and clothing. These clubs, the membership in which was approaching the one million mark nationally, had been in the forefront of child labor reform for some time.

West Virginia had child labor laws on the books as early as 1887, which I believe put us somewhat ahead of the curve. National redress was attempted with the Keating-Owen Act of 1916, but the Supreme Court overturned it.

As Nightingale's investigation discovered, enforcing whatever laws did exist was not easy, nor was it always a kindness to do so. Survival in a society with few safety nets took priority over the law.

United States Warplanes Sent to Bomb West Virginia Miners

November 28, 2004

F ollowing World War I, Brigadier General William "Billy" Mitchell desperately wanted to prove the military value of aircraft to skeptical politicians who had the power to fund or kill future development of the new weapon. His aircrews had demonstrated they could sink captured warships, but Mitchell needed something more.

About that time—August 1921—a minor war broke out between striking coal miners, mine owners and the local constabulary in southern West Virginia.

Quelling domestic disturbances. Yeah, that was the ticket. Airplanes could perform reconnaissance, strafe striking miners, drop a few bombs. In fact, Mitchell supposedly told a reporter exactly how to put an end to the violent clashes in Logan County.

"Gas. You understand we wouldn't try to kill these people at first. We'd drop tear gas all over the place. If they refused to disperse then we'd open up with artillery preparation and everything."

There is debate over whether Mitchell actually said that, but restraint was not one of his attributes. Within five years, he would be court-martialed for his public condemnations of top military brass.

Nor was he alone in wanting to use technology introduced in the Great War against domestic disturbances. Workers in Glasgow, Scotland, demanded a forty-hour workweek, which let to bloody clashes between the police and angry mobs. The British government sent tanks to settle matters, same as they did against strikers in Ireland, according to *Tank*, by Patrick Wright (Viking Penguin, 2000).

In South Africa, white miners from the gold fields struck to maintain racial barriers (thereby protecting wages). They fortified a Johannesburg suburb, so General Jan Smuts shelled them, then sent in infantry and a tank, which broke down before reaching the miners.

In these civil disturbances, and the one in West Virginia, the government position was that the strikes were actually Bolshevist uprisings. Some West Virginians more or less agreed. "Uncle Tolbert" Hatfield was quoted by a reporter as saying, "Them strikers ain't int'rested in recognition o' no coal mine unions ... Them fellers are just naturally hot-headed and lookin' for trouble."

In late August, some 7,000 miners assembled in Boone County to march through Logan County and drive off mine guards in Mingo County, hoping to force recognition of their union. The state's National Guard hadn't been reorganized since the war, so Governor Ephriam F. Morgan pleaded for federal troops, military aircraft, anything to restore order.

President Warren G. Harding was reluctant to make too great a show of force—such things could haunt a man at election time—but ultimately, he ordered the miners to disperse by September 1 or he would impose martial law.

Fifteen machine-gun armed DH-4B planes and some Martin bombers were dispatched to Charleston's airfield. One plane wrecked trying to land in the dark near Fairmont. Several others went down in mountain storms, killing at least three crewmen.

The people of Charleston were fascinated by the planes, bringing food, cigars and cigarettes to their crews. Reconnaissance flights reported all quiet on the West Virginia front, although ground reports claimed heavy fighting between miners and machinegun-armed guards.

No gas attacks were made. The Army claimed no shots were ever fired or bombs dropped by the planes, which sometimes returned with bullet holes.

Logan County officials had privately obtained some planes, however. Reportedly, it was one of those that dropped a bomb that "virtually shook the steep mountain hills" on August 31; another such attack on September 2 killed an undetermined number of strikers. A homemade bomb reportedly fell between two women washing clothes in their back yard but failed to explode.

The Mingo War soon ended. Mitchell was pleased. His crews had proven air power "can go wherever there is air, no matter whether they may be over the water or over the land."

Most of today's information comes from "Billy Mitchell, The Air Service and the Mingo War," by Maurer Maurer and Calvin F. Senning, *West Virginia History*, Vol. XXX, No. 1, October 1968.

A First-Of-A-Kind Parking Lot for Welch's Traffic Woes

December 9, 2007. I make reference to Green Stamps in this article. For read-ers too young to be familiar with that reference, once upon a time many gas stations, grocery stores and other businesses gave customers a number of S&H Green Stamps for each dollar spent, and books of the stamps could be redeemed for household items or other goods through the Green Stamp store. I still have a couple of water glasses obtained with Green Stamps. The company now oper-ates online as S&H greenpoints.

The opening of the new parking lot on Pike Street and the re-moval of some meters from Clarksburg's streets brought to mind the story of Welch and its bold move to alleviate traffic grid-lock some sixty years ago.

With cars parked on both sides of its streets, Welch's thorough-fares were narrower than the mind of a political talk-show host. On some nights and weekends, the city had to get help from Boy Scouts and hire extra police officers at 50 cents an hour to direct traffic. The city fire truck had a clearance of less than seven inches between the cars parked on both sides of a 19-foot-wide street.

A parking garage seemed an obvious solution, but you couldn't get one of those with Green Stamps. Such facilities existed in other cities; heck, what's believed to be the first public parking garage opened in Boston in May 1899, according to *Famous First Facts*, by Joseph Nathan Kane, et al (H. W. Wilson Co., 1999).

Back on April 13, 1918, the Clarksburg *Exponent* reported that Frank M. Powell and Camden Sommers planned to build a 100-car, three-story, "fireproof" garage here on West Main near Angle Inn. It was expected to cost $20,000 in 1918; by the time Welch was getting desperate for traffic relief in 1940, $20,000 wouldn't begin to do the job.

Every such garage in the country was a private enterprise, but no investors were stepping up down in McDowell County, so the people of Welch developed a novel idea: The city would pay to build and maintain a parking garage. It became the first community in America to do so, according to *Famous First Facts*.

Beno F. Howard had been elected mayor in June 1940 on a campaign for civic improvements. In addition to building sidewalks and straightening some curved streets, he proposed to issue $90,000 worth of bonds, along with a special tax levy, to erect a three-story garage. On August 30, voters approved the notion by a nearly ten to one margin.

A few months later, it was decided the structure should have four floors instead of three, and additional financing was secured.

Local architect Hassel T. Hicks produced a modernistic design that would have done George Jetson proud, a triangular shape with attractive, curving lines, open on all sides. Its 84,000 square feet could accommodate up to 350 cars.

Construction required fifty-three carloads of gravel, thirty-two of sand, and eighteen of cement, plus a whole bunch of steel. If all the material had been brought in on a single train, it would have required 125 cars, stretching more than a mile.

By late August 1941 it was open for business and was officially dedicated on Labor Day, decked out in flags and bunting.

How to best utilize its open-top fourth floor had been a matter of some discussion, the most entertaining suggestion being a "moonlight sparking garden" where couples could pitch a little woo 'neath the stars.

On Labor Day night, a round and square dance was held on that floor. In those days of segregation, the festivities were for white folks only, but Welch's black citizens got their turn on the fourth floor the following night, with entertainers coming from as far away as Cleveland.

This publicly funded facility allowed the city to prohibit parking on one side of especially congested streets. The meters that had been erected just two years earlier were relocated.

It was cheaper, too. A meter cost a nickel an hour; the garage offered four hours for eleven cents, and an attendant parked and fetched the car.

This first-of-a-kind structure is still in use. It recently underwent renovations. In the process, its original sign was discovered under paint and restored, so that once again the black lettering shows brightly on a curving side, according to City Clerk Robin Lee.

Most of today's information comes from the *Welch Daily News*, August 30–September 4, 1941.

An Aviator from Clarksburg Went Missing in 1939

October 12, 2008

The discovery of adventurer Steven Fossett's missing plane's wreckage out West is a reminder of the dangers inherent in solo air travel, even with today's advanced equipment. It was an even riskier proposition in 1939, when a young aviator who had grown up in Clarksburg went missing.

Aviation was still relatively new then. A May 18, 1939, article in the *Telegram*, datelined Washington, told of famed pilot Charles Lindbergh encouraging Congress to fund more aviation research. Another, in the May 28 *Exponent-Telegram*, reported the Institute of Public Opinion found that half the men and a third of the women queried would like to learn to fly. Locally, on May 26, the *Telegram* reported on the monthly meeting of the Mountaineer Aviation Club.

One former resident of Clarksburg had caught the flying bug at an early age. Thomas H. "Tommy" Smith, son of Mr. and Mrs. Harvey Smith of 514 Philippi Street, had slipped away from his parents during a trip to Buffalo, N.Y., when he was 10 and "squandered all of his $5 spending money on a short sightseeing flight over the city," according to the *Telegram*, May 30, 1939.

The family went to Florida when he was in his teens, where he enrolled in Miami High School and the Curtis-Wright flying school before returning to Clarksburg and graduating from Roosevelt-Wilson High School the following year.

At the age of nineteen, he opened a flying school "at the old Patton field on Buckhannon pike (sic)," the *Telegram*'s May 30 story said, where he trained a number of local pilots. Two of them later died in crashes, including Roosevelt-Wilson's former coach, Ted Leader.

In 1937, Tommy left for a job in Los Angeles, but on the night of May 27-28, 1939, he was in Old Orchard Beach, Me., firing up the *Baby Clipper*, a single-engine, silver-winged, Aeronca monoplane. Its cockpit was crammed with extra fuel tanks, enough to carry him across the Atlantic, according to the *Exponent-Telegram*, May 28.

At 3:47 a.m., after the tide went out, he roared down the hard-packed sand beach and disappeared into a night of fog and rain.

Just two weeks earlier, Swedish pilot Carl Backman had disappeared flying essentially the same route. Tommy had three compasses but, like Backman, he didn't have a radio, just three canvas bags he hoped to drop onto passing ships to show his progress.

The trip had not been cleared with the Civil Aeronautics Authority, nor had Tommy told his parents in Clarksburg about it; when they learned of it from news stories after his departure, they were "amazed." His goal was to demonstrate the feasibility of using small planes for long-distance flights.

On May 29, the *Telegram* carried a story from Londonderry, Ireland. Some people there thought they'd sighted the *Baby Clipper* overhead, but it never landed. Tommy Smith was officially missing.

His parents and their neighbors kept radios on constantly, hoping for news. Speculation had it that he might have landed in a rural area or some island off Ireland or Scotland. His mother was hopeful; his father, an attorney used to dealing with harsh realities, was less so.

"He carried only a few sandwiches and some bottles of fruit juice," Harvey Smith told reporters.

Eventually the radios were turned off, but as late as June 9 the *Telegram* reported an aunt in Parkersburg still held out hope. She said the British Air Ministry "wasn't entirely satisfied" the 24-year-old flyer hadn't reached England.

Two years later, the crew of a Canadian patrol craft spotted the wreckage of an Aeronca 65-C in a rugged, remote part of southwestern Newfoundland, according to "Mystery Cloaks Fate of Flier," Phil Mosher's Web site about Tommy Smith's last flight, http://www.geo-met.com/tommysmith/.

Inside the plane was a note Tommy had written, saying he'd been "iced down" at 10:40 EST on May 28 and was going to start walking through the sleet; he feared falling asleep and freezing to death.

His body was never found.

James-Kanawha Canal Was a Monumental, Futile Enterprise

February 22, 2004. Corridor H, a proposed, 130-mile, four-lane highway from Weston to the Virginia border near Front Royal, was authorized in 1965 and the first small section opened in 1972. As I write this in 2017, the Corridor is still incomplete.

Corridor H, the proposed highway to link Interstate 79 to the Shenandoah Valley, was back in the news recently. One might easily suppose this is the most controversial and longest drawn-out transportation project ever to enflame passions in these mountains.

One would be wrong. Let me tell you about a project that won support of presidents from George Washington to Ulysses S. Grant and involved building a waterway over mountaintops.

Today's information comes from "The James River and Kanawha Canal," by Harry E. Handley, *West Virginia History*, Vol. XXV, No. 2, January 1964.

The whole thing started as a gleam in the eye of George Washington, who proposed a bill in 1774 to the Virginia Assembly to improve navigation on the Potomac River. The Assembly turned it down, which was just as well since a little distraction known as the Revolutionary War came along a couple of years later.

After that war, Washington's name carried considerably more weight. When he brought up the idea again, the Assembly said yes, but residents of central and southern Virginia amended the bill to allow for improvements on the James River above Richmond as well. The bill, passed in 1784, authorized a private company to sell $100,000 worth of stock and required completion of the project within 10 years.

Yes, well …

Raising the money proved no problem, but the 10-year deadline was a mite optimistic. After a decade, locks had been completed around Richmond but not much else was done.

Still, an 1808 report to the United States Senate listed the James River Company's work among the most successful internal improvements in the nation, although critics howled over its failure to live up to its charter.

As population moved westward, the original concept expanded to envision improvements to the Greenbrier and New rivers, as well as building a turnpike connecting the James River to White Sulphur Springs. Cost estimates ranged from $160,000 to $600,000. That, my friends, is a wide-open range, but it was pocket change compared to what lay ahead.

The War of 1812 interrupted work, but in 1816 Virginia appealed to the United States government and opened negotiation with Kentucky, Indiana and Ohio for assistance to unite the Big Kanawha River with the James.

By 1824, the state had borrowed $830,000 and had only 34 miles of canal and 100 miles of "imperfect turnpike" known as the Kanawha Road to show for it. The governor said another $4.7 million was needed, and even then the James and Kanawha wouldn't be connected.

Eastern Virginia legislators voted against continuing the project and work on the canal halted, raising western residents' ire. (The 200-mile Kanawha Road turnpike was completed, however, from the mouth of Big Sandy to Covington, at a cost of $1.2 million.)

Some ideas refuse to die, and in 1832 a new private enterprise formed to finish the waterway. By 1851, construction costs had risen to $8,250,000, more than the cost of building the famed Erie Canal between 1817 and 1825, according to Handley.

Railroads had become serious competition to canals, but on March 29, 1861, the Virginia Assembly decided to have another go at completing the water project.

Unfortunately, the Civil War started just weeks later. Over the next four years, canal laborers were drafted into the Confederate army, Union cavalry damaged some locks, and the new state of West Virginia confiscated everything west of the mountains. Oh, bother. It's always something.

Hope and public works projects spring eternal, however. In 1870 and 1872 President Ulysses S. Grant implored Congress to complete the canal. New plans called for a nine-mile, summit-level tunnel through the mountains as part of a 1,333-mile waterway from Hampton Roads to the Ohio River and points west.

Iowa and other states supported the plan, but the vultures were hovering. On March 5, 1880, facing bankruptcy and a lawsuit, the James River and Kanawha Co. went out of business for good.

THE TANGLED HISTORY OF THE
NORTHWESTERN VIRGINIA RAILROAD

January 25, 2004

D id you see the article in this section two Sundays ago about the model railroad club and its exhibit at the Clarksburg library? I still remember the Christmastime train exhibits at Palace Furniture and Rex Heck when I was a kid. Model railroad displays have been gone from Clarksburg for a long time; I'm glad to hear they're back.

Reading about the modelers' plans to recreate in miniature the old railyards of area towns reminded me of the story of how the railroad first came to this region. It required some conniving and backroom deals.

Railroads were all the rage by the mid-nineteenth century. Any town that hoped to grow had to have rail or river transportation, preferably both. To connect the Atlantic Coast with Cincinnati and points west, a route had been surveyed for a railroad between Baltimore and the Ohio River at Parkersburg.

Problem was, folks in Wheeling wanted their town, instead of Parkersburg, to be the Ohio River destination for any choo-choo that chugged out of Baltimore. Thanks to some friendly legislators in Richmond, the Virginia Assembly changed the Baltimore & Ohio's route so Wheeling would be the western terminus, according to *The Story of the Baltimore & Ohio Railroad 1827–1927*, by Edward Hungerford (G. P. Putnam's Sons, 1928). You might say they railroaded the legislation through.

The citizens of Parkersburg didn't take this lying down. Some half-dozen of Wood County's luminaries organized a company to build the Northwestern Virginia Railroad, following the original route that had been planned for the B&O. The tracks would run from Parkersburg to connect with the B&O at the "three forks" of the Tygart River Valley.

Apart from massive constructions costs, the gentlemen from Wood County needed to come up with cash to purchase, maintain and operate locomotives and cars—rolling stock, as such are called. To raise the necessary funds, they proposed to sell bonds, a common method used in those days for railroad building.

Here's where the connivance begins.

The laws passed by the Assembly to favor Wheeling effectively prohibited the B&O company from constructing any other route elsewhere in Western Virginia. Nothing prohibited said company from investing in another company's railroad, however.

That was a loophole you could drive a locomotive through, and the businessmen of Parkersburg and Baltimore did exactly that. Parkersburg offered a more direct route than Wheeling did for connecting to the Ohio River trading city of Cincinnati, and Baltimore wanted that shorter route.

Total cost of building the road was estimated at around $5,400,000. (By comparison, I once heard an economic development official say constructing a single mile of interstate in West Virginia's mountains can cost $10 million today.)

To get this project going, the B&O guaranteed $1,500,000 worth of Northwestern Virginia Railroad bonds, according to *The Book of the Great Railway Celebrations of 1857*, by William Prescott Smith (D. Appleton & Co., 1858). The City of Baltimore matched that guarantee for another million-five. Oh, but it wasn't a B&O project. Heavens, no. The Assembly had prohibited that.

As construction neared completion, the executives of the Northwestern Virginia Railroad company faced the fact they had no rolling stock to roll on their rails. The B&O offered to provide and operate the necessary equipment. The two companies then discovered that, son-of-a-gun, the only practical arrangement was for the two railroads to operate under one management. Who would have thought it? They entered into an agreement to that effect December 27, 1856.

The people of Parkersburg and Baltimore, and the officials of the B&O, had successfully circumvented the General Assembly and Wheeling's friends therein. A connivance? Yes, but towns like Clarksburg, Salem, and Cairo reaped the benefits along with Parkersburg.

A new town grew up where the Northwestern Virginia met the B&O in the Tygart Valley. It was named Grafton. Some 50 houses were built in less than four months, according to a *Baltimore Sun* article reprinted in *Cooper's Clarksburg Register*, January 11, 1854.

HARD FIGHTING AT THE BATTLE OF THE TROUGH

June 24, 2007

S outhwest of Romney in the Eastern Panhandle, steep mountains rise up sharply from the South Branch of the Potomac, creating an area known as the "Stone Trough" or simply "the Trough."

Sometime around April 24, 1756, it was the scene of a bloody clash between Shawnee and white settlers. All accounts were written long after the fact, and details are sketchy.

Events apparently were set in motion when Shawnee abducted a Mrs. Brake and Mrs. Neff, which wasn't easily done. The two women reportedly had once killed from one to seven Indians at Baron's Castle near Brake's Falls.

By most accounts, Mrs. Brake, who was pregnant, was killed because she couldn't keep up, but there is some indication she may have survived. Mrs. Neff (or Neafe) escaped to Fort Pleasant that night (not to be confused with Point Pleasant on the far side of our state). She may have been permitted to escape in order to lure out a pursuit party.

Other versions say a small group of Shawnee made themselves visible outside the fort, fired a few shots, then moved off, which certainly suggests they were trying to provoke pursuit. Mrs. Neff's harrowing tale following her escape would have guaranteed white men would pursue into the Trough where several small bands of Shawnee were planning to rendezvous.

Among the volunteers chasing the Indians was a teenager named Parsons. His parents had forbidden him to join the pursuit, but he slipped out over the fort wall with a friend's help. Any teens reading this take note—pay heed when Mom and Dad tell you not to do something.

The white men found their quarry encamped near a spring in the Trough and prepared to ambush them. One story says a small dog that had followed the volunteers barked at a rabbit, alerting the Shawnee. Other versions say the Indians had deliberately chosen this spot in order to effect their own ambush.

Either way, the Shawnee hastened up a deep ravine that cut the north face of a steep slope rising from the area of the spring. They worked their way behind the white men, cutting them off from the fort and trapping them against the rain-swollen South Branch. The Battle of the Trough was on.

Over the next hour or two, half the white men fell in the desperate fighting. The survivors decided to try their luck swimming the swollen river. Some who were too badly wounded to make the attempt stopped at the bank and fought till they were overwhelmed, buying their companions time.

Young Parsons dove in and swam halfway across submerged. When he came up for air, bullets splashed all around him. He got across, tore through briars and a cornfield and barely made it back to the fort with his foes on his heels. Next morning, his mother, washing dirt and blood from his hair, found a small piece of shot lodged under the skin of his forehead. He was much luckier than most of his companions.

One account claims a company of British regulars was quartered at the fort, which was less than two miles distant, and clearly heard the raging battle. Their commander refused to send them out and ordered the gates barred to prevent anyone else from leaving. If this actually occurred, it probably was done to prevent a second ambush, which might have meant the loss of the fort and all its inhabitants.

Information for today's column came from *History of Grant and Hardy Counties, West Virginia*, by E. L. Judy (Charleston Printing Co.); "Battle of the Trough," taken from *American Pioneer*, Vol. II, No. V (May 1843), reprinted on the West Virginia Archives and History Web site; excerpts by Perry Brake from Richard K. MacMaster's *The History of Hardy County 1786-1986* at www.eg. bucknell.edu; and *A History of the Valley of Virginia*, Fourth Edition, by Samuel Kercheval (Shenandoah Publishing House, 1925).

LETTERS HOME FROM THE GREAT WAR

November 11, 2007

T oday is Veterans Day. Originally, it was called Armistice Day, celebrating the end of the Great War, the War to End Wars— later known as the First World War.

The Second World War has eclipsed the first one in the public mind, but the years 1914–1918 saw unprecedented slaughter as lethal technology far outpaced tactics. I am told that in some places in Europe to this day, the ground is still so saturated with poison gas that it oozes from fence posts after a hard rain.

In honor of those who served in that war, let us look at excerpts from letters they wrote to the folks back home. These originally appeared in the Grafton *Sentinel* around the end of the Great War and were reprinted in that paper as part of Charles Brinkman's Taylor County history columns after the next world conflict had begun in Europe and Asia. They appeared in what Brinkman referred to as chapters 554, 566, 571, 571-A, 572, and 601. Gene Larosa of Bridgeport shared his collection of these columns with me.

On September 30, 1917, Arlie Phillips wrote to his father, saying he was sending 70 photographs home. He'd set up a camera on top of a trench to capture images of No Man's Land, the desolate, shell-crater-pocked area between the lines. He could not lift his head up, as the enemy was just 50 yards away. The Germans fired five shells at the camera and missed by just six inches, he reported.

Engineer Leon Motter laid out highways and lot plats in Taylor County before he was drafted into the 18th Engineers Corps. He'd also been a "scene shifter" in Grafton, moving scenery and props around between scenes at the Opera House.

He was utterly unimpressed with France, including its water. He guzzled Vin Blanc "to allay my thirst, and relieve the hack resulting as the aftermath of a bad taste of (poison gas) William Bill Hohenzollern's (Kaiser Wilhelm of Germany) lively lads sent our way, and take it from Mot its effect was damn unpleasant and painful."

Underwhelmed by the renowned beauties of France, he felt the girls back home had them "skinned from Genesis to Exodus."

Schoolteacher Walter A. Wood wrote on October 18, 1918, of the magnificent sunsets he'd seen from the ship on his way to Europe.

Joseph J. Gerkin of the 314th Field Artillery wrote on November 14, 1918, to refute newspaper accounts that his regiment had been annihilated in battle just days before the armistice was signed. He said he and other Grafton boys in the unit were fine, except for the cold weather.

Lorain Painter wrote his parents on Thanksgiving Day, 1918, telling of the worry about U-boats during their ship's unescorted passage. Their training in France, under English officers, was cut short as they were sent to the St. Mihiel sector, where he and a captain set up a dental infirmary in the woods about three miles behind the lines.

During one advance, his unit held half the city of Grandpre, the Germans held the other half, and 157 wounded came through his aid station. Of 650 men who went into the line, only 240 remained when they were relieved.

Private William Scranage from Booth's Creek was displeased by his fellow soldiers' indulgence in strong drink, but he liked the YMCA at his camp. The men were treated to movies three times a week, and Sundays offered Bible class and preaching.

Corporal William Henderson, a sailor on the *George Washington*, attended a memorable religious service. He wrote his mother on December 10, 1918, to say President Woodrow Wilson had been aboard and attended services with them. Wilson debarked in France, and the ship returned home, carrying 300 troops and 900 wounded.

Estimates of combat deaths for West Virginians in the war vary from around 750 to about 1,100.

A 'Dented Skillet with Two Handles' in Combat over Europe

August 2, 2009

During World War II many aircraft were decorated with beautifully painted "nose art." The most common theme was a gorgeous, scantily clad woman. Remember what we're fighting for, boys.

Walt Disney's cartoon characters were popular, too; Mickey Mouse and friends flew into combat painted on the cowls of American, German, Italian, and Romanian planes and probably on those of other nationalities as well.

Then there was the nose art on the fighters flown by Robert "Punchy" Powell of Wilcoe, McDowell County, West Virginia To some folks, it might have looked like a badly dented skillet with two handles at forty-five-degree angles to each other. Actually, it was a very nicely rendered map of the Mountain State, and forward of it on the cowling was the name of Powell's plane: *The West by Gawd Virginian*.

The name and artwork first appeared on the P-47 he flew during approximately half of his eighty-three missions. When his fighter group received the longer-range P-51 Mustangs, he kept the map and name.

Photographs show two versions of the nose art. One with a pick and shovel inside the outline of the state can be found at www.352ndfightergroup.com. One also appears in *The Mighty Eighth: The Air War in Europe as Told by the Men Who Fought It*, by Gerald Astor (Donald I. Fine Books, 1997). Most of the information in today's column comes from that book.

By his own account, Powell was seven when he first took to the skies over Bluefield, where a barnstormer was offering flights for two dollars. The experience so enthralled the youngster that he forgot to get change from the five-dollar bill he'd given the pilot. His father was not amused.

When Powell was nineteen, with a year in college behind him, America entered World War II, and he became an aviation cadet. He got his wings and commission in January 1943 and went to Cross City, Florida, where his class became the first there to train in P-47 Thunderbolts. They didn't get to fire the planes' guns until arriving in England in April.

Assigned to the 352nd Fighter Group, Powell was flying combat missions by September. A few weeks later, he shot down his first enemy plane. He wrote about the incident to Paul Flowers, a West Virginia University School of Journalism professor with whom he corresponded throughout the war, according to "Blue Skies for Bob Powell," by Ronda Gregory Weese, "West Virginia University Alumni News," Vol. 22, No. 1, Spring 1999.

There were essentially two kinds of fighter pilots: those who learned quickly and those who didn't come home. Training in tactics came "on the job," Powell once said.

In a post-war discussion he told renowned German ace Adolf Galland, "I really didn't learn to fly until the first time one of your fighters got on my (tail)." Galland, by the way, was one of those who favored Mickey Mouse for his nose art.

Powell was in the air on D-Day, which he described as "probably some of the easiest (missions) we flew." Eighth Air Force fighters provided a semicircle of protection about fifty miles inland to prevent enemy aircraft from reaching the invasion beaches.

By war's end, he had a Distinguished Flying Cross with two Oak Leaf Clusters, an Air Medal with three Oak Leaf Clusters and other citations testifying to his success as a pilot. He returned home to marry his childhood sweetheart and finish a Journalism degree at West Virginia University . When the Korean War flared up, he spent another four years in a cockpit. His post-combat work was in the publishing industry, from which he retired in 1987 in Georgia, where he still resides. He penned a 1990 memoir, now out of print.

His P-51 has been depicted in at least three paintings: Troy White's *Punchy & Jack*; Robert Bailey's *Bluenoser Bounce*; and Ted Williams's *The West Virginian*.

Addendum

From a display at the National Naval Aviation Museum in Pensacola, Florida, I learned that Disney Studios prohibited the use of Mickey Mouse's image on United States bombers or fighters. He could be used on planes like transports that weren't designed to kill people. Disney's other characters could be and were used on combat planes. Of course, Axis pilots didn't care what Disney wanted.

Powell's nickname "Punchy" came from his days in Golden Gloves Boxing. He died June 22, 2016.

A 16-Year-Old from Charleston in the Korean War

April 14, 2013

G eneral William Tecumseh Sherman of Civil War fame is often misquoted as saying, "War is hell." What he told a group of cadets who were graduating from a military academy in July 1879 has been printed many times with slight variations in phrasing, but essentially his words were, "Young men think war is all glory; it is all hell."

A young man from Charleston — a teenager, actually — learned the truth of Sherman's statement during a month and a half in combat.

Rodney Allison Keller left Charleston High School after just one week of classes in 1949. He lied about his age, enlisted in the United States Army, and the same day he was sent to Fort Knox, Kentucky, for basic training.

On February 8, 1950, he began a fifteen-day ocean cruise to Japan at Uncle Sam's expense, where he was stationed with the 24th Infantry Division on the island of Kyushu. So far, his military experience had probably been what he had hoped for when he enlisted; he was getting paid to see the world. But he was about to learn the truth of another saying: "Join the Army, travel to exotic foreign lands, meet unusual and exciting people, and kill them" — to which should be appended the phrase, "while they're trying to kill you."

On June 25, 1950, the communist state of North Korea crossed the 38th parallel with 135,000 men and support weapons to invade South Korea. On June 30 American president Harry S. Truman ordered United States troops to South Korea. First to go were 540 men from the 21st Infantry Regiment, 24th Division, and an artillery battery from the 24th.

This small group, named Task Force Smith after its commander, Lieutenant Colonel Charles B. Smith, fought the first delaying actions. Near Osan, they faced nearly ten to one odds and the tanks of the North Korean Peoples Army (NKPA) but managed to delay the NKPA advance for about seven hours, according to "Task Force Smith honored at ceremony in South Korea," by Walter T. Ham IV, Eighth Army Public Affairs, on the United States Army's official homepage. It was published in Osan July 3, 2012.

An interview with young Keller in the *Charleston Gazette*, August 28, 1950, says he sailed from Kyushu with his regiment of the 24th Division to the port of Pusan at the southern end of South Korea. Since Task Force Smith was airlifted to Korea, that suggests he was not with the first troops to arrive. However, the article also says his unit was attacked the night after arriving on July 2; American troops first clashed with North Koreans on July 4 (July 5 in America).

Whenever they arrived, Keller and his buddies weren't expecting to have much trouble dealing with the North Koreans. He said they joked about the "futile" incursion of the NKPA. The jokes ended during their first night in combat.

According to Keller, during that first night mortar and artillery shells kept his battalion pinned down. Another battalion was cut to pieces by a Korean attack, and the following days were a series of defeats and withdrawals.

"Sometimes a man would become hysterical from fright and start running to the rear. Then the fear would spread to a few of his buddies until the whole outfit was running and the officers with them," he told the *Gazette*.

At one point he was in a jeep, checking a frontline communication wire with an officer when a shell exploded, flipping the vehicle over.

"I was too scared to think and just jumped to my feet and started running," he said. Men returning from patrols had told horrifying stories of NKPA atrocities against captured Americans.

Somehow, the Army learned Keller's real age. On August 9 near the Naktong River he was ordered home, arriving in Charleston August 26 and wondering why he had dropped out of school in the first place. He had learned the truth of Sherman's words.

EDUCATION
RECREATION
ANIMALS
HOLIDAYS

Field Schools Were the Region's Early Education System

August 27, 2006

As summer freedom gives way to textbooks and homework, let us remember the schools that provided education in this region's early years, schools that were out standing in their fields — literally.

They were called "field schools" because, well, they were built in fields.

"Down on the broad river bottoms, in the valleys of smaller streams, or among the hills where was a bubbling spring or rippling brook, a spot, in juxtaposition to half a dozen or more cabin homes was agreed upon by the heads of the families as a suitable place for a schoolhouse. It was an old 'clearing' which tradition said was made by a man who was killed by the Indians, lost in the woods and never afterward heard of, or, tired of the wilderness, had gone back over 'the Ridge' — the Blue Ridge.

"There, on the margin of that 'improvement' — an 'old field' — where half a dozen paths bisected, with the primitive forest in the rear and the plat of wild grass and tangled weeds in front, these men — advance guards of civilization — reared the schoolhouse," according to *The History of Education in West Virginia*, prepared under the direction of the State Superintendent of Schools (Tribune Printing Co., 1907).

As this column has noted before, Old Virginia was not a big supporter of public education. That was "a heritage from England," according to *A History of Monroe County West Virginia*, by Oren F. Morton (Regional Publishing Co., 1988 reprint of 1916 edition).

The Scot-Irish who comprised many of the early settlers west of the Blue Ridge were more inclined to see all children educated, an attitude fostered by their religious beliefs, according to Morton. Germans who settled in the Canaan Valley were also early supporters of public education.

The field schools met their needs, more or less, but many parents couldn't afford tuition. In 1809, Virginia finally created the Literary Fund to provide schooling for the poorest children. It was to raise $30,000 over seven years by means of a lottery.

Teachers were expected to travel around a county soliciting subscriptions to the school in the off-months and to "board 'round" during the school year, living with one pupil's family this week, another family next week, and so on, according to *The History of Education in West Virginia*.

In Monroe County, teachers received the princely sum of four cents per indigent pupil per day. The total paid there during the 1822–23 school year was $429.25, according to Morton.

The schoolhouse was a rude building of logs and chinking, often with just a dirt floor.

(We'll pause here while you tell your children how much better education was when the schoolhouse was rude and the students weren't. Feel better now? May we continue?)

Young scholars sat on long, log benches that might or might not have a rudimentary backrest. Wall pins supported broad, sloped, wooden slabs that served as writing desks. Pens were shaved from geese, turkey or sometimes eagle quills. Diffused sunshine through greased-paper windows provided light.

A dunce cap and a collection of hickory switches stood ready for pupils needing additional motivation.

Girls swept the room and boys hauled wood for the fireplace.

Field schools educated tens of thousands of pupils over several decades, according to *History of Education in West Virginia*, which lists some graduates who went on to exceptional success and the counties where they got their education.

The list includes: Alabama governor Reuben Chapman (Randolph County); two unnamed governors of Ohio (Berkeley); Jesse Quinn Thornton (Mason), who wrote Oregon's first constitution; Lorenzo Waugh (Pocahontas) who taught field schools in Harrison and Mason counties before he "gathered the first Methodist congregation ever assembled in the Sacramento Valley;" James T. Farley (Monroe), a United States Senator from California; Thomas Mullody (Hampshire), a tutor to the crown prince of Naples and president of Georgetown University; and Civil War generals Thomas "Stonewall" Jackson (Lewis) and Jesse Reno (Ohio).

MARSHALL UNIVERSITY'S EARLY YEARS AS A TEACHERS' COLLEGE

September 21, 2003. By happy coincidence this column ran the same week Marshall's football team knocked off a Top 20 Division I opponent for the first time, upsetting number six Kansas State 27–20 on September 20.

T his column has recently looked at public education in West Virginia's early history. To close out this series, let's look at the birth of West Virginia's first state-run teacher's college, called West Virginia State Normal School when it opened September 6, 1867. Today it has another name—Marshall University.

Today's information comes from "A Social History of Marshall University During the Period as the State Normal School 1867–1900,' by Victoria Ann Smith, *West Virginia History*, Vol. XXV, No. 1, October 1964.

The school's beginnings actually predate the state. A group of citizens from the Huntington area established an academy in 1837 to provide their sons with better educational opportunities. They named the new institution Marshall in honor of the late Supreme Court Chief Justice John Marshall. He had been a friend of John Laidley, in whose home the founders of the academy met to launch their new endeavor.

The school did well for more than a decade before falling upon hard times. The Conference of the Methodist Episcopal Church South then assumed financial responsibility for it and elevated it to college status before selling it during the Civil War years.

West Virginia, dedicated from the very beginning to providing education for all its citizens, suffered a dearth of qualified teachers. The legislature decided to establish "normal schools" to train educators in-state. Toward that end, it purchased the former Marshall College property from a family who was using it as their residence.

A lovely choice it was for establishing hallowed halls of learning. A four-story brick house with a two-story wing and several outbuildings nestled on eleven plus acres "overlooking a fine fertile country on both sides of the Ohio River."

It was more than just a college; indeed, the once and future Marshall consisted of three departments. The Primary Department educated children aged six to fourteen (thereby providing an on-site observation laboratory for the teachers-in-training). The Academical (sic) Department served as something akin to modern high schools, preparing older students for college or business. The Normal Department (Let's just leave that description alone, shall we?) was itself split: One section trained teachers for lower grades, and another part prepared educators to teach older students or to serve as county and city school superintendents.

Tuition for the Primary Department was $5; for the Academical Department, $10. Heck, piano lessons cost more that that—$14 for 12 weeks.

The real deal was in the Normal Department. Fees for tuition, books and apparatus were zero. Zip. Nada. Like I said, the state was desperate for teachers. (Let us observe a moment of silence for parents who read this after writing their kids' tuition checks.)

Out-of-state students could attend for a fee. Courses included most forms of mathematics, geography, botany, anatomy, physiology, music and the art of teaching. Those preparing to teach higher grades studied general history, American and English literature, mental and moral philosophy, logic and rhetoric as well.

The school provided a couple of dormitories where $3.20 a week got students food and a room with stove, bed, washstand, table, two chairs, pail, looking glass, lamp and window blinds.

The campus was co-ed, and both sexes took meals at Normal Hall. On Friday nights from 8–10 p.m. the ladies could receive male visitors, providing their parents had given prior consent.

In sports, baseball and croquet were quite popular, but the Thundering Herd football of today got off to a rocky start. The team disbanded in disgrace in 1891 after "some one had not enough manliness about him to pay for a broken window," according the school's paper, the *College Echo*.

Marshall established a debate and oratory society that explored such topics as "Resolved, That the Indian has been rightly treated by the white man." (Yes, well …) This led to a State Inter-Normal oratorical contest that brought the school closer association with other state normal schools in Fairmont and West Liberty.

PARTISAN BICKERING NEARLY DISMANTLED WEST VIRGINIA UNIVERSITY EARLY IN ITS HISTORY

January 14, 2001. The "Twang Town Trouncing" mentioned here was West Virginia University's surprising performance at Nashville's Music City Bowl in December 2000. After struggling through a 6–5 season, the 'Eers led Old Miss (7–4) 35–9 at halftime and were up 49–16 at the beginning of the fourth quarter. At that point, Old Miss put in a red-shirt freshman named Eli Manning who led his team to 22 unanswered points but came up short as time ran out. Despite that fourth quarter, West Virginia University played as it had not all season. This also marked the first bowl victory for the Mountaineers after eight straight tries under Coach Don Nehlen.

West Virginia without West Virginia University is nearly impossible to imagine. The U gives incalculable assistance to the state's economy and image. (By the way, did we ever find out who kidnapped the West Virginia University football team and replaced it with pros for the Twang Town Trouncing, aka the Music City Bowl?)

Surprisingly, West Virginia University was nearly abolished early in its history. The sordid story is told in *West Virginia*

University: Symbol of Unity in a Sectionalized State, by William T. Doherty, Jr., and Festus P. Summers (West Virginia University Press, 1982).

On February 7, 1867, the state legislature authorized the Agricultural College of West Virginia in Morgantown. The name was changed to West Virginia University December 4 of the following year. Its continued existence was soon threatened by lingering animosities from the Civil War.

Immediately following the war, Republicans ruled and Democrats, who had supported the Confederacy, could go whistle until, gradually, Reconstruction-era prohibitions against those who fought on the losing side were relaxed. Up in Morgantown, which had been Unionist during the Late Unpleasantness, turf battles began over the young university.

Morgantown's Rev. John Rhey Thompson, at the tender age of twenty-five, was put in charge after his predecessor resigned during an ugly brouhaha. Thompson, a liberal Republican and Methodist minister, was more or less acceptable to both parties and to the critically important Methodist Church, which had split over the slavery issue prior to the war and was heavily involved in forming the university.

Thompson spent eight weeks traveling through the state on a goodwill tour in which he was "surprised and startled that such ignorance and apathy, and suspicion, and distrust, and downright opposition should prevail among the citizens of West Virginia concerning their own University."

Thompson energetically courted the favor of the Methodist Church and won its glowing endorsement in 1877. As a result, enrollment jumped from 93 in 1876–77 to 132 four years later. He also convinced the Methodists to provide students with books at cost, secured free tuition for ministerial students and relaxed the harsh discipline of the preceding administration.

"The attempt to govern young men in attendance upon a State University by laws conceived in the same spirit as those which obtain in the conduct of reform schools and inebriate asylums is foredoomed to miserable failure," he declared. He rode and boated with his students and entertained them in his home, even as he fought to keep them out of the bars of Morgantown.

He advocated reforms for better education at all levels, not just at the university, and for a time he produced a newsletter that he sent to every member of the legislature to promote his ideas.

The Democrats were unimpressed. They approved more money for public education—"(T)he taxpayers have paid a mint of money for the erection of school houses and support of instruction," the Republican Wheeling *Intelligencer* wrote on August 9, 1875—but remained suspicious of the university. The *Hinton Herald*, on Christmas Day, 1880, proposed abolishing West Virginia University and converting its buildings "into a colored insane asylum." Others suggested turning it into a reform school. The *Morgantown Weekly Post*, December 11, 1880, demanded the president and all other Republican faculty members be removed and the professors' salaries reduced. The faculty itself was divided along politically partisan lines.

Thompson resigned January 1, 1881, and was replaced by ex-Confederate William L. Wilson, whose later success in establishing Rural Free Delivery was explored in this column last week. Wilson barely got the president's chair warm before he won election to the United States Congress. During his brief tenure, Wilson fought to preserve the office of university president and to prevent the conferring of honorary degrees.

He failed at both. Ironically, West Virginia University later awarded him an honorary degree.

The school operated without a president for a time, but as we all know, it survived, prospered and sprawled across Morgantown. How 'bout them 'Eers?

West Virginians' Long Struggle Over Public Education

August 17, 2003

A sk not for whom the bell tolls, kiddies. Soon it will toll for thee, summoning you from the freedom of summer to the confines of the schoolroom.

Not to rub salt in your wounds, but if some West Virginians had their way a century ago the state wouldn't have compulsory education and you wouldn't be dreading the school bell now. Of course, you also wouldn't have free access to an education costing hundreds of thousands of dollars.

The value of an educated populace is largely taken for granted today, but in 1897 the *Logan County Banner* editorialized against compulsory education: "We are so confident that the parent is the proper guardian for his child, that we hope never to see the day when the state shall assume such guardianship."

The *Banner* decried the notion "that the schools shall be filled up by force, that the sacred precincts of an humble home (sic) be entered by the officers of the law and children, half-clad, torn from their mothers."

Resistance to public education dates to an English tradition that maintained formal education wasn't essential "for the poor youth of the community." That attitude crossed the Atlantic and took root in the slave-tilled fields of Eastern Virginia, according to "Sectionalism, Slavery, and Schooling in Antebellum Virginia," by Thomas C. Hunt, *West Virginia History*, Vol. XLVI, 1985-86.

The Old Dominion's constitution of 1776 said nary a word regarding public education. Not until 1810 did the state establish the Literary Fund, which provided three months of schooling in reading, 'riting and 'rithmetic for indigent children. Virginia thus had a two-tiered system with nothing in the middle. Well-to-do parents paid for private education for their children. The indigent had the Literary Fund schools, although attending one was considered a disgrace. Families in between those extremes had few options.

Wealthy planters feared public schools would cause higher taxes on land and slaves. Other groups opposed state control of schools. Education was also a class distinction.

From the mid-1820s onward, the public school movement was further hindered by slavery issues. Massachusetts was leading the way in school reform, and Eastern Virginia slaveholders didn't cotton to northern teachers spreading New England abolitionist views in the Old Dominion.

Folks west of the Blue Ridge were more supportive of public education. In 1837, 1,047 of 4,614 men applying for marriage licenses in Virginia couldn't write their names, and westerners decided it was high time to do something about this appalling situation.

On September 8–9, 1841, Clarksburg hosted 113 delegates from 16 counties to discuss and agitate for a free public education system. Other meetings and conventions followed in Lexington and Richmond to no avail.

The state did establish the publicly funded University of Virginia, but by 1859 only seventeen of the University's 370 students came from west of the mountains. Westerners resented their taxes paying for a university for the children of aristocracy while their own pleas for general public education went unanswered.

When the western counties seceded from Virginia in 1861, the first constitution of the new state provided for establishing free schools for all white children. By 1867, separate colored schools were also provided for.

So why was there still opposition to mandatory public education at the turn of the century?

The school system of the time was so corrupt Boss Tweed would have been envious. Poorly trained teachers were hired by local good-old-boy school boards, the members of which voted themselves lavish salaries. Pupil attendance was low, not surprising in a state where travel was difficult and children were needed to work the farm. Ultra-conservative elements urged parents to keep the kiddies at home.

A compulsory attendance law was passed in 1901 and strengthened in 1908. School board corruption was gradually cleaned up, but today's flight from public schools to private ones and to home schooling may presage a return to a system like Old Virginia's, where public schools exist only for the poorest children.

KERMIT MCKEEVER, 'FATHER OF WEST VIRGINIA'S STATE PARKS'

July 26, 2009

S ummertime travel isn't what it used to be. Unemployment, high gas prices and economic uncertainty have many Americans staying close to home this year—enjoying "staycations," to use a currently popular term according to a plethora of news stories.

Fortunately for West Virginians, we don't have to drive far to find a pleasant getaway. For a small state, we have an abundance of state parks where visitors can swim, ride a steam train, or just enjoy nature for a while.

No one person can take credit for these parks. But if you've ever ridden the air tram at Hawk's Nest or the old logging train at Cass, if you've skied at Canaan Valley or played golf at some of our more upscale resorts, you should give a tip of the hat to Kermit McKeever, who the *Charleston Gazette* on September 10, 1995, called "the father of West Virginia's state parks system."

Our park system had its beginnings in January 1925, "when the Game and Fish Commission purchased 4,560 acres of sec-ond-growth timberland in Pocahontas County to develop as a wild-life and timber preserve," according to Donald R. Andrews, *The*

West Virginia Encyclopedia, edited by Ken Sullivan (West Virginia Humanities Council, 2006).

Ultimately, that land plus another 5,500 acres became Watoga, our first and largest state park.

In 1927, the legislature voted to acquire additional lands from which to create state parks, protecting those areas from commercial development.

Seventeen years later, in 1942, a graduate of West Virginia University's forestry program was named superintendent of Lost River State Park. His name was Kermit McKeever, and he hailed from Greenbrier County where he was born March 10, 1910, near Renick, according to an article by Maureen F. Crockett in the *Encyclopedia*.

Before going into forestry at West Virginia University , he had been a teacher in a two-room school in Greenbrier County, the *Gazette* wrote.

After two years at Lost River State Park, he was named superintendent of Watoga. Another four years, and he was in charge of the entire state park system.

McKeever understood something basic: Funding for parks was dependent on the good will of the legislature from whom all blessings flow. He encouraged his managers to pay attention to state politics, as he did himself, according to Crockett. That may help to explain his rapid rise in the system.

His understanding of the ways of politics helped him expand the state park system, both in terms of the number of parks and the amenities they offered to visitors.

In the 1950s he oversaw the creation of Blackwater Falls, Holly River and Grandview state parks, preserving these areas for posterity.

The 1960s saw changes in American culture and interests, and McKeever began expanding what the parks had to offer. He developed the "resort park" concept, adding championship golf courses, tennis courts and upscale lodging, according to the *Gazette* article. Among the most visible of these resort concepts was establishing the state's first ski resort at Canaan Valley State Park, increasing winter tourism in the state.

He initiated the idea of aerial tramways at Hawks Nest and Pipestem and turned an old logging railroad into the Cass Scenic Railroad State Park.

He was not without his critics. Budget-minded legislators and citizens complained the parks didn't pay for themselves and entrance fees should be charged, something McKeever vehemently opposed.

He responded that the parks had paid for themselves many times over by attracting millions of dollars worth of businesses and jobs, which resulted in more tax revenue for the state.

Apparently, many people agreed. He remained at the helm of the park system until he retired in 1978, a career of thirty years. During his tenure the number of West Virginia's state parks more than doubled, from fourteen to thirty-four, according to the *Gazette*.

McKeever Lodge at Pipestem State Park was named in his honor in 1991. Four years later, on September 8, he died at the age of eighty-five.

The Rhododendron Festival Flowered Briefly in Webster Springs

July 15, 2012

A while back, a reader of this column asked if I'd ever heard of an event in Webster Springs called the Rhododendron Festival. Not even my long-time friend from Webster Springs, the late Alan "Dusty" Hardway, ever mentioned any such thing to me.

The festival existed, though; it budded, bloomed and faded over the course of four years.

The first festival was held July 1–2, 1938. The 1930s saw the birth of many fests in the state: A story in the *Webster Republican* on May 12 of the following year claimed, "West Virginia Is Becoming Known As Pageant Section of Nation."

Apart from the Strawberry and Forest festivals and the Buckwheat Show, we had the Tomato, Apple Harvest, Tobacco, Ohio River, Potato, and the Spud and Splinter Festival. Each took some local aspect, such as crops like strawberries or potatoes, and built an event around it to draw visitors and their money.

Webster County had lots of rhododendron.

For the inaugural festival, thousands of feet of lumber were used to build bleachers and platforms. A forty-eight-page program was printed, the *Republican* said, and the Emerson Gill orchestra of Cleveland, with "the silver voiced offerings of Johnny Drake," provided the music for a dance on both nights. A "historical spectacle" called "The Rhododendron Trail" utilized hundreds of county residents.

Although the first festival lost money, it drew participants from several counties. In its parade, the United Mine Workers of Fairmont took first honors in the musical competition, but Clarksburg's Parsons-Souders department store edged out the UMW for best commercial float. Rain bedeviled the event but cleared in time for a crowd estimated at 20,000 to enjoy the two-mile long parade.

Heavy rain soaked the canvas during the first night's boxing matches, limiting the footwork of Clarksburg's Johnnie Folio and Fairmont's Carl Turner as Turner tried unsuccessfully to take back the state welterweight championship he'd lost to Folio earlier. While many places, especially south of the Mason-Dixie Line, prohibited interracial boxing matches, West Virginia apparently didn't: Folio was white, Turner black.

The other matches that night all involved pugilists from Clarksburg, Fairmont or Nutter Fort.

The following year, the festival expanded to three days: June 29–30 and July 1. It was second chronologically in a series of state fests that stretched from spring to autumn. The *Republican* of July 3, 1939, claimed a total of 60,000 visitors came.

Among the events that year was a coal-loading contest won by Paul Hunter of Bergoo who shoveled two tons into a car in five minutes, twenty-seven seconds. The state's wood-sawing champions, brothers Clyde and Lester Hamrick, also hailing from Bergoo, whipsawed through a twenty-inch log in less than forty-three seconds. There was also a fly-casting contest.

A problem arose in the coon dog trials when it was discovered Moonlight Dan of Dayton, Ohio, was a professional race dog and the world's champion in coon dog trials. The judges ruled he could compete for the $158 purse—he won, naturally—but not for the state championship, which went to a three-year-old local favorite, Trojan.

For two more years, the festival flourished. Bonds were sold to raise $14,000 to construct a community building that would hold 3,000 on the local athletic field. In 1941, Queen Rhodora IV was a Clarksburg girl, Elizabeth Romine.

The festival seemed to be rolling along nicely, but events far afield led to its demise. The rhododendrons wilted in the oily smoke roiling from the stricken battleships at Pearl Harbor. Wartime necessities led the federal Defense Transportation Director to ask that all fairs be cancelled for the duration.

On July 1, 1942, the *Republican* announced that the county fair would probably be held as usual at Camp Caesar. A strictly local display in a non-defense area, it wouldn't impact the war effort.

So far as I can determine, Webster County's Rhododendron Festival was never revived. Today, a Rhododendron Outdoor Arts and Crafts Festival is held in Charleston in June.

The Camp at Jackson's Mills
Became a Place for Friendships
and Memories

September 2, 2001. Today Jackson's Mills is referred to in the singular, "Jackson's Mill," but that is a fairly recent development. Cummings Jackson had both a gristmill and a sawmill there, and the location was known as Jackson's Mills. Old postcards show the plural form, and it was still known as Jackson's Mills at least into the 1970s.

This weekend thousands will stroll the grounds of Jackson's Mills State 4-H Camp near Weston during the annual Stonewall Jackson Jubilee of arts and crafts. Paved lanes wind through the camp's scenic grounds, past cabins built with funds raised by several of West Virginia's counties. A handful of other buildings, a man-made millpond, and floral gardens also grace the site now, but all that was once just a dream in the making.

On June 12, 1922, Morgantown's *The New Dominion* reported construction work was "going forward rapidly" to create permanent buildings for the world's first state 4-H camp, then referred to as Camp Stonewall Jackson in honor of the Confederate general who spent his boyhood there.

The assembly hall was nearly complete, a sewer system was being installed and wells sunk. A dining hall had been built the previous year, but sleeping quarters consisted of tents and a nineteenth century gristmill.

A full summer was planned, including a 10-day training session for 200 4-H boys, a similar one for 200 girls and another to prepare counselors to work 30-some camps around the state; then Harrison and Lewis would hold their county camps at the site. The first farm women's camp in the United States was scheduled August 21–26, and a few other meetings were planned before West Virginia University's football team moved in for their training camp.

Plans for the first permanent cottages were well underway. It looked like Harrison and Lewis counties would finish theirs first, but Marion and Webster were close behind. Wood and stone were the construction materials, but Webster County envisioned "something unusual in a log cabin which will be representative of the pioneer cabins of our forefather's days," the *New Dominion* wrote.

The United Daughters of the Confederacy wanted a monument erected to Stonewall, and what they most desired was to rebuild his uncle Cummins Jackson's home and turn it into a museum. The Sons of Confederate Veterans "heartily endorsed the proposition" and offered their services to make it so.

It never happened. Over the years, other organizations have attempted to raise money to rebuild the house, so far without success. The old mill serves as a museum, instead. A few items related to Stonewall's career are on display there along with materials related to early 4-H activities and general paraphernalia of years gone by, such as old saddles and farm tools, kitchen utensils and a buggy whip — the latter donated by my father, Harold, when I was museum attendant there.

Reconstructing the Jackson home remains only a dream, but the camp at Jackson's Mills has never been about its buildings.

Thousands of young people have learned new skills, found new confidence and made lifetime memories on its 35 acres. Friendships born around the camp's council fire continue to burn long after its ashes have scattered on the winds.

One such friendship is on my mind as I write this, one I formed with a fellow from Webster Springs named Alan "Dusty" Hardway, whom I met at some state 4-H camp at the Mills when we were in our teens. We shared a passion for history, a love of folk music, and a demented sense of humor. Over the course of several years and many camps, the friendship grew into a lifelong bond.

He married a wonderful lady named Sharon and stayed in-state, teaching social studies in Ritchie County while I went chasing dreams in otherwheres, but the three of us visited when we could. Then a couple of weeks ago, he came in from mowing his lawn one evening, sat down and, in poet Robert Penn Warren's words, "all-to-be-said is the done."

Adios, Dusty. Thirty-odd years of friendship weren't nearly enough, but thanks for all the memories. And thanks to the visionaries who, nearly a century ago, created a special place at Jackson's Mills where friendships like ours could be born.

The Naked Truth About Fun on the Monongahela River

November 14, 1999

Pleasure boating on the Monongahela at Fairmont. What a love-ly way to spend a Sunday afternoon, sharing the company of good friends, feeling the waves slap the side of the vessel, enjoying the scenery while moving slowly over the water.

And such scenery! Waterfowl taking to flight. Tree-lined banks rising up to become towering hills. And look over there; there's a group of fellows swimming. See, they're waving to us and — Avert your eyes, ladies!

They're nekkid!

Such was the raw crisis that faced Fairmont in the summer of 1909, as reported in the pages of the Fairmont *Times*, July 1 and 3.

Pleasure boating had become the thing to do that summer in Marion County. The number of people enjoying the river's cool breezes from aboard a boat increased with each passing week, the *Times* noted.

"The number of launches owned here is greater than that of any other West Virginia town located on the Monongahela."

Fairmont residents possessed at least fifteen private "power boats." More watercraft were also docked there, owned by aspiring admirals from Mannington and other land-locked towns.

Barnes and Harr, the only "boat livery" in Fairmont, had available for patrons' use a splendid new vessel that cost over $300. Around two dozen of the newfangled steel rowboats and numerous "large wooden picnic boats" were kept on the river. One Thursday evening at the end of June, 16 boats were afloat at the same time.

The Mon attracted swimmers, too. A fine, paved wharf sloped gently into the river downtown, and bathers could be seen taking advantage of it throughout the day, every day. Of course, they observed decorum and wore bathing suits, the newspaper added.

But there was trouble in river city, trouble with a capital T.

Swimmers taking a plunge downtown might wear suits, but nearby, boys and men were splashing about *au naturel*. Naked, I say, naked as a jaybird without its plumage.

And, by golly, the good citizens of Fairmont weren't going to put up with it.

On July 1, the newspaper issued a front-page warning. Due to numerous complaints, the minions of the law would begin patrolling the river on Sundays, arresting any swimmer without a bathing suit. They picked Sunday because that was the day of heaviest river use, both by pleasure boaters and skinny-dippers.

The officers planned to make frequent trips on the Mon from the downtown bridge (That would have been the Low Level Bridge, now closed; the so-called Million Dollar Bridge now being restored opened in 1921.) "up to the railroad bridge and down as far as the lower railroad yards."

Those who enjoyed a swim without donning a cumbersome bathing suit had only themselves to blame for the crackdown.

The July 1 story claimed the bare bathers were not only very careless about covering themselves when boaters approached, some of them deliberately attracted attention to themselves when boats filled with women floated by.

I can't help wondering if the naked swimmers weren't part of the reason so many women were going pleasure boating that summer. Human nature hasn't changed much since 1909, despite the romanticized notions we have about our ancestors' behavior.

This story reminded me of when I lived in Austin, Tex., and of Hippie Hollow nearby. Boaters of both genders on Lake Travis liked to steer as close as possible to the discrete little cove where people cavorted nude.

In Austin itself, women had to wear bathing suits on one side of the stream at Barton Springs, a city pool formed by the waters of Barton Creek, but could go topless on the other side.

As *Austin American-Statesman* columnist Townsend Miller once wrote, many visitors were highly offended by all this naked flesh—several drove hundreds of miles just to be offended.

And that's the naked truth.

Addendum

The "Million Dollar Bridge" that was being restored when this was written reopened on October 27, 2000, as the Robert H. Mollohan-Jefferson Street Bridge, although it still retains its old nickname. The reopening was accompanied by a one-day festival that ended with a fireworks display that night.

An Elkins Mayor Had a Beef with Certain Criminals in 1908

March 23, 2003

E lkins was plagued—plagued, I say—by marauding bands in 1908 who cared nary a tiddle for the law. They wandered where they would, with no regard for laws prohibiting trespass or for the property of others. What they wanted, they took.

These miserable miscreants often carried out wanton acts of destruction right in front of their victims, as if challenging them to do something about it. If one of them chose to block the path of a law-abiding citizen going about his business, it was far better to walk around than to try to push by. The reprobates made no distinction in whom they troubled. They showed disdain equally for men, women or children.

Like an Appalachian version of the leather-clad Lords of Flatbush, all of these thugs were juveniles, under the age of 20. Sullenly silent, often unkempt and in need of a good bath, they were a curse upon the community.

Who'd have thought cows could be such a problem?

Well, for one, A. M. Fredlock, the mayor of Elkins, had a beef with them. He'd had it right up to the top of the milk pail with people who let their cattle wander loose like so many prowling cats. No bovine was going to boss him around, no, sir. He wasn't easily cowed, so to speak.

One day in early October, he heard a report of five cows damaging the lawns of residents near the pail factory and decided that went beyond the pail—uh, pale. He ordered Chief of Police United States Davis to hasten to the scene of the crime and arrest every one of the perpetrators, according to *The Daily Inter-Mountain*, October 5, 1908. Let the chips fall where they may.

One can only imagine the scene that ensued near the pail factory. One imagines it with Don Knotts playing the role of the chief.

Perhaps the cows tried to pretend they were on legitimate business, testing pails at the factory. It was to no avail; in half an hour, the chief was back in the mayor's office, reporting success.

"Good," His Excellency the Mayor responded, according to the *Inter-Mountain*. "This thing of cattle running at large in the city must be stopped. I insist upon you and the other officers enforcing that ordinance. Whose cattle are they?"

Without batting an eye, Chief Davis replied, "Two belong to you, one to Councilman Daniels and two are not identified."

To his undying credit, Mayor Fredlock assessed the usual fine of a dollar a head and forked over two bucks to the city's coffers. Of course if he hadn't, come election time his opponent would have milked it for all it was worth.

That brings to mind another tale of farm animals and criminal activity, this one from *The Morgantown Post*, October 17, 1901.

A grand jury had indicted one Dick Collins on two counts of providing intoxicating liquor to a minor, and Deputy Sheriff Core (no first name given in the report) sallied forth to apprehend the accused.

Upon arriving at the home of Collins, the deputy was informed his quarry had taken off for the woods. Being a diligent lawman, Core conducted a search, but it proved fruitless.

He was just about to give up and return to town when he heard sounds of distress from a member of the porcine family. The deputy saw a pig scrambling back from a tree. Upon further investigation, Core found his quarry hidden behind said tree.

Seems the pig had long been a pet of the Collins family, so naturally it tried to cozy up to Dick Collins when it saw him. He unwisely kicked at the animal, precipitating the distress sounds that drew the deputy's attention to his hiding place.

Served him right. A dog can be trusted to be loyal, but Collins should have known a pig would squeal on him.

Laying it on the Lion: The Story Behind Alderson's Strange Leash Law

May 21, 2000

I n the town of Alderson, citizens were once required to have a collar and leash on any lion they took strolling upon the public thoroughfares. At the risk of seeming catty, here is the story of how it came to pass, as detailed in Thomas W. Dixon, Jr.'s *The Rise and Fall of Alderson, West Virginia* (McClain Printing Co., 1967)."

On October 3, 1890, French's Great Railway Circus played in Alderson. Following the performance, three cubs were born to one of the lionesses. Next morning, the lion keeper was carrying them to the river in a basket when he encountered Susan Bebout, wife of the town blacksmith, E. Bebout.

Whither with yon cubs? she inquired, or words to that effect.

The keeper explained no lion born in captivity lived very long. A mysterious stomach ailment did them in. Better to drown them now instead of leaving them to suffer.

Mrs. Bebout pleaded clemency for the cubs. Let me have them to see if I can raise them, she begged. Imagine the look on her husband's face when she introduced him to the family's new pets.

Being an unselfish woman, Mrs. Bebout shared her good fortune, giving one of the little Leos to her friend, Mrs. Henry Cook, but it ran afoul of the Cooks' rat terrier, which proved to be as efficient in dispatching African cats as American rats. The lion population in Alderson dwindled to two.

One of those soon succumbed to the strange stomach ailment, as prophesied. To save the remaining kitten, Mrs. Bebout sought advice from the town doctor, Dr. W. C. Beard. He prescribed a daily dose of castor oil.

As the saying goes, that which does not kill me makes me stronger. Any kitten that could survive swallowing castor oil every day has a good shot at attaining full-grown cathood. Mrs. Bebout's beloved little cub not only lived, he flourished. She named him French for the circus that brought him into her life.

French had the run of the house and roamed the streets like any young tabby. As the months passed, the good people of Alderson became a trifle concerned about a full-grown lion strolling their avenues. He was a frisky little dickens; many citizens turned around in the street to discover 400 pounds of jungle cat playfully barreling down upon them like a runaway locomotive.

To pacify the neighbors, the Bebouts built a tall wooden fence around their yard in hopes of confining their pet, like Wile E. Coyote holding up a tiny parasol to protect his head from a falling boulder. French discovered fence jumping was a cool way to get exercise.

Hence, the town council passed what is believed to be the only lion leash law in America, requiring all lion owners put a collar on their tawny pets and keep them tethered by a leash within the city limits.

Can't you just hear the Bebouts going into the local hardware store? Yeah, Sam, I need a cat collar that could fit around a lard barrel and gimme ten feet of that anchor chain while you're at it.

They set about finding a new home for their beloved leonine companion, but in the meantime they entered French in the Greenbrier Fair, where he won first place in livestock. One ponders whether there is now a Greenbrier Fair regulation prohibiting entrants from eating their competitors.

As luck would have it, the National Zoological Park at Washington needed a tame, housebroken lion and, wouldn't you know, there was a dearth of them on the market just then. The zoo happily bought French for $400. E. Bebout visited him there some years later, nearly giving other visitors apoplexy when he walked up to the cage and scratched the head of his former pet.

WESTERN VIRGINIA FOSSILS FASCINATED FUTURE PRESIDENT THOMAS JEFFERSON

October 8, 2000

T homas Jefferson was staring at a puzzlement. John Stuart, a former scout and Indian fighter, had sent him some bones. Big bones. There was part of a femur, a broken ulna, a radius, several foot bones and three large claws.

Jefferson was certain they came from a species never before identified. He had seen oversized, fossilized bones before. While working on his *Notes on the State of Virginia* in 1780, a statistical survey he prepared at the request of the French government, he examined remains of a mammoth found at Big Bone Lick in Kentucky country, then part of Virginia.

Stuart said the new fossils were found in a cave near his home in Greenbrier County (actually Monroe County) by saltpeter miners.

Jefferson, the future United States president, needed a thighbone to determine the mysterious critter's stature. One such bone had been part of the original discovery, but it had been lost in transit. Working with what he had, he determined the animal was similar to a lion, the largest clawed animal with which he was familiar.

He named it *Megalonyx*, "the Great Claw," and estimated it had been over five feet long and weighted a bit more than 800 pounds.

He also believed its species still existed in North America, prowling the wilderness of the West along with mammoths.

"Our entire ignorance of the immense country to the West and North-west, and of its contents does not authorize us to say what it does not contain," he wrote. "The movements of nature are in a never-ending circle. The animal species which has once been put into a train of motion, is still probably moving in that train. For, if one link in nature's chain might be lost, another and another might be lost, till this whole system of things should vanish by piece-meal."

As usual, Jefferson's views were ahead of his time, coinciding closely with today's environmental movement. His curiosity about what lay hidden in the Western mountains eventually led to the Lewis and Clark expedition during his presidency.

In March 1797, he packed his bones, picked up his prepared paper and headed for Philadelphia where he was to be sworn in as vice-president of the United States He intended to present his findings to the Philosophical Society there. Along the way, he happened to see a copy of the British *Monthly Magazine*. Inside was an engraving of the skeleton of a great clawed animal discovered in Paraguay and donated to the royal cabinet of natural history in Madrid. It had been named *Megatherium* and was determined to be a relative of the sloth.

Jefferson realized he had most likely erred in declaring his *Megalonyx* was a feline. Hurriedly, he revised his paper. He alluded to the British journal's article, but cautioned its representation of the sloth-like creature might not be reliable. Ironically, he forgot that he had a drawing of the *Megatherium* skeleton, with its exact dimensions, lying in a drawer at his home, Monticello. It had been sent to him eight years earlier by William Carmichael, Charge d'Affaires at Madrid. If he had not forgotten the drawing, Jefferson could have had the honor of identifying and naming the creature. He was honored in 1822 when a French naturalist named the creature whose bones were found in western Virginia *Megalonyx jeffersoni*.

Not everyone honored his work. In Jefferson's day, science was often equated with atheism, not much different from the evolution vs. creationism debate going on in schools and state legislatures today. He was vilified by press, pulpit and the poet William Cullen Bryant, then thirteen years old.

The public can see replicas of Jefferson's *Megalonyx* fossil bones at the West Virginia Geological Survey at Mt. Chateau, Cheat Lake, outside Morgantown.

Thanks to Ray Garton, curator of PaleoClones fossil reproductions in Barrackville, for providing me with copies of "Thomas Jefferson and American Vertebrate Paleontology," by Silvio A. Bedini, the source of today's information.

A Woman Recalls Her Narrow Escape from a Shoating Death

November 26, 2000

P eople say we live in dangerous times, and I suppose that's true, but prithee, what time wasn't dangerous? We've traded getting trampled by mammoths for getting flattened by speeding cars. Different method, same result.

Mrs. Myrtle A. Byers, for example, nearly expired when she was a child, around 1879, as the result of a shoating accident. No, there are no misspelled words in that sentence.

She told her tale in the Snyder (Texas) *Daily News*, October 14, 1956. The account is reprinted as Appendix X in *Where It All Began: The Story of the People and Places Where the Oil & Gas Industry Began, West Virginia and Southeastern Ohio*, Part One, by David L. McKain and Bernard L. Allen, Ph. D. (published by David L. McKain, in cooperation with The Oil & Gas Museum, Parkersburg, West Virginia)

When Mrs. Byers was five, her papa had a job tending six oil wells on another man's property near Volcano, West Virginia Papa considered himself lucky to have found a rental house a scant half mile walk from the boiler house where he watched over the well pump. It was too far to allow him to come home for a hot meal during his workday, however, and that was what nearly led to his little girl's demise.

Papa worked a twelve-hour shift, Mrs. Byers told the *Daily News*, from midnight till noon. He fetched his breakfast along with him in a dinner pail—sorry, make that a breakfast pail.

That worked fine in wintertime, but come summer, the food tended to spoil before he could eat it. What wasn't spoilt was often covered with ants, which have never been considered a delicacy in this part of the world.

Papa talked to Mama about the distressing situation, and they came up with a solution. Mama would fix a breakfast, and their five-year-old daughter could carry it over to the pump house while it was fresh. Mama would watch from the front porch to make sure the little girl got safely across a creek at the bottom of the hill. From that point on, Papa could watch her on her way to and from.

The system worked like a charm for a while. The problem came from a mess the oil company left after drilling for oil. There were no environmental protection laws then. Slush pit? Leave it be. Either that, or dig a ditch and let the dirty oil run downhill to the creeks. Made pretty rainbows when the sunlight hit it right.

Made the rocks slick, too.

One morning, as the little girl was doing her Red Riding Hood routine, cheerfully carrying a pail of goodies while her little black terrier dog, Frankie, trotted alongside, she slipped on an oil-slick rock in the creek. Applesauce, butter, bread, coffee, eggs and all the rest of a nineteenth century Grand Slam breakfast went flying about the landscape.

Now it happened that in this same country there was a herd of shoats—young pigs, that is—taking a drink at the creek. They charged toward all that manna from heaven like shoppers hitting the mall the day after Thanksgiving, totally oblivious to the little girl lying helpless in their path.

A wiry, black fury whizzed in among them. Frankie the Wonder Terrier sailed in, nipping and slashing at all that bacon on the hoof. Utter chaos reigned. If the girl tried to get up, a frightened pig would come along and knock her back down. Finally, her parents reached the creek and saved her. From that time on, Papa decided to work on the well that sat closest to the house every morning at 7:30. His little girl brought him breakfast there.

The family never again suffered a random shoating.

Idea of Holiday to Honor Mothers Received Only Laughs

May 10, 1998

On May 9, 1908, Senator Elmer Burkett, a Republican from Nebraska, asked his colleagues in the United States Senate to establish a national Mothers' Day holiday.

His bill was laughed off the floor.

Inaugurating such a holiday was the obsession of Anna (no middle name) Jarvis, a native of Taylor County, West Virginia. Her mother had often wished a Mothers' Day observance would be established. When Anna's mother died on May 9, 1905, Anna vowed that wish would be fulfilled, for her mother, Anna Maria Reeves Jarvis, had been an extraordinary person.

Anna Maria and her husband Granville Jarvis moved from Philippi to Webster, a railroad terminus near Grafton, in 1854. The new railroad brought prosperity and growth to Taylor County, but with growth came pollution, filth and disease.

It was a common problem. Even in major cities like the nation's capital, sewers were open ditches. Animal carcasses were left to rot in the open. Information linking decay to disease could found in writings as ancient as books of the Old Testament, but few paid heed. In the cultured city of New Orleans, 7,000 people died of illness in just the month of August 1853.

In burgeoning Taylor County, Virginia, Anna Maria Jarvis connected the unsanitary conditions around her to the deaths of three of her five children and the babies of many of her friends.

She formed Mothers' Day Work Clubs in communities throughout the county to clean things up and insisted every mother in the area belong to one of them. She recruited two physicians to teach the clubs about health and sanitation. Her organization bought medicine for indigent families and inspected water supplies and bottled milk.

Conditions improved, but that did little to help Anna Maria's own family. Eight of her twelve children died without reaching adulthood.

During the Civil War, she required all Mothers' Day Club members to swear an oath against allowing political divisions within the organization. In 1868, Anna Maria used the clubs in a public demonstration of unity that put the lid on festering North-South resentments in the county.

Small wonder, then, that Anna Maria's daughter Anna promoted a national Mother's Day with obsessive zeal. On May 9, 1908, three years after her mother's death, an observance was held in Grafton's Andrews Methodist Episcopal Church, and 15,000 gathered in celebration at Philadelphia. At the same time, Burkett's bill was placed before the United States Senate at the behest of the YMCA. It asked Senators to wear a white flower to show support for a Mother's Day holiday.

The bill "brought out a number of witty sallies and also created some bitter feeling," *The New York Times* reported. Legislators decried the attempt to "let down the legislative bars in honor of 'sisters and the cousins and the aunts.'"

The Senate of 1907–8 was not a holiday crowd. Their committees also recommended against letting Washington, D. C., have a holiday on Columbus Day, or permitting the capital city to officially celebrate the upcoming centennial of Abraham Lincoln's birth on February 12, 1909. Sen. Burkett warned his colleagues they would "be sorry" for voting against his Mother's Day bill, though.

Women didn't have the right to vote, but they were working on it. The growing woman's suffrage movement took up Jarvis's cause. The International Mothers' Day Association took pains to point out the celebration of this day was in no way connected with woman's suffrage. The Association was "friendly to the suffrage movement where it may benefit the home," however.

Anna Jarvis raised an army of supporters faster than Napoleon ever did. Suffragettes kept beating the drum. Ministers appealed from pulpits. Very soon 45 states officially observed the holiday, and Congress got on the bandwagon *de facto*.

Exactly six years after Burkett's bill was ridiculed, President Woodrow Wilson proclaimed May 10, 1914, as Mother's Day and directed all government buildings display the flag "as a public expression of our love and reverence for the mothers of our country." Wilson's Secretary of the Interior was John B. Payne, son of Dr. Amos Payne who had been one of the physicians that worked with Anna Maria's Mothers' Day Clubs.

In New York state, suffragettes used the holiday to appeal for the right to vote.

Grafton's churches put on their most extensive Mother's Day display yet, according to the town's *Sentinel* newspaper. The Baptist Church saw 507 worshipers turn out to hear Rev. Leland J. Powell preach "The Motherhood of the Father." The Jarvis Memorial class of Andrews M. E. Church held special services in the evening. The Lutheran and United Baptist churches opted for a Parents' Day service.

Within days, the *New York Times* received a letter from a New Jersey reader suggesting a Father's Day with red, white and blue lapel ribbons. This prompted a wag to propose 12 holidays from Maiden Aunty's Day when bleeding heart blossoms would be worn to Household Pet Day with catnip corsages.

Regardless, Mother's Day soon became the third most widely observed holiday in the Western world. Jarvis hated the commercialization that followed, such as the 1928 ads urging men to say love on Mother's Day with a Darlo dishwasher. Buy one for your wife, too, "if you're feeling generous," they added.

Commercialized or not, Jarvis had kept the promise she made at her mother's graveside, and had done it in record time.

Father's Day Began in Spokane Although First Service Was in Fairmont

June 21, 1998

W ithin two months of the first Mother's Day church service in Grafton, the first known Father's Day sermon was preached twenty miles away in Fairmont. Unfortunately, Marion County isn't known as the birthplace of Father's Day.

Grace Golden Clayton was inspired by the May 9, 1908, Mother's Day services to propose a Father's Day to her pastor, Rev. Robert T. Webb of Williams Memorial Methodist Episcopal Church, South, in Fairmont.

Clayton wanted to honor her own father, Fletcher Golden, a Methodist minister, but she was also aware too many children in the area had become fatherless the previous year when 361 men perished in a mine explosion at Monongah.

Clayton and Rev. Webb chose July 5 for the service. Coming during the Independence Day weekend, what might have been a simple event before a small congregation became part of a carnival atmosphere, according to the account written by Harold L. Goff.

Fairmont's streets were crammed with 12,000 visitors, come to see a hot air balloon ascension and a daredevil who would thrill them with death-defying feats atop a spiral tower. For the more intellectual, Dr. William Spurgeon of London, England, was scheduled to deliver his world-famous lecture, "Popular Follies and Common Mistakes" Saturday evening. The doctor had pledged a cash award to the person in attendance who had submitted in advance a written contribution concerning "man's worst folly."

In the midst of this hubbub, Williams Memorial Methodist Church sat with quiet dignity at the corner of Second Street and Fairmont Avenue. Above its entryway, a tall, wide tower rose to a point high above the sanctuary's roof. Inside, sheaves of wheat graced the altar. The pews were filled to overflowing with worshipers who turned out to hear this first Father's Day sermon. (Today the church is Central United Methodist at 301 Fairmont Avenue, which holds special services each Father's Day.)

Perhaps because the event was tied closely to the recent Monongah tragedy, Grace Clayton did not push for a national holiday the way zealous Anna Jarvis did with Mother's Day. If she had, West Virginia might claim the birthplace of both events, but a Washington woman's name is connected to the holiday we now observe.

The concept of a day to honor fathers was widespread, occurring in many places. Virtually all the stories of the day's origins, however, indicate it grew out of the movement for a national Mother's Day.

Within days of Woodrow Wilson signing the Mother's Day bill in 1914, an unidentified New Jersey man wrote the *New York Times* proposing a similar event for fathers. He suggested red, white and blue lapel ribbons, reflecting the patriotic military service so many fathers had rendered to the country.

According to Maymie R. Krythe's book *All About American Holidays* (Harper Collins, 1962), Mrs. Walter H. Burgess patented the name National Father's Day Association in 1932. Burgess said that in 1919 when she was 15 years old and living in Drewry's Bluff, Virginia, she had written to a newspaper proposing a day to honor fathers. In 1921, she convinced Virginia's governor to proclaim a Father's Day. She withdrew her claims as the holiday's founder when she learned a woman on the other side of the country had been several years ahead of her.

Sonora Smart Dodd of Spokane, Washington, thought of Father's Day while listening to a Mother's Day service in 1909. (Although national recognition took six years, Jarvis's concept to honor mothers spread rapidly, carried by daughters, ministers and suffragettes.)

Dodd's father, Henry Jackson Smart, had raised her and her five brothers after the death of her mother. While Dodd's minister, a Dr. Rasmus, was praising mothers, she kept thinking about her father's efforts and sacrifices.

When the sermon ended, she spoke with Dr. Rasmus who offered enthusiastic assistance. The following year, Dodd asked the Spokane Ministerial Association to select one Sunday in June "to remind their parishioners of the appreciation owed fathers." She had chosen June because that was her father's birth month.

The ministers agreed, the YMCA got involved, the mayor of Seattle issued the first Father's Day proclamation, and Governor M. E. Hay set the third Sunday in June for a statewide observance. News of the event appeared in the Spokane papers and spread across the country. Soon even the renowned William Jennings Bryan was praising Dodd for her efforts.

In 1916, Woodrow Wilson pushed a button in the White House to unfurl a flag in Spokane, kicking off the day's events there. The usually reticent President Calvin Coolidge praised the day in 1924, saying the occasion would strengthen the relationship between children and fathers and impress upon the latter their obligations to their families. Coolidge, like Warren G. Harding before him, refused to create a national holiday though. Both feared commercialization like that which had followed the creation of Mother's Day.

Dodd, on the other hand, encouraged giving gifts to fathers and suggested Spokane merchants put up special displays. She steadfastly refused personal profit, rejecting hundreds of offers to endorse products. In 1953, she offered her views on how the day should be spent.

"It should include family attendance at church, a little gift for Dad, and some tender words you've always longed to say to him."

Anna Jarvis was moved to create Mother's Day when her mother died. Dodd's father lived long enough to celebrate Father's Day nine times.

Did a Headless Ghost Once Stalk the Entrance to Goke Hollow?

October 25, 1998. This column began my tradition of exploring folklore instead of history at Halloween.

In the spirit of fun that will accompany All Hallows Eve next Saturday, let us put aside the history books this week. Stack those battle maps next to the biographies, and let us wander where stark branches of long-untended trees scrape like bony fingers against windowpanes.

Come visit in a place where tomes of archaic lore lie piled beneath the dust of centuries, where cobwebs cluster and things best left unnamed skitter past dark corners.

But enough about my housekeeping …

Halloween celebrations are a mixture of pagan harvest festivals interwoven with a Christian celebration honoring all known and unknown saints, according to Maymie R. Krythe's *All About American Holidays* (Harper Collins, 1962). Among Druids, autumn festivals included rituals to placate the Lord of Death, who allowed the spirits of those who had died during the preceding year to return home, warm themselves at the fire and enjoy aromas of food cooking on the fireplace.

For centuries, children gathered round their parents or other family storytellers to hear spine-tingling tales of h'ants that walked the night. Such family storytelling has largely been been supplanted by gathering at the VCR to watch *Friday the 13th, Part 127*.

But not so long ago, West Virginia's children dived into bed, pulling the covers over their heads for protection after hearing about the Cull Betts ghost or The Sobbing Woman in the Hollow.

One story in particular served to keep me awake as boards creaked in the former schoolhouse we lived in a few miles from Clarksburg. It wasn't enough we had the cemetery just across the road at the Center Branch Baptist Church, with crumbling head-stones dating back to the early nineteenth century.

No, Dad had to make the night a little darker, the wind a little spookier by relating the tale of a headless ghost that prowled the railroad cut near our home.

To quote my father, this story was told to me for the truth.

Around the time of World War I, a miner stopped at a store then located near the railroad trestle between Stonewood and Route 20 South. It was payday, and he was on his way to Clarksburg for a little liquid recreation, but first he bought a sack of flour at the store, asking that it be left where he could pick it up on his way home.

Sometime after midnight, someone saw him walking up the railroad tracks into Goke Hollow, the sack of flour slung over his shoulder.

The railroad curved through a steep cut behind a white mansion where the Coca-Cola plant now stands. In the wee hours of the morning, a locomotive was pushing coal cars up the tracks through that cut to the tipple a quarter mile or so away.

As the engine, bringing up the rear, entered the cut, the engineer thought he saw something lying on the tracks.

After getting the cars to the tipple, he went to investigate. Lying in the darkness was the body of a miner. The train wheels had severed his head from his body and burst a sack of flour, the white powder giving a ghostly appearance to the macabre scene. Locals speculated the man had been knocked out, robbed and left laying on the tracks

The engineer flatly refused to take his train over the bloody rail. Huh-uh. No, sir. He pulled the coal cars back out of the hollow only after the rail had been replaced.

Soon, people walking the tracks or the road above them at night began to see a spectral vision in the area of the railroad cut. It appeared to be a man. A man without a head.

No one got close enough to make certain of that, mind you.

In fact, my father always finished the story by relating the experience of a cousin who headed up Goke Hollow one night to visit Granddad. As the cousin walked along the dirt road, he saw someone in the shadows of the cut below, keeping pace with him. If he sped up, the figure sped up. If he slackened his pace, it slowed down.

Was it the miner, seeking vengeance for his murder or perhaps looking for a head to replace the one he lost?

The road dipped down toward the tracks. Soon, our cousin would be forced to meet the shadow that paralleled him and learn what it wanted.

He turned around and walked over the hills to visit family in Philippi rather than find out.

The ghost in the cut hasn't been seen in many years. Perhaps it was put to rest when the rail on which the miner died was buried.

The rail laid by the side of the tracks until 1944, when it was used with other materials to shore up the high bank above Turkey

Run near the tipple. My father recalled the year because he was one of the workers on the job.

Was there anything unnatural in that cut? Or was it like the ghostly apparition that haunted the site of Harry Powers's murder farm at Quiet Dell, which turned out to be an owl two boys had tied to a cord and outfitted with a cloth dipped in luminous paint?

Our continuing pleasure in ghost stories says something about our need to believe things exist that our science "can explain not," to borrow a line from Bram Stoker's *Dracula*. The last comment I ever heard my father make about ghosts, after a lifetime of scoffing at his own stories, was that he regretted he had never seen one.

Happy Halloween. Next Sunday, we'll return to our usual haunts.

Remembering Santa's Workshop of the Ohio Valley

December 17, 2006

I f you were a child who bounced out of bed on Christmas mornings anytime from the 1950s to the early 1970s, you knew the name Louis Marx almost as well as you knew Santa's. He was a real subordinate Claus. His company reportedly produced twenty percent of all toys sold in America during the 1950s, from train sets to Sindy dolls.

Marx began his career working for toy maker Ferdinand Strauss but was fired in 1919 for advocating mass production, so he set up his own company on New York's Fifth Avenue. Initially, he found ways to produce toys more cheaply for other manufacturers but soon began producing his own.

All businesses have their ups and down, but that had new meaning with Marx—he sold 100 million copies of his version of the yo-yo in the 1920s.

Louis Marx & Company always operated under two overriding policies, according to www.marxtoys.com. They were, "Give the customer more toy for less money," and "Quality is not negotiable."

A factory at Erie and another at Girard, Pennsylvania, poured out dolls, toy soldiers and the like, but Marx needed more manufacturing capability. In Glen Dale, West Virginia, near Wheeling, he found a recently closed, quarter-mile long manufacturing plant that belonged to Fokker Aircraft. (Yes, history buffs, Fokker, the company that made the Red Baron's famous World War I triplane, once had a factory in West Virginia.)

Glen Dale became the manufacturing home for large, heavy-gauge metal vehicles of the Marx toy line, according to an article written by Harold Malcolm Forbes in *The West Virginia Encyclopedia*, edited by Ken Sullivan (West Virginia Humanities Council, 2006).

The company prospered even during the Great Depression, but World War II stopped the production lines. The Glen Dale plant shifted to producing materials for the war effort.

At the close of hostilities in Europe, General Dwight D. Eisenhower asked Marx to become an Industrial Advisor for rebuilding the ravaged continent's manufacturing.

Back home, his company became the unrivaled world leader in toy production. Less expensive items filled counters in the nation's five-and-dime stores, while more upscale playthings were sold through Sears and Montgomery Wards stores and catalogs.

Plastic emerged as a revolutionary element for toy making and played a significant role in the expansion of the Glen Dale plant.

The company entered its golden years. In December 1955, *Time* magazine dubbed Louis Marx "The Toy King."

The arrival of television led to new product lines based on popular series. Letters to Santa included requests for Johnny West figures and Fort Apache playsets.

(And Santa brought me the Fort Apache I asked him for, bless his jolly old soul.)

In the mid-1960s, the company scored a real knockout with Rock 'Em, Sock 'Em Robots, a red and a blue plastic "robot" that boxed each other as players controlled their movements with pushbuttons on plastic joysticks. The robots were later produced by Mattel.

The last great, gotta-have-it toy Marx developed was the Big Wheel tricycle in 1969, which rolled out of Glen Dale in huge numbers during the early 1970s.

Some 2,000 employees worked at the Panhandle plant at its peak. Then, in 1972, 76-year-old Louis Marx sold his company to Quaker Oats, which owned the Fisher-Price toy line. Quaker sold Marx Inc. to a British firm, Dunbee-Combex, which filed for bankruptcy and liquidated in 1980. The wonderful toys that lit up so many children's eyes on Christmas mornings were no more.

In 1995, however, an entirely new entity, Marx Toy Corporation, began production of some classic Marx playthings. In the age of video games, they may not amaze like they once did, but they're still making children happy.

Louis Marx was an initial inductee into the Toy Hall of Fame. His plaque there declares he was the "Henry Ford of the Toy Industry."

For over a quarter century, he made Glen Dale, West Virginia, into Santa's workshop of the Ohio Valley.

OTHER STORIES
I WANT TO
SHARE WITH YOU

A Birthday Salute to West Virginia's Longest-Running Newspaper

August 24, 2003

Happy birthday to you. Happy birthday to you. Happy birthday *Intelligencer*. Happy birthday to you.

Today marks the 152nd birthday of a newspaper, the name of which frequently appears as a source of information in these columns. Wheeling's *The Intelligencer* is West Virginia's oldest newspaper still publishing, and thank heaven someone decided to preserve virtually all of its issues. They are a boon to researchers like myself because at times they are the only source of information on events in the state's past.

Today's information primarily comes from the *Intelligencer's* August 24, 1867, edition. The paper turned sweet 16 that day, and its editors, in looking back on tumultuous years that had significantly reshaped their publication (and reshaped Virginia and the rest of the United States as well) reprinted its original statement of purpose.

From the get-go the *Intelligencer* was a daily, in a time when weeklies were the norm. The paper began as a Whig political organ intended to "antagonize the course of the *Wheeling Daily Times*," a more liberal Whig publication. The new kid in town was based on "the late declaration of the Baltimore Whig Convention, as containing the great and essential elements of harmony, development and prosperity."

(The nation had nearly been ripped in two over slavery-related issues in 1850; hence, the Whigs' call for harmony. We'll examine that situation more closely in this column next month. The Whig party favored a strong central government that promoted internal improvements such as railroads, canals, telegraphy and banks. It supported industrialism and the growth of an entrepreneurial middle class. The Democrats of the day generally opposed everything but the harmony idea.)

The *Intelligencer* might be partisan, but it wasn't utterly dogmatic about its political attitudes. "While these are our present views, we hesitate not to say that we are open to conviction, and if our Democratic friends can convince us that our principles are wrong, we are willing to renounce them at once, and embrace those which we may then think 'right.' Nor are we so blind and bigoted as to suppose that the Whig platform will prove a political panacea for all time ... *The measures of any people must change with the wants and necessities of the community. What is at one period expedient and proper in the government of a country, may at another period, from an entire change of circumstances, become inexpedient and improper.*" (*Intelligencer*'s italics.)

True to its word, the paper became a Democratic publication in 1856, after the Dems nominated Pennsylvanian James Buchanan for the presidency. He was the most conservative candidate, compared with Millard Fillmore, standard-bearer for the declining Know-Nothing Party, and anti-slavery John C. Fremont, the first-ever presidential candidate from the new Republican Party. Whiggery was gasping its last breaths by that time, anyway.

After just a few months in the Democratic camp, the paper was sold on October 18, lock, stock and ink barrel to its city editor, Archibald Campbell (nephew of the founder of Bethany College). He promptly made it a Republican paper, although anti-Republican mobs had recently filled Wheeling's streets. (According to some sources, the *Intelligencer* was the only paper in Virginia to support Republican Abraham Lincoln for the presidency in 1860.)

It was a complete reversal for the newspaper, which was begun in order to "break the force of the Anti-Slavery sentiment in West Virginia, (but) it became in a few very brief years the friend and advocate of that sentiment."

In observing the *Intelligencer*'s sixteenth birthday in 1867, the editors concluded by saying it would continue to support anti-slavery sentiment "until every logical necessity resulting from the destruction of slavery is fully and firmly established throughout the land."

Slavery by then had been outlawed by the 13th Amendment, but Ku Klux Klan members in Wheeling threatened death to those who advocated racial freedom. The *Intelligencer* reprinted some of those threats. Its 1867 position on slavery required more courage than is obvious in our time.

A Trip Through the Scrapbooks as the Twentieth Century Says Adios

December 26, 1999

O ne more column, a few more days, and the twentieth century is history. As the saying goes, if I'd known I'd be around this long, I'd have taken better care of myself. Maybe. I've been looking at the last half-century from a personal standpoint, opening mental scrapbooks to see what faded snapshots fall out.

I recall standing in line with my parents during the Great Coal Depression of the 1950s to get "commodities," canned food and powdered milk provided to out-of-work miners. I'm sure the canned goods helped feed our family, but we had a cow and powdered milk is atrocious. Wrapped in paper sacks, though, it made nifty toy hand grenades.

When John Kennedy was assassinated, Mrs. Elsie Shepherd's fifth-grade class at Norwood Junior High School was at recess. A student with a transistor radio (Remember when those were the golly-gosh of modern technology?) said the president had been shot. I happened to be standing beside her. She waited for the news to be rebroadcast, then called us all inside. A radio was hooked up to the public address system and we sat silently at our desks, listening until a solemn voice announced, "Ladies and gentlemen, the President of the United States is dead."

A few days later, I was playing at a friend's house when his mother rushed through the living room to turn on the television, shouting, "They shot Oswald," the man charged with Kennedy's assassination. Even to a fifth-grader, the notion an armed man could slip through police guards and conveniently kill the accused assassin before he went on trial seemed awfully coincidental. Pity there weren't any fifth graders on the Warren Commission.

Early in the 1960s, news reports said international troops were being sent to the Belgian Congo to quell a bloodbath. I had brothers in the Marines and feared America would be at war in Africa. I shoulda been worrying about a different continent. Ten years later, all the guys in my dorm at Fairmont State College gathered to listen as draft numbers were called. Whenever someone had to leave for class, we'd write down his name and birthday in case his ticket to Vietnam was announced while he was gone.

A montage of images swirl around Christmas time in downtown Clarksburg during the 1950s and 60s. Crowded streets with snowflakes coming down. The mechanized display in Parsons-Souders window. Salvation Army bells mingling with the tinkling sound of a bell on the cup held by a blind man who sold pencils in front of the ten-cent stores.

When NASA put the first man on the moon, I was working at Jackson's Mills State 4-H Camp. The staff watched the event on a TV in the offices under the dining hall. When the *Challenger* shuttle exploded many years later, I saw it on television at a trade show in Chicago. Our normally boisterous magazine staff had a long, subdued flight back to Washington, D. C., that week.

Although great events make the history books, it is the people who touch us on a personal level who probably have the greatest effect on our lives. Many snapshots shake out of the scrapbooks of friends in West Virginia, Texas, Washington, D. C., and Tennessee. Dancing through the memories is a laughing, dark-haired woman from La Feria, Tex. We thought we'd grow old together. We did, but not the way we planned. Get your annual mammograms, ladies. If you won't do it for yourself, do it for someone who loves you.

Now, another 100 years beckons for us to make new memories. Some will fall on us like summer storms, some will drift in slowly like snowflakes. May the good ones outnumber the bad, and may we have the sense to realize they do.

See you in the next century. Wake me up for meals.

A Tale of California Red's Infamous Binge and One Unlucky Viper

January 2, 2000. As the 1900s slid into the year 2000 there were all sorts of apocalyptic predictions. One major concern was that older computers weren't programmed for dates after 1999, and there were fears that would cause electric grids to shut down and create other problems that would destroy life

as we knew it.

In the introduction to this book I mentioned that before codes of journalistic ethics were created reporters, or "correspondents," sometimes made up news stories from whole cloth. This may be an example of such a story, but it's fun.

Well, I presume we made it. If you are reading this, we didn't regress to techno levels of medieval Europe at midnight on December 31, and the world has not fallen under the domination of the Antichrist, Bill Gates, or Pinky and the Brain.

Welcome to 2000.

I suspect that, with all the celebrations and all the fears, more people than usual were imbibing too much on the late New Year's Eve. Many probably reached a condition that used to be called "snake bit." And that brings to mind a tale.

The late comedian W. C. Fields, whose capacity for alcohol was legendary, once responded to a question about his liquor consumption by saying, "I never drink. I merely keep handy a flask of medicinal alcohol in case I should encounter a venomous snake ... which I also keep handy."

Old bulb-nose Fields may have known what he was talking about, if an article from the *Buckhannon Delta*, June 29, 1899 (reprinted from the *State Journal*) has any truth in it.

A hairy-legged soul known in the oil fields as "California Red," went on a drinking jag near the town of Waverly. I do not mean he imbibed too much one evening nor even that he had a "lost weekend."

Nay, verily, California Red had been keeping distilleries in business almost single-handed for weeks. Red surpassed even Mark Twain's description of the time when he, Twain, had a dreadful cold and two people separately recommended he drink a quart of whiskey to treat it.

Twain wrote, "That made a half a gallon. I have been drunk before, but that was a masterpiece!"

But Red had surpassed even that. The newspaper article declared, "It is said that for several long weeks he has been on a hard old batter, but yesterday he had an annual dose. Old liquor seems to have oozed through his epidermis perforations, and beneath the cuticle, river(s) of boose (sic), old, new, good and bad, seemed to float. Some of his friends took him out and placed him under the shade of a tall oak to sleep off the latest contribution to the protracted jag."

Undoubtedly, their decision to move Red to the great outdoors had much to do with trying to get upwind of him. At any rate, they left him slumbering beneath the oaken boughs and returned to their temperance meeting, or whatever.

Eventually, someone decided they ought to check on old Red, so back they went. They discovered him still motionless at the base of the oak tree, but one look at his face horrified them.

His skin was discolored. Shades of deep red, dark blue and grayish black painted his face like it was an Easter egg for the Addams family. One cheek was swollen to five times its normal size.

No one among them had ever seen alcohol do this kind of damage. They tried to shake him awake, but to no avail. He was breathing, but oblivious. They sent for a doctor who discovered what they had not observed.

Fang marks. Several of them.

Red had been bitten by a snake while he was lying there already snake bit. Talk about a lack of professional courtesy; next thing you know, sharks will start biting lawyers.

As the crew was about to pick their friend up and carry him to more comfortable lodgings, they noticed a dead reptile lying 10 feet away. They deduced old Red had so much booze in his bloodstream the snake died of alcohol poisoning after it bit him.

California Red survived. "One poison was merely greater than the other," the news story said. There is no indication he woke up singing "Fangs for the Memories."

A cautionary conclusion to this venomous tale: More people die from alcohol poisoning each year than from snakebites. Don't keep flask and snake handy.

A 'Yankee Lawyer' Found a Way Around the Law

Not previously published

A popular story claims that one day a friend found the curmudgeonly comedian W. C. Fields, a staunch atheist, reading the Bible. When the friend asked what he was doing, Fields replied, "Looking for loopholes."

The story is probably apocryphal, although it is the sort of one-liner the former vaudevillian was known for. Ah, yas, m'little chickadee. Looking for loopholes is more in the realm of attorneys than of comedians, but a Connecticut Yankee who wanted to hang out his lawyer's shingle in Old Virginia found a loophole that makes for an amusing story. Hu Maxwell related the tale in *The History of Barbour County, West Virginia* (The Acme Publishing Co., Morgantown, 1899).

After completing the study of law in Connecticut, young Spencer Dayton packed his valise with an extra suit of clothes, stuffed a few hundred dollars he'd saved into his pockets, and turned his feet toward Dixie in 1847. He'd heard the South was a fertile field for men wanting to practice law, though why Southerners may have been more litigious than New Englanders is not in the record at hand.

He stopped at Winchester but decided not to stay there. Maxwell did not give Dayton's reasons for traveling on, by stage and by foot, to Lewisburg in Greenbrier County. He heard court was going to be session soon in Nicholas County, so he set out once again, in hopes of plying his profession at Summersville.

There he encountered Judge Edwin S. Duncan, "one of the ablest lawyers and jurists of the first half of the (nineteenth) century," according to *Bench and Bar of West Virginia*, edited by George Wesley Atkinson (Virginian Law Book Company, 1919). Born in the Shenandoah Valley, he'd studied law in Randolph County before relocating to Clarksburg, with a second office at Weston.

Duncan served a term in the state senate beginning in 1820 before being appointed United States District Attorney for the Western District of Virginia four years later. In 1831, he was elected Judge of the General Court of Virginia and of the 18th District. *Bench and Bar* describes him as "truly a learned lawyer and an incorruptible judge."

Dayton, the young attorney with the New England accent, was granted license to practice law in Nicholas County. When the court convened in Braxton County, he applied there as well and received permission—for about five minutes. Judge Duncan had suddenly recalled that Virginia law required a one-year residency before an attorney could practice within the state.

Believing he was the victim of prejudice because he was from New England—the hot disagreements between North and South were already getting warm by the late 1840s—Dayton resolved not to take this lying down. He did what any competent attorney would do. He looked for a loophole.

He found one in the understanding of reciprocity that existed between Virginia and Pennsylvania: an attorney licensed to practice in one of those states was considered to be licensed in the other.

Obtaining a copy of the order that allowed him to practice in Nicholas County—apparently no one bothered to tell the clerk there Judge Duncan had rejected his application in another county—he hied himself off to the Keystone State. Based on the Nicholas County license, a judge in Somerset County, Pennsylvania, granted him license to practice in that state.

Dayton then returned to see Judge Duncan again, who by that time was holding court in Randolph County. Presented with the *fait accompli* of Dayton's stamp of approval from Pennsylvania, the judge had no choice but to honor the reciprocity agreement between the states, though he wasn't happy about it.

He warned the people in the court, "If any of you have any dealings with this young Yankee, I would advise you to look out for yourselves."

Despite this inauspicious beginning, the two men became friends, according to Maxwell's account. Dayton settled in Philippi and became the law partner of John S. Carlile.

Clarksburg's Early Theatre Caused Unexpected Controversy

May 17, 1998

Clarksburg was swimming in culture during the waning days of 1819, and some people were upset about it.

In mid-December, Colonel David Hewes announced a traveling "museum" exhibit at his tavern. Admission was two-and-a-half cents for adults, children half-price, but with cash scarce after the disastrous Panic of 1819, even that was out of reach for many.

The display featured a panoramic view of Rome, with an accompanying index that identified 407 churches, ancient ruins, bridges and other points of interest. Along with this magnificent painting were wax figures of generals George Washington and Andrew Jackson; Commodore Oliver Hazard Perry, hero of the 1813 Battle of Lake Erie; and an exciting diorama depicting the goddess Liberty supporting the late Capt. Wilcox while a soldier bayoneted a 'barbarous looking Indian" poised to take the captain's scalp.

In contrast, figures of a "fond mother with three beautiful children;" a Sleeping Beauty with her infant; and the renowned Virginia beauty Charlotte Temple honored family life and the fairer sex. If all that wasn't enough, there was also a twelve-foot long sea serpent skin to amaze and astound.

The traveling exhibit apparently came and went without arousing comment from the citizenry, but when a local theatre (to use the spelling of the time) opened a week later, controversy screamed in Clarksburg's newspaper, *The Independent Virginian*.

The Thespian Society of Clarksburg offered a Friday evening's pleasure on Christmas Eve, presenting a tragedy called *Revenge*, accompanied by a three-act farce, *Animal Magnetism*. The society promised a Spanish dance exhibition, and a comic song as well, all for five cents, half that for children.

In its advertisement, the Thespian Society stated it had been established for charitable purposes. In subsequent articles, the group was presented as being comprised entirely of young men from the best part of society. Most had never performed as actors before, although they were said to be blessed with musical talent.

Entertainment, a bit of culture on the frontier, and all for the sake of charity: Who could find fault with that?

The problems started on January 5, 1820, when a correspondent calling himself "A Spectator," wrote the newspaper praising the thespians and the "beautiful scenery" they had obtained at their own expense. He hoped the public would offer liberal support, and expressed his opinion this theatre would turn citizens away from less admirable pastimes, presumably drinking and gambling.

On January 12, one "Amicus Rationi," (A Friend of Reason, loosely translated from Latin), responded by stating in no uncertain terms few things were "apt to produce more deleterious effect upon the community, than those plays, in which obscenity, murder and suicide form the most striking parts."

Good thing the Thespian Society never performed Shakespeare's *Hamlet*; A. Rationi would have suffered apoplexy.

The *Independent Virginian* called upon A Spectator to take Rationi to task in their pages for his narrow-minded views. If he failed to do so, the newspaper itself would "exert every talent we possess to unmask a hypocrite and expose a bigot."

A Spectator returned on January 19, wielding a poison pen like Excalibur. For a column-and-a-half, he praised the young men of the Thespian Society and ripped A. Rationi as one of those "ignorant, superstitious, fanatical bigots (who) disapprove by turns almost every thing necessary for the convenience and happiness of man."

Jerry Springer would have had a field day with those two.

Things didn't end with the Spectator-Rationi feud. The society continued to perform new plays every couple of weeks, usually a comedy accompanied by a farce. *Animal Magnetism* was held over for a second run. Then came criticism from a new corner.

"Miss Ann M. Twister," of Muckletown wrote to a newspaper questioning whether the Thespian Society actually existed for charitable purposes and accusing the society of contributing to drinking and boxing.

On March 1, a member of the thespians answered hotly in the *Virginian* the society had not yet received enough income to pay for the scenery, largely because "the Beaux's of such a lady, herself, the gentry of Muckletown and many others, rudely take seats without paying a cent." Any drinking or boxing, he averred, "belongs alone to my lady's Muckletown friends."

Not long after, references to the Thespian Society dropped from the newspaper. It likely was done in not by ardent opposition, but by apathy and a lack of cash among the citizenry. For a little while, though, the Clarksburg Thespian Society provided as much entertainment in the pages of the newspaper as it did on stage.

A special thanks to the staff at Fort New Salem for their help in preparing this week's column.

A Mother, a Grave and a Romantic Legend

August 30, 2009

I n Westlake Cemetery near Ansted in Fayette County is a grave steeped in history and legend. The person whose body lies there would not be remembered today—indeed, the grave would not even have a headstone—but for one thing: she was the mother of Thomas "Stonewall" Jackson.

Julia Beckwith Neale was born at Peach Orchard, near the town of Aldie in Loudoun County, Virginia. Her father relocated the family to Parkersburg where he prospered as a merchant, and in 1817, she married an attorney, Jonathan Jackson, and they made their home in Clarksburg. Her husband died in 1826, when young Thomas was but two years old.

The 28-year-old widow with three small children reportedly taught school and did sewing work to support the family. In 1830, she remarried and soon her new husband, Blake Baker Woodson, was named clerk of Fayette County. He never cared much for his stepchildren, and they were sent to members of Julia's family to raise when she and Woodson moved to Fayette County. Thomas was seven at the time.

He only saw his mother once more. In November 1831, he and his sister Laura were summoned to her bedside for "her farewell and blessing." She had given birth to another child in October, her constitution had been weakened, and she was dying of tuberculosis, according to *Stonewall Jackson: The Man, the Soldier, the Legend*, by James I. Robertson, Jr. (Macmillan Publishing, 1997).

The children returned to their relatives at Jackson's Mills and were not present when Julia Neale Jackson Woodson passed away on December 4, 1831, nor did they make the long trip to attend her funeral. She was buried in the rain at a new seven-acre cemetery on a farm outside Ansted.

There, a legend began. It was recounted by J. T. Peters and H. B. Carden in *History of Fayette County, West Virginia* (Jarrett Printing Co., 1926).

As the story goes, a stagecoach was passing through Ansted just as the Rev. John McElheny of Lewisburg was delivering the eulogy over Julia's grave. The coach's passenger bade the driver to stop long enough for him to pay respects to whomever was being interred. That passenger, according to legend, was President Andrew Jackson.

A poem by one J. L. Cole, "The Old Fayette School-House," devotes several verses to the event, one of which recognizes, "This may be all a fact or may be partly fiction."

Was one famous Jackson actually present at the burial of the mother of another soon-to-famous Jackson? Anything's possible — that's why I keep buying lottery tickets — but this coincidence is almost certainly romantic legend.

First, there is the question of why Jackson would be passing along that route. His journeys between Nashville and Washington would have been greatly shortened by taking a boat up the

Cumberland and Ohio rivers to Pittsburgh, followed by a carriage ride to the capital — which is exactly what he did on his first inaugural journey.

What seems to truly dispel this legend is the date of Julia's death, December 4. In November 1831, Jackson didn't even attend his son's wedding in Philadelphia, remaining in Washington to prepare his annual message to Congress, which reconvened on December 5, according to *Andrew Jackson and the Course of American Freedom 1822–1832*, by Robert V. Remini (Harper & Row, 1984). It's exceedingly unlikely he was gallivanting around the Kanawha Valley at that time.

Julia's son Thomas visited her grave during a trip to Western Virginia in 1855. He found it sunken and unmarked; her husband, in financial straits when she died, never erected a headstone and a wooden marker had rotted away. Thomas intended to have one erected but never did.

After the Civil War, a member of his old command, Confederate captain Thomas R. Ranson of Staunton, Virginia, arranged for a marble marker to be placed on the grave. It erroneously gives her death date as September 1831.

LEMUEL CHENOWETH'S MATHEMATICAL MIND DESIGNED MANY BRIDGES

January 18, 2004

Have you noticed the news stories lately about the debate concerning students using advanced calculators while taking exams in higher math, such as calculus?

Some instructors say use of these electronic aids is realistic since the students will be using them when they take their skills into "the real world." Opponents maintain the developing scholars will not learn the underpinnings of advanced mathematics if they rely on a computerized abacus to do calculations for them.

Personally, I side with the traditionalists, although I acknowledge that six calculators and tutoring from Albert Einstein probably wouldn't have helped me with higher math. This kid's brain ain't wired that way.

A couple of West Virginians did have calculating minds, so to speak, with math mentalities to the nth degree.

One was Nobel laureate John Nash, the subject of the movie, *A Beautiful Mind*. The other didn't win any prizes, but his monuments have stood for over a century.

Lemuel Chenoweth was the preeminent bridge builder of Western Virginia. The preserved covered bridge at Barrackville was one of his structures. His greatest work was the span he designed and constructed at Philippi, the only two-lane covered bridge west of the Alleghenies and the only covered bridge still in use on a United States highway, according to *Lemuel Chenoweth and Family – Building Bridges*, by Barbara Smith, former Chair of the Division of Humanities, Alderson-Broaddus College (City of Philippi Convention & Visitors Bureau publication, 1997).

Chenoweth was born in Randolph County in 1811. Opportunities for formal education in that time and place might charitably be called limited. The so-called "pauper schools" held session irregularly and usually for only a couple of months at a time, according to Smith. These schools were intended for indigent children and shunned by many, so young Chenoweth may have been schooled at home.

However he was educated, he displayed a talent for mathematics. According to Jim Comstock's *West Virginia Heritage Encyclopedia*, Chenoweth met up with a surveyor named James H. Logan, who was laying out the Staunton-Parkersburg road, and asked Logan to teach him about math. Logan handed him an algebra textbook and told him to study the first two pages. A few days later, Chenoweth recited 60 pages to his mentor. Within three months, he had digested every mathematics book Logan could offer.

The budding mathematician grew to manhood and applied his knowledge to the carpentry trade, building furniture, wagons, houses and those indispensable wooden commodities, coffins. With his brother Eli, he built the Presbyterian Church in Huttonsville that was still in use at the time Smith wrote her account of Chenoweth's life.

He also put his knowledge to work as an inventor, creating a saw that cut up-and-down and back-and-forth. In his later years, he toyed with such concepts as underwater cable.

Bridges were his greatest legacy, though. He won several contracts to build them along the Staunton-Parkersburg road his friend Logan had surveyed. Most of these were small, utilitarian affairs, but he also landed contracts for larger, covered bridges, including those at Beverly, Rowlesburg and Barrackville.

His bridge designs made liberal use of the Burr truss, named for its creator, Theodore Burr. It combined the arch with a truss for greater stability, allowing construction of bridges at least 350 feet long without support piers.

When bids were let for a bridge to be built at Philippi, Chenoweth built a sectioned model and set off on the long trip to Richmond. At the end of the bid day, he was the last of a goodly number of men vying for the contract, according to reports.

He assembled his model sections, stretched them between two chairs, then stood on the model to demonstrate its strength. He got the contract.

In 1852, the Philippi bridge was completed at a cost of $12,181.24. A fire destroyed much of it in 1989, but Chenoweth's sturdy foundation and the primary timbers survived, and the rebuilt bridge still bears heavy use every day.

INDEX

A

abolitionists 2–4, 5, 15, 254

Adams, Jean 145

Agricultural College of West Virginia 250

Ahenakew, Mary 192

aircraft (airplanes, planes) 63, 215–17, 221–23 236–38, 293

Alderson 271–3

All About American Holidays 286, 288

Allen, Bernard L. 37, 277

Allshouse, —— Rev. 167

Ambush, W.E. 2–3

American Coal Company (Consolidation Coal) 34

American Miners' Association (AMA) 208

American Pioneer, 232

American Society of Newspaper Editors (ASNE) xiv

Andrew Jackson and the Course of American Freedom 1822–1832 313

Andrews, Donald R. 256

Andrews Methodist Episcopal Church 281

Andy Griffith Show 103–04

Angell Treaty 188

animals

    dog 231, 261, 270, 278–79

    horse 7, 18–19, 22, 54, 63, 67, 69, 78, 81, 113, 132–33

    lion 271–73, 274

    pig 70, 278–79

    snake 108, 130, 303–04

Ansted 311–12

Antietam, Battle of 21–23

Arden 99

Arlington, Lizzie (Elizabeth Stroud) 178–80

Arms, Clarence C. 122–24

arsenal 14–16, 68

Ashby, Turner 15

Associated Publishers 183

Association for the Study of Negro Life and History 182–83

Astor, Gerald 237

Atkinson, Gov. George W. 56, 306

Austin American-Statesman xiii–xiv, 267

Avis, Oza 172

Awada, Hanady M. 185

Aylor, Arthur 165

Aylor, Pearl Hitt 165

Aylor, Raymond Jr. 165

Aylor, Raymond Sr. 165

B

Baby Clipper 222

"Back to the Mountain: Emigration, Gender, and the Middle Class in Lebanon" 185

Bagby, Lucy 2–4

Bailey, Minter 116

Bailey, W.W. 135

Balboa Amusement Producing Company (Balboa Studios) 93–95

Balboa Films: A History and Filmography of the Silent Film Studio 94

Ball, Christian 54

Ball, William H. 54

Davis, United States (police chief) 269–70

Dawson, James 66

Dayton, Spencer 305–07

Deel, Emma Stalnaker 137

DeKalb 52–54

Dell, William E. 85–86

Democratic Party 11, 12, 62, 116–17, 129, 152, 251, 297

Democrats 12, 34, 116–17, 250, 297–98

Dempsey, Celia 172

Dempsey, Hiram 172

Dempsey, W.H. "Jack" 172–74

Devil's Saddle 86

Diez (Dietz, Dies), Eugene W. 51

Dixon, Thomas W. Jr. 271

doctors 108, 109–11, 112–14

Dodd, Sonora Smart 286–87

Doddridge County 31, 49–51, 157, 163

Doddridge, Joseph 133

Doherty, William T. Jr. 250

Douglass, Frederick 183

Drew, Harvie 24

Duckworth, —— Miss 50

Duncan, Judge Edwin S. 306–07

Dunkards 138–40

Dutch Ridge 62, 63

E

Easter 144, 154, 166–68

Eastern Panhandle 31, 83, 85, 100, 147, 210, 230

Eckarly, Thomas 138–39

Eckerlin, Samuel 139–40

education xiv, 37, 78, 98, 120, 121, 133, 154, 181, 243–255, 315

Edwards, James 87–88

Eldred, Jarvey 104

Eljer Company 201

Elk River 196

Elkins 40–42, 92, 268–69

Elkins, John Rush 73, 74

Elkins News 41

evolution 128–30, 276

F

Fairmont 18, 33, 109, 110, 146, 159, 167, 177, 217, 248, 260, 265–67, 284–85

Fairmont Free Press 41, 80

Fairmont General Hospital 114

Fairmont State College 300

Fairmont Times 265

Fairmont West Virginian 146

Fansler, Homer Floyd 90, 91

Farley, James T. 245

Farm Women's Camp 114, 263

Farmington 12

Father's Day 33, 106, 108, 283, 284–87

Faulkner, Col. C.J. Jr. 210

Fayette County 8–10, 159, 182, 311

Fenton, Frank L. 203–205

Fenton Glass 203–205

Fenton, John W. 203–204

Ferguson, Judge James H. 110

festivals 56, 186, 259–61, 267, 288

field schools 243–45

Fink, Mike 135–37

Fink Creek 137

Mexican War 152

Middlebourne 36

Mighty Eighth 237

military units

1st Virginia Cavalry Regiment, CSA 17

3rd West Virginia Cavalry Regiment, USA 19

7th West Virginia Infantry Regiment, USA 21–23

8th Ohio Infantry Regiment 21–23

8th Virginia Cavalry Regiment, CSA 25

9th Virginia Cavalry Regiment, CSA 24

14th Indiana Infantry Regiment 21–23

18th Engineers Corps 234

21st Infantry Regiment 240

24th Infantry Division 240

132nd Pennsylvania Infantry Regiment 21–23

314th Field Artillery 234

352nd Fighter Group 237

Cabell County Border Rangers 25

Miller, Thomas C. 57

"Million Dollar Bridge" 266, 267

Mineral County 86

miners 68, 101, 129, 173, 182, 196, 206, 207–208, 215–219, 274, 289–90, 299

Mingo 190

Mingo County 60, 236

Mingo (County) War 216–17

Mingo Flats 190

Mingo Knob 190

Mingo Run 190

Minnie Post Office 81

Minnora 136

Mitchell, James R. 201

Mitchell, Brig. Gen. William "Billy" 215–17

Moatsville 96

Mockler, R. Emmett 5

Monongah mine disaster 284–85

Monongahela Republican 196

Monongahela River xv, 17, 206, 265–67

Monongalia County 22, 142

Monroe County 244, 245, 274

Monument to and History of the Mingo Indians 190

Moore 90

Moore, Maj. ——45

Moore, Henry 165

Moore, Phoebia Gean 113–14

Moore, Phyllis Wilson xii, 92

Moorefield 25, 187

Morgan, Aaron 81

Morgan County 75, 88

Morgan, Gov. Ephriam F. 216

Morgan, John G. 36, 69

Morgan, Sarah 82

Morgan, Col. Zackquill 33

Morgantown 17, 22, 23, 32, 33, 103, 104, 105, 110, 128, 139, 142, 167, 175, 176, 196, 250, 251, 252, 262, 276

Morgantown High School 105

Morgantown Post 269

Morton, Oren F. 244

PaleoClones 276

Parkersburg 37, 38, 51, 64–66, 116, 159, 223, 227, 228, 229

Parkersburg: An Early Portrait 66

Parkersburg Sentinel 59

parking garage 218–20

Parsons, —— (at Battle of the Trough) 231

Parsons-Souders 260, 300

"pasteboard capitol" 68

Patteson, Gov. Okey L. 62

Payne, Amos 282

Payne, John B., Sec. of the Interior 282

Pemberton, Israel 149

Pennsboro 85, 180

Peters, J.T. 312

Philadelphia Centennial Exposition 56, 185

Philippi 99, 280, 290, 307, 315, 316

Phillips, Arlie 233

Phillips, Pvt. Joseph 23

Pickens 159

Pierpont, Gov. Francis H. 18, 27, 33–35, 37

Pinnell, D.S. 110

"Planting the cedar tree" 185

Pleasantville (Rivesville) 110

Pocahontas County 190, 245, 256

Pocahontas Times 191

poets 72, 90–92, 264, 276

Point Pleasant 230

Point Pleasant, Battle of 191

Polsley, Lt. Col. John J. 19

Potomac River 14, 31, 139, 224, 230

Powell, Frank M. 219

Powell, Rev. Leland J. 282

Powell, Robert "Punchy" 236–38

Presbyterian 150, 151, 315

Preston County 138–40, 144

Preston County Journal 188

Price, Andrew 191

Prichard, Arthur C. 114

Prichard, John 176

Prospect Hill (Quincy Hill) 64

Q

Quakers (Religious Society of Friends) 147–49

Quick Years, The 91

Quiet Dell 164, 165, 291

R

"Railroad Recollections" 50

railroads 14, 31, 33–34, 49, 80–83, 188, 194, 196, 209–211, 226, 258, 227–29, 280, 289–90, 297

Rainelle 73

Ramsey, J.W. 110

Randolph County 142, 190, 191, 245, 306, 307, 315

Raspberry, William xiii

Rathbone, William P. 197–99

rebel yell 24–26

Red Cross 68, 146, 158, 136–38

Reed, Mrs. Charles 24–25

Reed, Harrison 96

Reed, Ida L. 96–99

Reed, Louis 197, 199

Reed, Nancy Willard 96

Reeves, James Edmund 109–11

religion xiv, 144–56, 166

T

U

V

W

Illustration Credits

Cover photograph: Autumn along a country road. Photographed by author, date unrecorded.

West Virginia placemap: Map of outline of state and counties created by National_Atlas.gov - http://www.nationalatlas.gov, modified by author

Slavery, Civil War, and Statehood: The burning of the U.S. arsenal at Harpers Ferry, 10 P.M., April 18, 1861. Sketched by D.H. Strother. Library of Congress, LC-USZ62-134477

Crime, Politics, and Other Disasters: A deputy with a gun on his hip during the September 1935 strike in Morgantown, West Virginia. Photographed by Ben Shahn. Library of Congress, LC-USZ62-67517

West Virginia Women, the Arts, Medical Matters, Social Change: Housewives in Tygart Valley, West Virginia, have weekly group meetings in home economics. Here they are quilting. Photographed by Marion Post Wolcott, September 1938. Library of Congress, LC-USF34-050077-E

Pioneers, Religion, Weather, Sports, Mountain Melting Pot: Negro schoolchildren, Omar, West Virginia. Photographed by Ben Shahn, October 1935. Library of Congress, LC-USF33-006191-M2

Industry, Labor, Transportation, West Virginians At War: Train-load of ore and miners outside Davis Coal and Coke Industry. Photographed by G.V. Buck, ca. 1904. Library of Congress, LC-USZ62-41100

Education, Recreation, Animals, Holidays: Baseball game, homestead school. Dailey, West Virginia. Photographed by Arthur Rothstein, December 1941. Library of Congress, LC-USF34- 024408-D

Other Stories I Want To Tell You: Tygart Valley, West Virginia. Photographed by Carl Mydans, August 1936. Library of Congress, LC-USF33-000718-M1 [P&P]

About the Author

Gerald D. Swick's writing has been recognized with a Literary Fellowship in Nonfiction and a Lifestyles excellence in journalism award. In addition to a weekly column that ran in the *Clarksburg Exponent Telegram* his work has appeared in *The West Virginia Encyclopedia* (West Virginia Humanities Council, 2006), *The Encyclopedia of World War II: A Social, Political and Military History* (ABC CLIO, 2005), and in *American History, America's Civil War, Armchair General, Blue Ridge Country, Travelhost, Wonderful West Virginia* and other magazines. His coffee-table book *Historic Photos of West Virginia* (Turner Publishing, 2010) was authored as a gift to his  native state and its people. For several years he served as web editor for the sites of Weider History Group, world's largest publisher of history magazines.

He and Donna D. McCreary solved the 70-year mystery of why Robert Todd Lincoln, eldest son of Abraham and Mary Lincoln, is not buried with the rest of the family. They shared their findings in the Summer 1998 edition of *Lincoln Lore*.

His short fiction has appeared in the *Mist on the Mon* and *Dragons Over England* anthologies and *Appalachian Heritage* literary quarterly. Two of his poems were included in *Wild Sweet Notes: Fifty Years of West Virginia Poetry, 1950–1999* (Publishers Place, 2000).

Born in Clarksburg, he grew up in nearby Stonewood and graduated from Roosevelt-Wilson High School and Fairmont State College.

Gerald has been a featured speaker at national gatherings including the Association of Lincoln Presenters conference, Celebrate History!, and Women in the Civil War. He was interviewed on NBC Radio and PBS, not for his knowledge of history, but for his multiple victories in the annual O. Henry Pun-Off in Austin, Texas.

Apart from inflicting puns on his friends, his hobbies include photography, playing guitar and historical wargaming.

Visit him at his website, geralddswick.com.